30th Octr. 1907 –

Rd/

MEMORIALS OF THE COUNTIES OF ENGLAND

General Editor : REV. P. H. DITCHFIELD, M.A., F.S.A.

MEMORIALS OF
OLD ESSEX

THE BARTLOW HILLS.

MEMORIALS OF OLD ESSEX

EDITED BY

A. CLIFTON KELWAY, F. R. Hist. S.

AUTHOR OF

George Rundle Prynne

&c.

WITH MANY ILLUSTRATIONS

LONDON

BEMROSE & SONS LIMITED, 4 SNOW HILL, E.C.

AND DERBY

1908

DEDICATED
BY KIND PERMISSION
TO THE
RIGHT HONOURABLE
THE EARL OF WARWICK
LORD LIEUTENANT
OF
ESSEX

❧

PREFACE

THE plan of the general series to which this volume belongs is simple and understandable. It is to produce books which, while they do not assume to be detailed historical records of any one county, shall gather together the principal episodes of a county's history, and afford prominence to some of its outstanding characteristics and features. Thus in the present volume, dealing with a part of our land which, by reason of its geographical position, was necessarily the scene of frequent and exciting struggles for supremacy between Briton and Roman, considerable space has been devoted to the fascinating record of those far-off days. Again, the almost unique association of Essex with the Royal Forests of England, of which small fragments now remain, renders such a study of the Forest Records as Dr. Cox contributes of especial interest. And so, too, in regard to such widely different subjects as the Religious Houses of the county and the Monumental Brasses which are still contained within its churches, Essex, with few exceptions, stands at the head of all other counties. In common with other counties, Essex has her roll of famous sons; and this great home county has been the site of many a historic house, the rise and fall of which would furnish ample material for thrilling chapters in the nation's story.

The Editor desires to express his thanks to all who, by their literary or artistic co-operation, have assisted in the production of these Memorials, especially to Mr. Miller Christy, F.L.S., and Mr. R. C. Fowler, M.A., whose advice on various matters has been of the utmost value; and to Mrs. Godman for her kind permission to use several plates from the late Mr. Ernest Godman's admirable work on *Norman Architecture in Essex.*

A. CLIFTON KELWAY.

Corringham Rectory, Essex,
August, 1908.

CONTENTS

LIST OF ILLUSTRATIONS

xi

HISTORIC ESSEX

By the Editor

SSEX, by reason of its position in the south eastern corner of England, its contiguity to the Thames and to the metropolis, has had no small share in the general history—especially the earlier periods—of the country to which it belongs Naturally a maritime county, washed on its eastern shores by the North Sea, bounded on the south by the Thames, and pierced by three tidal rivers—the Lea, the Stort, and the Stour—Essex is the tenth in size of the English counties, being rather smaller than Kent and a little larger than Suffolk, between which two counties it is geographically situated. With Suffolk and Norfolk it forms the largest area of comparatively level ground in the whole of England, and in it there is but little waste land, Essex to-day being one of the leading agricultural counties in the kingdom.

The very beginning of Essex history would take us back to early days indeed, possibly to the Pre-glacial period—of which some traces are believed to have been found in the county; certainly to "ages so remote that no approximation of date is possible." But leaving the Palæolithic and Neolithic periods—traces of which have been discovered and preserved in the county—and passing to the Bronze, Essex has proved a mausoleum of weapons, ornaments, implements, pottery, and other relics of antiquity, the existence of which throws considerable

B

light on the dim ages to which they belonged. The
shape of the barrows containing the dead, and the
distinctive characteristics of the remains found within
them, point to the entry of an alien race—generally
regarded as the first of the Celts to reach our shores,
coming oversea from the Continent—forming in this
district one of their earliest settlements, and driving the
Neolithic men from the more temperate and fruitful
parts of the land. It is thought by Sir John Evans
that the Bronze period may have commenced here *circa*
1200 to 1400 B.C., and endured for well-nigh ten centuries,
namely, to 500 B.C.; but some scholars place its dawn at a
still earlier date.   There can be no doubt that these early
British inhabitants of this district, the Trinobantes or
Trinovantes, were a powerful, numerous, and considerably
civilized people, who met their Roman conquerors with
bravery and some degree of military skill.   This portion
of our county's history, however, is considered with
sufficient detail in the immediately succeeding sections
of this volume,[1] and only calls for passing reference here.
Mr. Maynard's map (page 44) affords interesting evidence
of the extent to which the Romans developed our district,
placing in it their first British colony, Camulodunum
(Colchester), creating one great road across the whole
length of the county, building their camps, forming
their stations, and after such bloody struggles as that
which finally broke the power of the Iceni, settling down
alongside the ancient Britons they had conquered.

Upon the evacuation of Britain by the Romans in
410, our island presented an inviting field to those
northern tribes who were roving about various parts of
Europe, notably the Angles, the Jutes, and the Saxons.
Of these invaders the Angles obtained possession of
the eastern district, which was called East Anglia, and
to them fell the honour of giving their name to all

---

[1] See Mr. Guy Maynard's articles on " The Britons of Essex," p. 19,
and " Roman Essex," p. 33.

England—at first called Angle-land, or in French, "Angleterre." Successive hordes of the northern tribes invaded different parts of the coast, and ultimately eight kingdoms were formed, called the Anglo-Saxon Octarchy, the kingdom of East Saxony, or Essex, being probably founded A.D. 527, and occupied by the men whose name it still bears, the East Seaxa. It is admittedly difficult to be entirely exact concerning the arrival of the East Saxons; indeed, Lappenberg, in his *History of England under Anglo-Saxon Kings*, remarks that no territory ever passed so obscurely into the hands of an enemy as the north bank of the Thames, where the kingdom of the East Saxons comprised the counties of Essex and Middlesex. Of affairs in this part of Britain generally during the fifth and sixth centuries we have very little information. We know, however, that London was selected as the capital of the new kingdom, thus depriving Colchester of the proud and important position it had held for nearly four centuries under the Roman dominion. Erkenwin, who is by some accounted to have been the first ruler of the Saxon kingdom, died in 587, and was succeeded by his son, Sledda. In the reign of Sæbert, his successor, the light of Christianity began to shine through the gloom of Paganism—not, it is believed, for the first time, however. Upon this point Dr. Cox, in his *Ecclesiastical History of Essex*, says :—

"With regard to the religious condition of the district afterwards known as Essex, previous to any English settlement therein, it is scarcely possible to state anything more definite than that early Christianity must have had a considerable hold during the latter part of the Roman occupation. Of the numerous legendary metropolitans of London of the British Church, only two have any substantial foundations, namely, Restitutus, who attended the Council of Arles in A.D. 314, and Fastidius, who was a Bishop of Britain in A.D. 431."[1]

During Sæbert's reign he embraced the Christian faith, Mellitus being appointed by St. Augustine to preach the

---

[1] *Victoria County History of Essex*, vol. ii., p. 1.

Gospel to the Pagans of the East Saxon kingdom. But under Sæbert's successors, Mellitus was driven out, the new religion banished, and Paganism again prevailed. It was not until 643, when Sigebert the Good was king of the East Saxons, that Christianity was once more and finally restored, Cedd, the brother of St. Chad, being sent from Northumberland to preach and baptize in Essex. Returning to Bishop Finan at Lindisfarne with a good report of his missionary labours, Cedd was consecrated bishop of the East Saxons, amongst whom he subsequently worked with evangelistic vigour, ordaining clergy, building churches, and in every way strengthening and extending Christianity throughout the kingdom. According to the Venerable Bede, the principal centres of Cedd's authority were at Ythancestir and Tilbury. The former has been identified with the site of the Roman fortress of Othona, near Bradwell-juxta-Mare, where the ancient chapel of St. Peter's-on-the-Wall, "a pre-Conquest church built of Roman materials," still exists. Tilbury, or "Tilaburg," Cedd's other and more monastic centre, assumes to-day an importance by no means ecclesiastical. During the period of the several kingdoms, until their union under Egbert, Christianity was re-established, Earkenwald, who was consecrated bishop of the East Saxons in 675, exercising vast influence for good upon his flock in Essex. The story of his monastic foundation at Barking is referred to elsewhere in this volume.[1]

Towards the middle of the ninth century the Danes, for some time settled in the north, descended into Essex, and, overcoming its inhabitants, rapidly made it one of their strongholds. Frequent conflicts between Saxon and Dane culminated in the emphatic victory of the latter at "Assandune"—possibly Ashingdon, near Rochford—in 1016, when Essex came under the

---

1 See "Monastic Houses of Essex," p. 110.

domination of Canute, the Danish king. The Saxon supremacy was restored in 1041, under Edward the Confessor, at whose death, in 1066, the throne was seized by Harold, Governor of Essex, son of Earl Godwin, and last of the Saxon kings. The tragic and disastrous end of this brief reign is well known. For Essex there is a note of deep personal interest surrounding the ultimate disposal of the body of the vanquished king:

> ". . . whom death, and not the Norman Duke,
> Had conquered; him the noblest and the last
> Of Saxon kings; save one the noblest he;
> The last of all."

From the monk of Malmesbury down to our own great historian of later times, Freeman, the belief has been firmly held that the body of the slain king, after it had been for a brief while interred in the sands of the sea-shore, was brought to Waltham Abbey, and there buried within the stately church " which he let himself rear." A careful study of the numerous authorities, ancient and modern, who have dealt with this much controverted matter, tends to confirm this belief.

The subsequent period, dating from the day when Harold's crown and kingdom were wrested from him by the victorious William of Normandy, was a momentous one for Essex, as, indeed, for the whole of England. Crowned on Christmas Day, 1066, William I. would not reside in London until a new fortress—the Tower of London—had been built for him. He therefore retired to Barking Abbey, and there received the homage and allegiance of several English nobles. From this moment England afforded the strange spectacle of a native population—not by any means easily overawed—with a foreign sovereign, a foreign nobility, and a foreign hierarchy. The king was a Norman despot, having no Saxon blood in his veins; the bishops and principal abbots were Normans; and, after the death of Watheof, every earl and powerful vassal of the Crown was Norman —prodigal indeed, but rapacious and oppressive. That great and exhaustive survey of England taken by William I. A.D. 1086, and known as the *Domesday Book*, dealt in a special and detailed way with the county of Essex, and affords a valuable picture of local circumstances and conditions at that period. Mr. Horace Round's admirable study and painstaking exposition of that portion relating to Essex opens this storehouse anew.[1] Reference to the *Domesday Book* shows that some ninety landowners of Essex were deprived of their lands by the Conqueror, the spoils of the county—lands, and slaves attached to them—being handed over to various Norman nobles, conspicuous among whom was the king's brother, Odo, " the mitred plunderer," Bishop of Bayeux, who succeeded in obtaining close on forty of the Essex lordships. " In Essex," Mr. Round observes, " as in other counties, the Survey teems with proofs of this grasping prelate's encroachments on the lands of others." He seems to have clutched the holdings of a multitude of small men rather than the possessions of any great English landowners. To awe the conquered people, and to secure safety for themselves and their possessions, the Norman lords built great fortress-residences or castles, of which a few massive fragments still remain, as at Colchester and Hadleigh. Not castles only, but numerous churches, monasteries, and other religious houses, sprang up throughout the county at this period; indeed, as stated elsewhere in this volume, about two-thirds of our Essex churches are computed to contain evidence of Norman work, while the Eastern Counties, as a whole, are richer in Norman remains than any other part of England. Remembering the nomenclature of so many places in this county, with their suggestive suffixes, often so reminiscent of Domesday lords, we must agree with

---

[1] *Victoria County History of Essex*, vol. i., p. 333.

Mr. Round that probably the imprint of the Norman Conquest is found more clearly in Essex than in any other English county.

With the Conquest there came undoubtedly a considerable development of civil and ecclesiastical government throughout England, and, for Essex in particular, a greater measure of freedom both from outside attacks and from internecine strife. Moreover, the influx of many husbandmen from Flanders, France, and Normandy tended to improve agricultural methods and to develop our lands. East Anglia was a wild uncultivated region of heaths, bogs, and swamps, Essex being largely forest; the majority of the people were the tenants and slaves, or *villeins*, of their lords, who had absolute power over them; while money was nearly ten times its present value. The cultivators of the land were bondmen, and could be sold, with their wives and children, by the lords.

Passing to the thirteenth century, we come to a period when the comparative freedom attained under the Plantagenet dynasty contrasts strikingly with the tyranny which prevailed during Norman rule. Early in this century Essex was the scene of strife resulting from the quarrels between King John and his barons, the castles of Colchester and Hedingham being besieged and captured by Louis, the French Dauphin, whom the barons had summoned to their aid. The desire for greater freedom which animated the barons in the twelfth century, and secured the Magna Charta for our land, slowly but surely permeated the lower classes, leading up to the great and terrible stroke for freedom commonly known as "Wat Tyler's Rebellion," which is intimately associated with Essex. In the third year of his troublous reign (1380), Richard II., needing money to prosecute his wars with France and Scotland, imposed a poll-tax of "three groats per head on every male and female of fifteen years of age, except beggars." This new and

strange impost, which was farmed out to collectors in each
county, caused grave discontent among the lower classes
of England, and led to the famous rebellion of 1381.
One John Ball, who styled himself "St. Mary's priest
of York, and now of Colchester," had thoroughly
prepared Essex for the insurrection, preaching equality
for all, and inveighing throughout the county against
the insolence of one class in assuming superiority over
another. Thus incited, the men of Essex rose
simultaneously with their brethren of Kent, and, mustering
in their thousands, marched through Romford and
Stratford to Mile End, taking up a position on the
north side of the Thames, while the Kentish rebels
assembled in a vast multitude at Blackheath, awaiting
the promised interview with their king. What followed
is a matter of history—the disappointment of the Kentish
insurgents, their attack on London, and the ghastly
excesses committed by them in their rage. Meanwhile,
the Essex rebels appear to have remained quietly at
Mile End, where the king and queen met them, listened
to their petitions, and granted them full and free
pardon. The men made no impossible requests, but
contented themselves with asking for the abolition of
slavery, a fixed rent instead of the services of villanage,
freedom to buy and sell in all market towns, and a
general pardon. These requests granted, the mob
dispersed. When they had done so, however, the king
recalled his proclamation, and marched an army into
Essex to suppress the revolt, which had grown to serious
proportions. "The disaffected, on their side, mustered in
vast force at Billericay, where they unanimously resolved
to retain their half-fledged freedom or die in the conflict.
A distracted and undisciplined mob, however, was no
match for mailed knights and men-at-arms, and when
the king's force came up they were surrounded, smitten
down, and scattered in all directions. . . . A court
was opened at Chelmsford for the trial of the offenders,

and it is stated that five hundred persons, who repaired
to that town and threw themselves at the king's feet,
obtained pardon; but the county wore the aspect of a
common slaughter-house. Cruelties of the most horrible
description were accompaniments of the executions. Men
were half strangled at one corner of a street, and then
taken to be hanged at another. In this way some were
'hanged four times at the corners of towns.'" Thus was
this rebellion quelled by such drastic methods as we in
these days can with difficulty conceive. More than thirty
years later Mile End was again the camping ground of
Essex men thirsting for freedom, but upon Cade's defeat
they dispersed without achieving their object. In spite
of these reverses, however, the tyranny of centuries was
slowly, but none the less certainly, being broken down,
a great and powerful agent in this direction being the
creation of a middle class, or body of yeomen, whose
uprising was due to the political necessities of the times
and the changed conditions of the country.

The fifteenth century, with its contending dynasties,
and correspondingly great and far-reaching changes for
the country generally, concerned Essex closely from the
religious standpoint. The county early began to be
prominent in the annals of Nonconformity, and during
the first part of the fifteenth century several Essex men
suffered martyrdom for their religious beliefs, which were
held to be contrary to those of the Church of Rome.
The annals of Nonconformity in Essex relate many
instances, including the burning of Thomas Bayley, "a
valiant disciple and adherent of Wycliffe," in 1430, and
of Richard Wyche, priest of Hermetsworth, on Tower
Hill, in 1440. In the religious struggles of the following
centuries Essex amply proved its pre-eminence in earnest
and determined Protestant Nonconformity, outrivalling
even Northamptonshire in this direction. David's *Annals
of Evangelical Nonconformity in the County of Essex*
(1863), and the less exact but more highly coloured

narrative of Fox's *Book of Martyrs*, furnish fuller
evidences of Puritan Nonconformity, and the punishment
meted out to it, than we can give. The full storm of
the Marian persecution fell upon Essex. When, upon
Bonner's reinstatement, the celibacy of the clergy was
enforced, eighty-nine of the Essex clergy were deprived
of their benefices, only one contemptible cleric, Hodgkin,
of Laindon, consenting to separation and public penance
as a means of rehabilitation. He was rewarded with
the living of St. Peter's, Cornhill. At Coggeshall,
Horndon-on-the-Hill, Braintree, Maldon, Colchester,
Rayleigh, Manningtree, Harwich, Rochford, Ardleigh,
Stratford, and Saffron Walden in the county, and at
Smithfield, Essex men, priests and laymen, yielded up
their lives in defence of their religious belief, and were
for the most part burnt at the stake. In Brentwood—
where William Hunter, the brave young silk weaver, met
his death in 1555—Colchester, and at Horndon-on-the-
Hill, tablets commemorate the revolting persecution which,
under the name of our most holy religion, wreaked such
horrible vengeance upon Essex men. As Dr. Cox
observes, in no other part of England were the horrors
of the Marian persecution brought so home to the people
at large as in the county of Essex. The number of
victims belonging to Essex was seventy-two, and its
prominent share in the long struggle against the claims
of the Church of Rome is the most striking feature in
the ecclesiastical history of the county.

It is unnecessary here to do more than mention the
dissolution of the religious houses (A.D. 1538), the effect
of which was necessarily more keenly felt in Essex than
in many another county of England. Although the
remains of these foundations are few indeed to-day, the
part these establishments played in the history of the
county was important and considerable. In addition to
the dissolution of the monasteries and the confiscation
of their property, the subsequent transference to the

Crown of the chapels, chantries, and colleges of the land brought about tremendous changes in Essex. And of more general consequence than any, perhaps, because its results admitted of few exceptions, was "the great pillage" of the parish churches which took place under Edward VI., at a moment when, as Dr. Jessopp says, "the lust of gain in the spirit of Cain was master of the situation, and men in high places, of high birth, and even of high culture, found the spirit of the age too strong for them." The tremendous havoc which was wreaked during those eventful six years of the boy king's reign was responsible for the irretrievable loss of priceless treasures from the ancient churches and parishes of Essex. To mention only one result—before the close of the reign of Edward VI., every church bell in the county was assigned to the young king's use, not a single bell being exempted from this demand except that of the almost ruined church of Fobbing.

With the accession of Elizabeth (1558) there was still persecution for conscience' sake, submission to the Acts of Supremacy and Uniformity by the clergy being insisted upon on peril of deprivation. The eventual ejections and sequestrations for refusing to subscribe were far greater in Essex than in any other part of the diocese of London, twenty-six incumbents being deprived at once, and others later. Recusants, too, were hunted out and punished, imprisonment and exile being inflicted upon them, and sometimes even severer punishment. The record of days when "priest-harbouring" was counted worthy of such an awful punishment as the *peine forte et dure* (Widow Wiseman, 1598) is a humiliating story, and one which we would gladly forget but for the moral which it so impressively conveys. The sickening catalogue of afflictions, imprisonments, confiscations, maimings, burnings, and the rest, belonging to the Marian and Elizabethan reigns, is the best corrective to any who to-day may be tempted

to indulge the spirit which prompted such things
of old.

The striking figure of Elizabeth is perhaps one of
the most prominent in the whole history of Essex, from
which it stands out boldly during the critical days of
the attempted invasion of our shores by the King of Spain.
In 1579, little more than twenty years after her accession
to the English throne, Elizabeth, riding on horseback,
made a tour of the Eastern Counties, and, being very
favourably impressed with the hospitality she received,
tarried long in the houses of the Essex nobles.
Undoubtedly Her Majesty was entertained with much
pomp and a certain degree of splendour. At Colchester,
for example, whither the Queen proceeded on Sept. 1st,
1579, the bailiffs and aldermen received her, riding
upon "comely geldings, with foot-clothes in damask or
satin cossacks or coats, or else jackets of the same, with
satin sleeves in their scarlet gowns, with caps and black
velvet tippets." The Queen received much, and gave
little in return. Nevertheless, her popularity was very
great, especially in the Eastern Counties. "Wherever she
came she was received with enthusiasm. The people were
prepared to submit to her will, and to die in her defence.
When the country was menaced by the Spanish Armada,
even the Roman Catholics enrolled themselves as
volunteers in the army. . . . The people of Essex,
expecting the enemy to land on their coast, furbished up
their old arms, and all the able-bodied men, even youths,
applied themselves to practise with the matchlock and
the pike. Colchester supplied three ships of war, all
well manned by hardy sailors. Maldon contributed a
small war craft, filled with sons of the sea. Arrangements
and preparations for defence were made along the eastern
coast."

But it is Tilbury and its ancient fort that are for ever
most intimately associated with the memory of the great
threatened invasion, for there the vast camp of defence

was formed, where the heavy guns of Tilbury fort could command the Thames, and thither the Queen came, riding her charger, and addressed her soldiers in words which made such apt and impressive appeal to her " faithful and loving people." To Tilbury thronged the levies from all parts of England, until around the blockhouse erected there by Henry VIII. was gathered a vast multitude of armed men, Catholic and Protestant, Papist and Puritan—22,000 foot and 1,000 horse—all united in the hour of national danger to defend their country and their Queen. The temper of the vast army at Tilbury has been thus described by Stow :

" It was a pleasant sight to behold the soldiers as they marched towards Tilbury, their cheerful countenances, courageous words and gestures, dancing and leaping wheresoever they came, and in the camp their next felicity was hope of fight with the enemy ; where of times divers rumours were of their foe's approach, and present battles would be given them ; then were they joyful at such news, as if lusty giants were to run a race."

The issue of the threatened invasion is too well known to need recounting. Of the vast and hastily formed camp of defence at Tilbury no trace remains, but the memory of those stirring happenings which called it into being forms one of the most impressive in our long and eventful history. During the later years of Elizabeth's reign Essex suffered heavily from the plague which raged so awfully throughout England, and in 1604, the opening year of James I., Colchester experienced the force of its dread power. Later, this town was similarly visited, four thousand seven hundred and thirty-one of its inhabitants being swept away before it in 1665 and 1666. The reign of the first James, with its years of famine, its dread plague, and deep-laid plots, was not a happy one for Essex. Two of its principal sons, Lord Grey and Lord Cobham, were implicated in Sir Walter Rayleigh's conspiracy against James, and the letter which led to the discovery and frustration of the Gunpowder Plot was addressed to

an Essex landowner, Lord Monteagle, of Great
Hallingbury Hall. This Catholic nobleman promptly
disclosed the warning to the Secretary of State, thus
saving the Protestant family and the Protestant
Parliament from a terrible fate.

Although fairly prosperous in the early days of the
Stuart dynasty, Essex was far from contented. The levy
of "ship money" by Charles I. in 1634 aroused the
strongest feeling in the county, which was expected to
contribute £8,000. Colchester, having first refused,
eventually paid a portion of its share; Maldon, £80;
Harwich, £20; and Thaxted, £40. In matters of faith
and religion, Essex, truly termed "the headquarters of
Puritanism," was ill-disposed to acquiesce in the measures
laid down by Charles I. and that strong-willed prelate,
Laud, in whose diocese of London the county was at
that time included (1628-1633). Upon the elevation of
Laud to the primacy, his further efforts to secure
conformity aroused deep resentment, and about this time
several notable Puritan preachers—Hooker, John Eliot,
Thomas Shepard, John Wilson, John Norton, and others—
fled to America from Essex in order to escape Laud's
clutches. The High Court of Commission, appointed to
enforce uniformity of worship in every place, caused
the arrest of a pronounced Puritan, John Bastwick, an
Essex man, and a physician at Colchester. He was first
fined £1,000, then excommunicated and imprisoned, and
eventually, by order of the Star Chamber, had his ears
cut off in the pillory in Palace Yard. In this way did
the unwise monarch create martyrs of his opponents,
and excite that wave of indignation which eventually
brought about his own tragic downfall. The part which
Essex played in the disastrous days which immediately
succeeded is dealt with by Mr. Kingston in this
volume.[1]

---

1 "Essex and the Civil War," p. 158.

During the Commonwealth period, notable Essex Puritans like "Master Steven Marshall of Finchingfield, and Master Obadiah Sedgewik of Coggeshall," were prominent both here and in London in their efforts to reform or abolish many things with which they did not agree. The first-named cleric was the chief promoter of the Presbyterian system, which succeeded the downfall of royalty and the overthrow of the episcopate. So venerated was he in his party, that at his death he was buried in Westminster Abbey—only, however, for a time, his bones being cast out again at the Restoration as unworthy of so honoured a resting-place. Strange and distressing scenes were enacted at this time in many an Essex church. The Vicar of Leyton, for instance, adopted the military uniform in church, and preached in a buff coat instead of a surplice. Strife was waged between the rival factions in matters religious. And just as the bitterness and persecution of the Marian reign was rivalled by that which was displayed under Elizabeth, so now, when opportunity arose, the narrow bigotry and fierce tyranny of Laudian days was easily matched by the sturdy defenders of religious freedom. "A Testimony of the Ministers in the Province of Essex to the Truth of Jesus Christ, and to the Solemn League and Covenant," sent up to their brethren in London in 1648, contains some genial sentiments. For example, these worthy men state their determination to "preserve and transmit that Sacred Despotism, as much as in us lyeth, unto all posterity." Desiring to "deal tenderly with the tender consciences of Dissenting Brethren," they proceed to declare that "from our soules we doe utterly detest and abbhor as all former cursed doctrines of Popery, Arminianism, and Socinianism, so likewise the damnable Errors, Heresies, and Blasphemies of these present evil times, whether of Anti-Scripturists, Familists, Antinomians, Anti-Trinitarians, Arians, Anabaptists, and whatsoever is found contrary to sound doctrine and the power of Godliness." As a conciliatory expression of tender dealing in matters of conscience, the whole document is instructive. So, too, is " The Agreement of the Associated Ministers of the County of Essex," put forth about ten years later, in the hope of securing " the Churches Peace," wherein the " Orthodox " ministers declare that language fails them to depict the extent and growth of " damnable Heresies and vilest practices, often also attended with hellish blasphemies."[1] As Dr. Cox observes, although the form of religious toleration had its rise in the days of the Commonwealth, " it was a tender bloom, that merely extended its mercies to Independents and Baptists, in addition to orthodox Presbyterians, for members of the Church of England, as well as those of the Church of Rome, and Socinians and Quakers, were more or less actively persecuted." In fact, a study of the ecclesiastical history of Essex, where the force of intolerant and bigoted persecution was so cruelly exercised by parties that successively gained the ascendancy, is an admirable corrective of undue partisanship in regard to the several schools of religious thought which have so long existed. The fierce contention of rival factions which was exhibited during the Commonwealth doubtless proved how unfit they were to carry on the civil government of the country, and thus prepared the way for the restoration of the monarchy in 1660. This event was hailed with gladness in Essex, Sir Harbottle Grimston, one of the members for the county, voicing the feeling of his supporters in a fulsome speech at Whitehall Banqueting House. The consequences of the Restoration, however, were serious for many an Essex incumbent, a very large number of Essex benefices being rendered vacant by the ejection of ministers under the Act of Uniformity (1662). Shortly after his restoration, Charles II. cast longing eyes upon

---

[1] *King's Pamphlet*, E., 953, 2.

Audley End, which speedily became a royal residence, while New Hall was the seat of General Monk, the famous Duke of Albemarle.[1]

A striking illustration of the ignorance and superstition that prevailed in Essex in days not long prior to those of the Restoration is furnished by the career of Matthew Hopkins, the witch-finder, a native of Manningtree. This wretched impostor, trading upon the credulity and ignorance of times when a belief in witchcraft was very generally held, assumed the title of "Witchfinder General," travelling the Eastern Counties regularly in pursuit of his disgusting profession. His favourite methods of satisfying himself concerning his unfortunate victims are too revolting to relate. In one year he haled twenty-five poor old women before a special court at Chelmsford, charged them with being witches, and secured the execution or death of all save one. In another year he is credited with having brought sixty unfortunate creatures to the stake; and, altogether, he was responsible for the cruel death of hundreds before he himself ended his career of murder and money-making at the hands of an enraged populace in Suffolk in the middle of the seventeenth century.

During subsequent reigns Essex has ceased to play any very important part in history, though the records of days when a Napoleonic invasion was thought to be imminent, or, later, of the struggles associated with such legislation as the Reform Bill of 1832, show the county aroused to activity and excitement in common with the whole of England. When war broke out between England and France, volunteers, as well as supplementary militia, were enrolled in large numbers in Essex; and at the resumption of the Napoleonic war, after the Peace of Amiens, there was renewed activity, the Parliamentary returns of 1803 showing a total establishment of 6,335

---

1 " Historic Houses," p. 192.

C

foot in the county. Indeed, Sir William Hilary's force of 1,700 men, raised when the French invasion was expected in that year, was, it is said, the largest private force in the kingdom.

Ecclesiastically, much has happened during the last half-century. From the earliest founding of the see of London, at the beginning of the seventh century, Essex came under its jurisdiction, the county forming one of the four archdeaconries into which the diocese was divided. Colchester was created a suffragan bishopric by Act of Henry VIII. (1534), a clerical pluralist, William Moor, Rector of West Tilbury and Bradwell, and Vicar of Witham, being its first occupant (1536-1540). After a lapse of over two centuries, this bishopric was revived, and Dr. Blomfield, son of Bishop Blomfield, of London, appointed to it in 1882. In 1846, however, the county of Essex, saving nine parishes, had been cut off from London and made to form part of the see of Rochester, an episcopal residence for the Bishop of Rochester being provided at Danbury. When, in 1863, the nine parishes previously omitted were transferred to the Rochester diocese, the whole county passed under the spiritual direction of a bishop south of the Thames! So things remained until, in 1875, an Act was passed creating the new bishopric of St. Albans, and allotting to it the two counties of Essex and Hertford. This arrangement has continued up to the present, when, the required endowment having been raised, Parliamentary consent is being sought to the formation of a distinct see of Essex, the seat of which, it has been decided, shall be the historic town of Chelmsford.

THE BRITONS OF ESSEX AND THE ROMAN CONQUEST

BY GUY MAYNARD

WHO were the British inhabitants of Essex at the Roman Conquest? What was their culture and social organization; what chain of events brought them there; and, finally, what was the nature of the changes which occurred, socially and industrially, during the four centuries of the Roman rule? These are questions which confront every Essex student who seeks to apply the general statements of early British history to his own locality. The answers rest in great measure upon indirect and perhaps inconclusive evidence. All that the following pages can attempt is to trace the general outline of such recorded facts as bear upon the history of the county during the remote period in question.

Research shows us the Trinobantes, or Trinovantes—those Britons mentioned by the Roman historians as occupying the district north of the Thames, which we may broadly identify with Essex—not as aboriginal natives, but as one link in a chain of racial and social changes, the beginning of which reaches far back into prehistoric times.

The flint tools from our Essex gravel beds and surface soils, the bronze swords and celts, and the corroded iron spear-heads, enable us to accept the conclusions based upon evidence from much wider areas, and to say with confidence that the old Stone Age hunter of mammoth

and reindeer once roamed our Essex forests—that the men
of the later Stone Age, with their sun and nature worship
and rude husbandry, were here also; and that, as time
passed on, the knowledge of metal-working spread through
our valleys, and a Celtic race came in from the mainland
somewhere between 2000 and 1200 B.C.   Again, still
later there came a second wave of Celtic immigration,
perhaps five centuries before the landing of Cæsar, and
with these tribesmen came the general use of iron, new
styles of ornament and new ideas in pottery-making
gradually filtering into these western islands from the
culture-radiating areas of South Central Europe.   Almost
down to Cæsar's own time the process had gone on, for
the tribes south of the Thames—Cantii, Regni, Atrebates,
and Belgæ—were certainly nearly related to Cæsar's
opponents in North-Western France; and thus the great
Roman found in Britain a mixed people, with a long
record of civil strife behind them.

We may accept the Trinobantes[1] of Essex as a Celtic
tribe, who were comparatively late comers into Britain.
Their territory was clearly marked out by natural frontiers
—the Thames, the Stour, and the range of hills on the
north-west.   The Iceni, or Iken, to the north of Essex,
may represent a nearly parallel stage of the last great
immigration wave; while, west of the county, the Cassii
and Catuvellauni of Hertfordshire and beyond may
have belonged to an earlier stage—Celtic tribes once
settled on the coast but now pushed inland by others
following; and still further westward lay the earliest
Celtic invaders and the remnant of the Stone Age race.[2]

It is certain that we must concede a much greater
degree of culture to these south-eastern Britons than was
at one time allowed.   The large numbers of war chariots

---

[1] " Battle piercers "—from the Welsh *trin*, a conflict.—*Prof. Rhys.*

[2] Tacitus states that the western Britons (*Silures*) were short, dark,
and curly-haired; while the eastern tribes resembled those of the mainland,
tall and red-haired.

LATE CELTIC POTTERY.
Found at Braintree.

LATE CELTIC POTTERY (BRONZE UTENSILS).
Found at Colchester.

in the British array point not only to roads or recognized tracks, but to wide expanses of fairly open country. The dense population mentioned by Cæsar could not have been supported by a wholly forest region.

Gold and bronze coinage, struck a century before Cæsar's invasion, indicates a fixed standard of value for commerce, and the rude imitations on these coins of the designs upon Greek coinage prove that trade routes with the Mediterranean were open. Gold and bronze armlets and neck-rings, enamelled bronze brooches and pendants, show the skill of the Britons in artistic metal-work. They had, of course, iron weapons and tools, sword, spear-head, knife, axe, etc. Stone spindle whorls point to woven material for garments, which were probably dyed in brilliant colours by the use of vegetable agents ; and, finally, it is established that they possessed pottery as finished and artistic in style as anything produced by Romanized Britain. A series of these late Celtic urns, which in many cases show, by their swelling curves and graceful pedestal feet, that they were modelled upon the type of bronze vessel produced by an earlier period of South European culture, has been discovered at Shoebury,[1] Great Chesterford,[2] Skitts Hill, Braintree, Earls Colne, Colchester, and elsewhere in the county. Some of these " finds " are illustrated herewith.

At the time of Cæsar's invasions the Trinobantes were disturbed by a dynastic struggle. Cassivellaunus, King of the Catuvellauni (Caswallon), slew Immanuentius, ruler of the Trinobantes, and made himself king of that tribe also. Mandubratius, son of Immanuentius, fled to Gaul, and may have been largely responsible for Cæsar's invasion ; at any rate, he returned with the Romans.

---

[1] See plate, etc., *Essex Archæological Society's Transactions*, vol. vi. (n.s.), and originals in Colchester Museum.
[2] A few are at Audley End in Lord Braybrooke's collection, and in the Saffron Walden Museum.

Cæsar's narrative of his British campaigns only allows us to say that very probably his forces entered the county of Essex. In his first reconnaissance (55 B.C.) Cæsar did not advance inland. But returning the following year with about 30,000 men, after securing his base camp and ships, he marched inland, defeated the united tribes under Caswallon, forced the passage of the Thames, and pursued the British leader into his own territories. Caswallon, finding that his followers were no match for the legions in the open, retained only a large force of chariots, with which he retired to the thick forest country, and, by rapid movements and intimate knowledge of the woodland tracks, managed to continually vex and harass the Romans.

Probably Cæsar was now in or on the borders of Essex, for the Trinobantes threw off their allegiance to Caswallon, and opened negotiations with the invader, begging the restoration of their prince, who was in the Roman camp, and offering their own submission. Cæsar grasped this opportunity of breaking up the tribal confederacy, and agreed, on condition that forty hostages and supplies of corn were forthcoming. This action by the Essex tribesmen had a marked effect on the campaign. Other tribes deserted Caswallon, and at last the position of the chief's " town " was disclosed to the enemy. Cæsar stormed the place, and the Britons, abandoning their homes and cattle, hastily dispersed. The site of this " town " is very doubtful. Cæsar merely alludes to it as a large area of forest (probably partly cleared) enclosed by ditch and bank. Wright, in his *History of Essex*, suggested Ambresbury Banks, the British earthwork in Epping Forest; while Verulam, near St. Albans, in Hertfordshire, has often been selected. The campaign ended by Cæsar accepting the advances of the British leader. The summer was fast departing, and so, after receiving a number of hostages and fixing the annual tribute to be paid to Rome, and also warning Caswallon not to interfere with the Trinobantes or their ruler, the Romans withdrew to Gaul.

During the ninety-seven years between Cæsar's second campaign and the invasion of A.D. 43, the Britons, although left to themselves by Rome, must have advanced in many ways. Gaul was rapidly Romanized, and the civilizing influences could not fail to cross the narrow straits. Cæsar's victories opened up the island to the world, and it is significant that soon afterwards the British coins, which previously had no legend, were struck with inscriptions in Roman characters, consisting of Romanized versions of the Celtic names of the kings.

The dynastic events of the Trinobantes and their neighbours, the Cassii, so far as they can be traced by comparison of the legendary accounts of Geoffrey of Monmouth and other chroniclers with the inscriptions on the coins, appear to have been, briefly, as follows[1] :

Although Mandubratius was restored to the chieftainship of the Trinobantes by Cæsar, yet Caswallon remained King of the Catuvellauni, and retained his general authority over the group of central and eastern tribes. Geoffrey of Monmouth states that Cassive Manus (Caswallon) was succeeded by Tenuatius. This Tenuatius would appear to be identical with the Tasciovanus whose name is found on British coins discovered in Eastern Britain. "After him Kymbellinus, his son, was advanced to the throne, being a great soldier and brought up by Augustus Cæsar."

Kymbellinus is certainly the " Cunobelin," whose coins, bearing his name and abbreviations of the names of the towns in which they were struck, are found in numbers in Essex and in adjoining counties. Many of Cunobelin's coins bear the letters TASC. F. (abbreviation for Tasciovanus Filius—son of Tasciovanus), thus supporting the traditional account.

---

[1] It seems that the southern tribes were in constant touch with Gaul, and, indirectly, with Rome, during this period.

Tasciovanus succeeded Caswallon about 30 B.C., while his son Cunobelin seems to have come to the throne about A.D. 5.   But there is evidence that during his father's life the Trinobantes were again subdued, and that Cunobelin ejected a certain Dubnovellinus (possibly the successor of Mandubratius) from the chieftainship. This prince is recorded on the Ancyra tablets as appealing to Augustus Cæsar under the name of Damno Bellaunus.   The mint marks show that after the fall of Dubnovellinus Cunobelin ruled, and that he struck coins in the royal city or Oppidium of the Trinobantes—Camulodunum, probably at or near the modern Colchester.   The coinage of this reign shows increasing Roman influence.   The types are copied from Roman coins, and Roman divinities are represented.   We may assume that this was accompanied by the adoption of many Roman fashions in furniture, dress, and social usage.

Cunobelin's reasons for selecting Camulodunum as his capital are obvious.   Its position—too far up the tidal river to be easily raided from the sea, yet so conveniently placed for communication with the Continent; its defensive qualities—perched upon the peninsula between the Colne and its tributary, the Roman river, so that a rampart drawn from one stream to the other enclosed a large area; and the fact that the presence of the paramount ruler would tend to keep the Trinobantes quiet, must far have outweighed the claims of the more central position of Verulam (St. Albans).

Although little positive evidence exists, yet there can be no doubt that Grymes Dyke, the long earthwork which once stretched from the Colne across Lexden Heath to the Roman river, represents the main defence of British Camulodunum.[1]   A little within this ran a second almost

---

[1] See Dr. H. Laver's article, *Essex Archæological Society's Transactions*, vol. vi., p. 17.

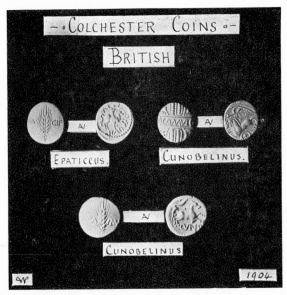

BRITISH COINS MINTED AT COLCHESTER.

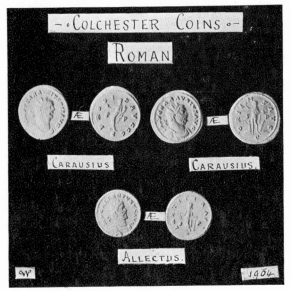

ROMAN COINS MINTED AT COLCHESTER.

parallel line of earthworks, and other entrenchments flanked the main defence at each end. Portions of these works still remain in a good state, and the line of the destroyed portions can be traced; but otherwise the destruction of centuries has been so complete that, save for a few British burial urns and many coins, all trace of the British occupation has been lost.[1]

We know little of the state of Essex during this period. No doubt the low parts of the sea coast and the river estuaries were unembanked and fringed with marshes. We must, however, concede broad ranges of forest, where the red deer, the wolf, the badger, the marten, and the wild cat made their home, and where human inhabitants were few. But between swamp and forest there must have been the wide grazing grounds and the corn land of the natives. Here and there were great entrenched camps commanding frontiers and road lines, or affording shelter to the inhabitants of exposed areas. It is very difficult to select the British sites out of the many Essex earthworks; but beside the western frontier camps of Ambresbury Banks and Loughton, in Epping Forest; Wallbury, near Bishops Stortford; and Ring Hill, or Starbury, Camp, near Saffron Walden, which may possibly have been defences against the Cassii, the large oval or rounded camps such as Uphall, near Barking (forty-five acres), Asheldham (oval, sixteen acres), South Weald (seven acres), Pitchbury Ramparts (oval, six acres), near Little Horkesley, a circular entrenchment and other slight works near Hatfield Broad Oak, and the semi-natural hill camp in Harlow and Latton parishes, may possibly be British. The settlements were probably thickest along the great trackways which crossed the county to Camulodunum (Colchester). We may accept one as following the general

---

[1] Sir J. Evans: "The numismatic evidence for identifying Colchester with Camulodunum seems overwhelming." More of Cunobelin's coins bearing Camulodunum, or abbreviations thereof, have been found here than on any similar area.

line of the present Colchester-Chelmsford-London road, and leading up from the Thames, where it communicated with the important roads to the south coast, through Essex to the country of the Icken, or Iceni. It seems also necessary to assume that Camulodunum and the British city of St. Albans were joined by a roadway, probably on the line of the Roman and still existing Stone Street, through Braintree, Dunmow, and Bishops Stortford. Beside these there must have been many local tracks leading through forest and waste from one settled area to another.

The settlements themselves probably consisted of groups of circular, timber-framed, wattle and plaster-walled huts, with high conical thatched roofs; there may have been a few larger, perhaps oblong, structures serving as communal buildings, the whole enclosed by a slight ditch and palisade. The royal houses at Camulodunum, however, may have been much more elaborate edifices.

Such was the Essex over which Cunobelin reigned for forty years, so far surpassing in glory and prosperity any native prince before his time that the memory of his splendour was carried down the centuries in chronicle and legend, until it was enshrined by Shakespeare in the story of the radiant Cymbeline.

Cunobelin died between A.D. 40 and 43, and was succeeded by his sons, Caractacus—or Caratacus—and Togodumnus. Somewhere about this time a dispute broke out which enabled the Emperor Claudius to interfere in the affairs of the island. Bericus, a British prince, driven into exile by an insurrection, appealed to Rome. Bericus has been identified with one VERIC. COM. F. REX.—" Veric son of Comius King "—probably ruler of the Atrebates of Hampshire, where his coins are found. But this is doubtful, and Professor Rhys and Sir J. Evans think Bericus possibly an expelled leader of the Iceni. Claudius determined to place Britain under Roman rule, and an expedition of four legions, with auxiliaries, crossed over from Gaul to the south coast in A.D. 43. The Britons, led by Togodumnus and Caractacus, avoided a decisive conflict, and clung to the shelter of difficult country. After some unsuccessful skirmishes they retired behind a river, where they were surprised and defeated in a two days' battle. The invaders then followed the Britons across the Thames, near its mouth, and in a fierce engagement, in which Togodumnus was slain, thoroughly routed them. Numbers of the Roman troops, however, were cut off in their too headlong pursuit, or were drowned in the marshes.

Although thus far successful, Aulus Plautius, the Roman general, now called for the support promised by Claudius should occasion arise. The Roman losses, the unshaken determination of the natives, and the risk of advancing inland in face of an enemy of unknown strength, were probably his reasons. Claudius accordingly landed in Britain with heavy reinforcements, and, joining the army on the Thames, marched against the enemy—who were assembled in great strength—and totally overthrew them. The site of this important battle was certainly in Essex. Its immediate result was the fall of Camulodunum and the submission of the Trinobantes and other neighbouring tribes. Claudius, after giving orders for their government and disarmament, returned to Rome, from which he was only absent about six months, and it is said that of this period he was only sixteen days in Britain—a fact which, considering the movements of large bodies of heavy infantry, points to good lines of communication and fairly open country.

With the years of campaigning that followed, when Vespasian, the future Emperor, gained his first laurels in the south-west, and Aulus Plautius pushed back the irreconcilable Caractacus beyond the Severn, we are little concerned. However, in A.D. 47, Ostorius Scapula took over the command, and the hostile Britons of the west seized upon the pause in operations consequent upon the change in leadership to raid the territory of the subdued and friendly tribes. After repulsing the raiders, Ostorius, besides throwing up a line of forts across the island, attempted to disarm some of the friendly tribes. The Iceni resisted, and a dangerous situation arose. Ostorius, however, stormed the camp of the assembled natives, and dispersed them with heavy loss. It has been suggested that this fight took place at one of the long earthwork dykes which run from the hilly north border of Essex down to the Cambridgeshire fens, several miles to the north, and which appear to be defences of the Icknield Way, leading from the Iken country to South Britain. This, and other disturbances amongst the Brigantes of Lincolnshire, showed the necessity of establishing a base on the east coast from which reserve troops could hold the subdued tribes in check while the army was in the west; and it was probably owing as much to this reason as to the orders of Claudius that the first colony of Roman veterans was founded at Camulodunum. The title of the colony, "Victrix," or "Victoria," seems to be derived from the twentieth legion, which took part in the Claudian invasion. This body of troops bore the cognomen "Valeria Victrix," and the fact that two inscriptions to centurions of the twentieth legion have been found at Colchester seems to strengthen the theory.

The exact relation of the "Colonia" to the British town Camulodunum has been greatly debated, but most probably the latter consisted of scattered settlements covering a large area of ground in rear of the great dykes at Lexden, and the Roman colony was planted practically upon the site later enclosed by the Roman walls at Colchester. The name Camulodunum is considered by Professor E. Hubner and other authorities to be derived from the deity Camulos, who, amongst the Gauls and Britons, was the god of war. Camulodunum may thus be translated as the Hill of Mars.

After the rising of the Iceni in A.D. 47, Essex enjoyed unbroken peace for fourteen years. We may assume the rapid Romanization of the district—the scientific construction of hard roads on the line of the rough British trackways ; the building of bridges and culverts ; the paving of fords, and the establishment of posting-houses, inns, and small military posts on the main roads, some of which were the beginnings of later populous towns. There was undoubtedly a steady influx of Roman or Romanized settlers, who were planted out on the confiscated territories as year after year went by and the Roman grip on the land and its late owners became more sure. Probably, too, each season saw an increased area under corn, which soon became an important article of export.

Londinium was swiftly rising to great commercial importance. Camulodunum was already an important Government centre, with large public buildings, Senate house, temple, theatre, and many stone and timber houses, built in the style adopted by the Romans for this northern province—a range of rooms opening from one side of a corridor, or arranged round a courtyard, and warmed by hot air. Settlements were springing up here and there near the roads, and throughout the district Roman civil officials, contractors, speculators, and financiers flourished amazingly.

During these years there was continual fighting in the west against the Silures. Caractacus had been captured and sent to Rome, but the struggle continued, and more than once the Britons achieved considerable successes. Ostorius died, worn out by the campaign, and there was a lengthy pause in hostilities, until under the great Suetonius Paulinus a determined effort was made to crush the resistance of the Silures. The four legions of the army of occupation were concentrated towards the west, the nearest to the east coast being the ninth, placed on the borders of the Iceni and Brigantes, perhaps in

Lincolnshire. Essex was thus devoid of troops, except for a few scattered detachments under the Procurator of the province and employed in the Imperial Revenue service. While Suetonius was overrunning North Wales the Eastern Britons made a last desperate effort for freedom. The extortion of the Roman officials had driven the Trinobantes and other subject tribes to desperation, and the treatment of Boadicea, or " Budicca," the widow of Prasatagus, King of the Iceni, showed the friendly nations who, like the Iken, had made terms with Rome, that, sooner or later, they would all be reduced to one level of subjection. Prasatagus, thinking to save a portion of his wealth for his family, had willed half of it to the Emperor ; but on his death his kingdom and palace were seized by the officials as spoils of war. Boadicea, his widow, was scourged when she protested, his daughters were outraged, and his relatives enslaved. The whole kingdom was overrun, and the nobles stripped of their possessions.

The Iceni rose in rebellion, and the Trinobantes and other peoples joined them. The first blow fell upon the veterans at Camulodunum, where the Romans had neglected to fortify the settlement. Tacitus thus describes its fall : —

"Meanwhile the statue of Victory at Camulodunum, without any apparent cause, fell down, and the face turned round as if she yielded to the enemy. The women, too, worked up to frenzy by their fears, prophesied that destruction was at hand. The circumstance of murmurs in a foreign tongue being heard in their Council Chamber; that their theatre rang with howlings; and that in the mouth of the Thames was seen the appearance of a colony in ruins; that at one time the ocean assumed an aspect of blood; and when the tide ebbed, the prints of human bodies were left;—all these things the Britons interpreted in confirmation of their hopes, the veterans of their fears. But, because Suetonius was at a great distance, they sought succour from Catus Decianus, procurator of the province, who sent them no more than two hundred men, nor these completely armed; and in the colony itself was but a small number of soldiers. The veterans not only relied upon the shelter and strength of the temple, but being frustrated in their measures by secret accomplices in the revolt, they neither protected themselves by a ditch and palisade, nor removed their women and old men, reserving only the youth for their defence. Unguarded, unprepared, as if in the midst of peace, they were surrounded by a host of the barbarians. Everything else in the colony was reduced to ruins in their fury, or was consumed by fire; but the temple, whither the soldiers had retired in a body, after two days' siege was taken by storm."[1]

This account, doubtless originating with the fugitives from the sack of the colony, shows that the gathering storm was not unobserved by the Romans, and we know also that Petilius Cerealis, commander of the ninth legion, hastened to the rescue, only to meet the insurgents fresh from the sack. His force was routed, the infantry destroyed, and Cerealis, escaping with some cavalry, was only saved by the shelter of his entrenched camp. The alarm spread rapidly. The Procurator, whose rapacity was responsible for the rebellion, fled oversea to Gaul; but a dreadful fate met thousands of Roman subjects for whom there was no escape. Fire and sword consumed Verulam (St. Albans), and doubtless numerous other smaller posts. Suetonius heard the news, and hastening by forced marches from the west, found London threatened by the enemy, and decided to abandon it. Some few of its inhabitants he was able to take with him; the rest perished with the city. Dion Cassius estimated that 80,000 of the Romans and their allies were slain.

Suetonius had only the fourteenth legion, the veterans of the twentieth, and auxiliaries, to the number of about 10,000 men, when he was confronted by the hordes of natives eager for his destruction. It is impossible to decide exactly where the great conflict took place. Tacitus simply alludes to the spot as a defile, or narrow valley, protected on rear and on both flanks by a thick forest, and opening out into a wide plain. Marks Tey and the vicinity of the Loughton or Ambresbury camps in Epping Forest have been suggested as Essex sites, and it seems

---

[1] *Annals*, xiv., 31 and 32. (Bohn's edition: Oxford Translation, 1854.)

very possible, at any rate, that the battle took place in the county.[1]

The Romans fought for some time, clinging to the shelter of their valley, and presenting only a narrow front to the enemy; but at last they charged out into the heart of the British masses, and routed them with tremendous slaughter. Many of the women and children of the natives were with their waggons in the rear of the battlefield, and all alike were included in a hideous carnage, the memory of which effectually prevented any further rising in the south for many generations. Boadicea, the soul of the movement, disappeared after this defeat. She may have been slain, or possibly she died by her own hand, and it can only be a picturesque legend which has connected her name with the great burial mounds at Bartlow.

With the failure of this great effort Essex and the rest of Eastern Britain passed finally into the power of Rome for well-nigh four centuries. Many a hard campaign was fought out amidst the wild hills and forests of the north, but the struggle left the south of the island practically untouched until the tide of Roman power began to ebb.

---

[1] Battle Bridge, or King's Cross, near London, is also traditionally the site.

ROMAN ESSEX

By Guy Maynard

HE large number of sites upon which Roman remains are found in Essex clearly shows that the district shared in the general prosperity which followed the Roman settlement of Southern Britain. No less than thirty-five churches are mentioned in Mr. Miller Christy's most useful *Guide to Essex* as having Roman tiles in their walls, showing that ruins of Roman buildings must have been adjacent when these churches were built. Archæological journals and museum catalogues contain references to the discovery of Roman remains in over one hundred and fifty parishes of the county, and no doubt this list could be largely added to, for it is certain that much evidence has been destroyed by carelessness and ignorance in the past.[1]

The part of Essex in the provincial economy was agricultural and commercial rather than official or military. As far as we know, it had no fashionable pleasure or health resorts, like Roman Bath, nor any great centres of learning such as flourished in Romanized Gaul; but it had upon its borders the most important commercial city of Britain— "Londinium"—which could not fail to influence the adjacent parts of our county through the country estates and villas of its wealthy citizens. Camulodunum, although

---

[1] " Probably the rural population was never larger than in the third and fourth centuries until its great development in the nineteenth."— Rev. C. Coneybeare in *Roman Britain*.

a place of official importance early in the Roman occupation, sank in relative position as the frontiers were pushed further west and north. It was not the standing headquarters of a legion, as was Cærleon or Gloucester; nor the seat of provincial government, like York; and, therefore, it had not the important public buildings and magnificent private residences of those places. Still, there is abundant evidence that Camulodunum was a wealthy and populous Roman town of the first class in the enormous quantity of Roman remains found there, and in the size and extent of its walls, which enclosed about 108 acres, and were one mile and three-quarters in circuit.[1] The date of these walls is uncertain. There are no inscribed stones to help to a solution; they appear to have been erected by local effort rather than by a large body of troops, who would have left some record behind them. They may have been built immediately after the Icenian rebellion; but it has been argued from the discovery within the walls of urn burials, with one of which was a coin of Domitian (A.D. 96), that they could not have been erected until after that date, as the Roman regulations against burials within walled towns were very strict.

The poverty of Essex in building stone makes the erection of these walls a remarkable achievement. The sea cliffs were quarried for the concretionary nodules of hard carbonate of lime, called septaria, which are found in the London clay. These were transported to the town and cut into rectangular blocks. Enormous quantities of thin bricks or building tiles had to be made, each of which, so it is said, taking in the various processes of moulding, burning, and drying quite five years to perfect. Ruined buildings were demolished to provide rubble for the

---

[1] For details of the Roman walls of Colchester, sketches, plans, and measurements, see Memoir on same by Dr. P. M. Duncan, *Essex Archæological Society's Transactions*, vol. i., 1858. Also Cutts' *History of Colchester*.

interior of the wall; and lime, pebbles, brick dust, broken tiles, sand, and grit had to be furnished in vast quantities and mixed together in careful proportions to produce the time-defying Roman mortar. The foundations—a dense mass of flints, septaria, and mortar, three feet thick and eleven feet wide—were carefully laid on the gravelly soil of the site. Above this the wall was built eight to ten feet thick and over twenty feet high. The facing of the wall was composed of four courses of squared septaria, separated by three courses of well-burnt tiles. On the west, south, and east sides the wall was backed by a rampart of earth. The north wall had no earth backing for some distance; but what is now low ground between the town wall and the river Colne was probably marsh, or covered by tidal waters, when the defences were built. The walls form an irregular parallelogram, about 1,000 yards east and west by 500 yards north and south. The north wall, facing the Colne, stands at the foot of the hill, and the enclosure slopes up the hill to the south. Away from the river "the hillside was scarped perpendicularly for ten feet, and faced with the wall eleven feet thick, below which the hill was again scarped to form a glacis and ditch."[1] The wall was then carried up above the earth backing for about five feet, and surmounted by a thinner parapet, with a crenellated top, thus giving a total height of about twenty feet.

The streets of Colchester still run partly upon the lines of the Roman ways through the city. One great thorough-fare crossed from east to west, and is still represented in part by the High Street. Another crossed from south to north, near the western end of the enclosure, on the line of Head Street and North Hill. This was probably the only main road through the town in this direction, owing to the position of the ford on the north side. There

---

[1] See Cutts' *History of Colchester* for account of Roman defences and antiquities. Also vol. i., New Series, *Essex Archæological Society's Transactions*.

were, of course, many other narrow streets or lanes cutting
the area into rectangular blocks of buildings. Near the
centre of the town, probably in and around an open space
at the crossing of the main streets, must have stood the
official buildings, Senate house, temples, and markets of
the colony. The statements of Tacitus clearly show that
several important edifices were in existence when the city
was sacked by the Iceni. The wall foundations of the
Roman houses and the tesselated pavings of their floors
have often been discovered buried a few feet below the
present surface. The want of good building stone is seen
in the absence of broken columns, capitals, or carvings
which can be recognized as parts of important buildings,
such as Camulodunum was bound to possess. It has been
suggested that the exteriors were finished with moulded
cement, as is known to have been the case with the great
Norman columns of St. Botolph's Priory Church. A
gilded bronze letter V, six inches long, and evidently part
of an inscription, may possibly have come from some
important edifice. The terminations of the main streets
were defended by arched gateways and guard-houses.
Parts of the main western gate, known from Saxon times
as the Balkerne Gate, still exist. It had a central arched
gateway, eleven feet wide, for wheeled traffic, with smaller
side entrances for foot-passengers, and was protected by
a massive semi-circular bastion containing two guard-
rooms. (A view of the remains of this gate is shown in
the accompanying plate.) The eastern gate was destroyed
in the eighteenth century, and the principal southern and
northern entrances have also disappeared. Beside these,
there were several smaller postern gates, which were
defended by square towers on the inside of the wall.
Additional strength was given to the south-eastern angle
of the defences by strong semi-circular bastion towers
built up against the outside of the wall. The wall itself
still remains in good condition for the greater part of its
circuit, rising to considerably over ten feet in height, and

THE BALKERNE GATE, COLCHESTER.

it is certainly in many ways the most perfect example of
Roman city defences now existing in Britain. Roman
pavements discovered outside the walls show that scattered
suburbs existed; and probably the wealthy citizens had
many villas in the neighbourhood. Beyond the gates also
were the cemeteries, fringing the road sides.

Very numerous Roman burials have been found on
either side of the London Road on the west, and near
Butt Lane on the south. As usual in Roman burials, the
cremated remains of the dead were contained in an
earthenware urn, which, with other vessels containing
offerings of food, drink, ointments, and perfumes, were
placed in a shallow pit. In some cases, to protect the
sepulchral vessels, large tiles were leaned together, forming
a roof, over which the earth was placed, or they were
enclosed in a square tile-built pit or in a wooden chest.[1]
In one remarkable burial a small tile chamber had been
built to contain a number of delicate glass vessels, and
then filled in with fine sand. One group, which numbered
thirty-seven articles of glass, Samian and other Roman
pottery, and a series of grotesque but well-executed figures
of men and animals in glazed clay and pieces of carved
bone, in addition to thirty-six middle brass coins of
Agrippa and Claudius, was contained in a chamber
carefully built of tiles. Coffins of lead have also been
found, and in the Butt Lane cemetery, where the coins
were of a late date, mainly of the Constantine group, many
burials had been made in large wooden coffins. These
indicate a Christian element in the population; but there
is very little supporting evidence, although the early
Church must have had many converts here by the time
of the Diocletian persecution (A.D. 303).[2]

---

1 See plates with Mr. Wire's article on " Urn Burials at Colchester,"
Journal British Archæological Association, vol. i. Also vol. v., C. R.
Smith on " Roman Urn Burials." Plate of typical tile tomb.

2 The discovery of a Roman pavement *beneath* Stanstead Montfichet
Church suggests that the absence of early Christian remains from Essex may
be largely explained by the building of later churches upon the sites of those of
the Romano-British period.

A few memorial inscriptions have been discovered at Colchester. The most important is the finely sculptured stone bearing the effigy of a Roman centurion, clad in richly decorated armour, and holding the staff of authority. Beneath is an inscription:—

M . FAVON · M· F· POL · FACILIS · > · LEG · XX · VERECVNDVS · ET · NOVICIVS · LIB · POSVERVNT · H . S · E —" *Marcus Favonius, ' Facilis '* [the good natured, or courteous], *son of Marcus of the tribe Pollia, a centurion of the* 20*th Legion. Verecundus and Novicius, his freedmen, placed this* [*memorial*]. *He lies here.*"

The centurion was evidently a man of wealth, by his freedmen dedicating such a beautiful memorial to his memory. The work has been pronounced by Hubner to be probably of the age of Vespasian.

Few relics connected with classic or pagan worship have been found. They comprise a series of small bronze statuettes of Jupiter, Mercury, Venus, and Apollo ; a bronze head of the disreputable Silenus, and a fine bust of Caligula, which may have figured in the rites due to the deified emperors ; and also a stone altar inscribed to the Matres Sulevæ, or mother goddesses, whose worship was common in the German provinces, and was evidently practised in Britain. A human-headed sphinx, worked in stone, has also been found, and it has been suggested that the sphinx was the badge or emblem of Camulodunum, as that creature occurs on some of Cunobelin's coins. Amongst the pottery and glass discovered are many pieces of interest, chief of which, perhaps, are the well-known Colchester vase, discovered many years ago—a black Caistor ware vessel, with raised figures of gladiators fighting, dogs chasing the stag, and what appears to be a combat between a barbarian and a wild beast (bear ?); and the beautiful embossed vessel of white glass now in the British Museum. The Colchester

Memorial to Centurion of the XXth Legion, at Colchester.

Museum contains, besides most of the objects before mentioned, a large and valuable series of Roman articles of personal and domestic use—bronze vessels, silver upon bronze mirrors, bronze fibulæ or brooches, rings, armlets, stylæ or pens, tweezers, iron tools, many types of bone pins, knife handles, iron and earthenware lamps, and pottery of all descriptions.

Much of the enormous quantity of Roman pottery found was locally made, as several baking kilns[1] have been discovered. But the bright red Samian ware, and some of the glass, was probably imported, the former from the Gaulist potteries; and it is proved that the Colchester potters imported the best productions of Italy to serve as models. The Upchurch potteries in Kent and the great potteries at Caistor in Northamptonshire also found a ready market in Camulodunum.

The town was most probably governed according to the common type of Italian municipal organization, with some special modifications relating to the subject native population.[2] The supreme magistrates were the two Duumvirs. There was an administrative council of one hundred—the Senate, chosen from the colonists, who were the dominant class. The important public officials were drawn from this body, which managed the ordinary business of the community; but it was subject to the veto of the Procurator of the Province or of the Emperor. Beneath the Senate were smaller administrative bodies, dealing with parochial business and religious celebrations; and doubtless local politics swayed men's passions as to-day, and on many a blank wall stood in paint-daubed letters the election addresses of the candidates. In the Vatican Museum is an inscribed stone of the third century, to "Gn Munatius M. F. PAL, Aurelius Bassus," a distinguished Roman, who, amongst many other offices,

1 *Essex Archæological Society's Transactions*, vol. i., New Series. Plates and article (Joslin).
2 Cutts' *History of Colchester*.

was "Registrar of the Roman Citizens of the Colonia Victricensis, which is in Britain, Camulodunum." [1]

We know nothing of the later story of Camulodunum; [2] but this brief account of its remains, culled from the records of many patient workers, may help us to a faint realization of the vanished city, as it stood far off through the dimness of bygone time, with its strong stone walls, red-banded with Roman tile; its massive gates and bastion towers; its busy streets, lined with low-built, tile-roofed houses; its public square, where stood the local Senate House, the district courts, the Basilica or meeting hall, the temples, and the banks; the market, where bargained men from every corner of the Empire; the shops, where the dainty glass and brilliant Gaulish pottery were set out before the tempted eyes of country visitors; the workshops of the craftsmen in wood and bone, bronze, iron, and gold; the well-built houses of the wealthy, elegantly decorated and furnished, and warmed by hot air in winter; and the narrow hovels of the poor. There was the joy of life and the traffic of the world within its walls; and day by day there rose beyond its gates the thick smoke of the funeral pyre, as yet another citizen passed to his last resting-place. On the roads were the swift chariots of the landholders and the heavy wagons of the farmers; and in the tidal river beneath the city walls were the broad-beamed corn barges taking in their cargoes for the mainland ports.

Let us turn to the general condition of Essex during the Roman period. We know that it was crossed by at least four main roads. The Icknield Street, from London to Colchester, and leading on to the Iken country of

---

1 Given in I. C. Gould's pamphlet on *Site of Camulodunum*, with Mr. Dalton's translation. See also *Essex Review*, vol. xii., plate and translations, pp. 233-8, and notes by W. G. Benham.

2 Space will not allow mention of the stories of King Coel, the marriage of Constantius with Helena, and the birth of Constantine the Great at Colchester. These seem to have no historical basis, except that Constantius probably did marry a British lady, and that Constantine probably was born in Britain.

GN·MVNATIVS·M·F·PAL
AVRELIVS·BASSVS
PROCAVC
PRAEFFABR·PRAEF·COH·III
SAGITTARIORVM·PRAEF·COH·I·ERMI·
ASTVRVM·CENSITOR·CIVIVM·
ROMANORVM·COLONIAE·VICTRI
CENSISQVAE·EST·IN·BRITTANNIA·
CAMALODVNI·CVRATOR·
VIAE·NOMENTANAE·PATRON·EIVSDEM
MVNICIP·FLAMEN·PERPETVS·
DVVMVIR·ALI·POTESTATE
AEDILIS·DICTATOR·II·I·

STATUE OF AURELIUS BASSUS IN THE VATICAN.

Suffolk; the Stane—or Stone—Street, from Colchester
to Bishops Stortford, and thence by Braughing, an
important Roman site, to St. Albans (*Verulam*); the
Via Devana—this term probably of much later date—
from Colchester up the Colne Valley, by Halstead,
Hedingham, and Haverhill to Cambridge, and thence
north-west to Chester. From London a road is thought
to have passed through Leyton, Harlow, and Bishops
Stortford to Great Chesterford and Cambridge. A branch
of the Ermine Street, the great London-to-the-North
highway, left Braughing, in Hertfordshire, and crossed in
almost direct line over the north-west corner of Essex to
Great Chesterford, where it took up the track of the
British Icknield way leading to Caistor, near Norwich.
A short portion of the raised mound of this road still
exists between Brent Pelham and Neasden, and a little
further on it is represented by a long, straight green lane,
now little used, between Butt Green and Cooper's End.

Mr. Napper claims a road from Caistor (near Norwich)
to Old Sarum,[1] which he considers was made by the
Romans to replace the British Icknield Way, which skirts
the north border of the county. He states that this later
road traversed Essex from Clare and Ridgewell (where
it crosses the Via Devana) in the north-east to Bishops
Stortford in the west, by way of Thaxted, and beyond
the county passed through Ware, St. Albans, Henley,
Reading, and Silchester. However this may be, the
following notes may be of interest. In some maps part of
the road between Steeple Bumpstead and Hempstead is
called High Street. This is in the general line of the
above road, and fairly direct through Wixoe and Baythorne
End to Clare. This High Street followed south-west
through Hempstead to the Radwinter-Sampford road,
not by the present road, but by bridle paths, which are
marked as wide lanes on old maps. It will be found to

---

[1] *East Anglian Notes and Queries*, vol. vi., N.S., p. 162.

nearly coincide with a narrow path known as Spooner's Lane, which leads to Little Brockles Farm. From Little Brockles Farm also a line of wide lanes and by-roads is marked as running westward through Wimbish Green, Elder *Street*, and Debden, and pointing to Newport, on the London-Cambridge road. Mr. W. Myhill, of Saffron Walden, whose family has long resided in the Hempstead district, informs me that in his youth Spooner's Lane was a very wide green road. I am also told by old farm hands in the district that their fathers have told them that in their own youth Spooner's Lane was used as a pack-horse road by which corn was taken to Bishops Stortford, *viâ* Henham and Stansted, where they struck the London-Cambridge road. Many of the parallel hedges marking these old road sites have been stubbed up in recent years.

From Chelmsford a Roman road seems to have run northwards, which, dividing near Little Waltham, sent a branch north-east through Braintree into the Colne Valley near Halstead, and continued on through Sudbury into Suffolk and Norfolk, possibly to Bury St. Edmunds, and to Caistor, near Norwich. The other branch continued northward through or near Pleshy, Dunmow, Thaxted,[1] and Radwinter,[2] to the county boundary at Bartlow. At Ridducks Hill, between the two last-named places, evidence of an ancient road of great width exists in the narrow meadows enclosed out of the roadside waste, and upon which quit-rents are still paid for encroachment; and in the presence of the old side ditches. Road ballast is also found in the fields by the modern roadside. There is still a tradition in the locality that "the great road came along there in the old days." Roman pottery has been found near this spot, which is not marked in Mr. Codrington's

---

1 From Thaxted very probably a road struck directly north-west through the Walden Valley to Great Chesterford.
2 Investigated by Mr. R. M. Christy, 1906.

Roman Roads in Britain. This road probably led into or across the Via Devana, just beyond the county border, and thus opened direct communication between central Essex and Cambridge, Godmanchester, and Leicester, and the direct roads to the north and west.

At Bartlow a road also came in from Great Chesterford, parts of which, still existing (1906) as a wide graded green lane on Great Chesterford Common, were pronounced by Richard, Lord Braybrooke, to be the finest example of a Roman road in the county. Such an important Roman centre as Billericay must have been well served with roads. Probably highways led through it from Tilbury to Chelmsford (or Cæsaromagus) on the one hand, and from the Shoeburys and Rayleigh across the Icknield Street to Ongar on the other. The long, straight High Roding Street is probably a surviving section of a Roman road, which, leaving London on the north, crossed the Lea at Woodford and passed through Ongar and Dunmow. Very probably it continued on through Finchingfield and Ridgewell to Clare on the Suffolk border. This appears to have been the track by which the relics of St. Edmund were in after years carried for safety to London from Bury St. Edmunds.

A well-made road ran from Colchester to Mersea Island, and beside the ways already mentioned there must have been a network of local roads of which little evidence remains except the occurrence of the significant term "street" and the discovery of Roman remains in localities distant from the main road lines. The accompanying sketch-map shows some of the suggested connections.

There has been much controversy over the site of five "stations" mentioned in the *Antonine Itineraries for Britain* (schedules of routes and distances compiled for the whole Roman Empire), which may safely be regarded as lying within Essex. The Roman mile was shorter by about one-tenth than the English, and the Roman mileage, too, was probably not strictly accurate; but the distance between Colchester (which, as the most important Roman town in Essex, we may identify with Camulodunum— Colonia, despite rival theories[1]) and London—fifty-two miles—corresponds so nearly to the mileage of the present direct road that we may assume the stations mentioned to have lain on, or near, the modern road line.

"Villa Faustini," a station mentioned in *Iter. V.*, has been placed at Dunmow, and Icianos identified with Great Chesterford by many writers, but the distances seem hopelessly at variance. Thus—*Iter. V.*, Colonia (Colchester) to Villa Faustini xxxv. M.P. (Colchester to Dunmow twelve miles!). Villa Faustini to Icianos xviii. M.P. (Dunmow to Chesterford fourteen miles!). And, worst of all, Icianos to Camborico (by most identified with Cambridge on name similarity) xxxv. M.P. (Chesterford to Cambridge twelve miles!). It thus seems very doubtful if these two stations can be claimed for Essex. (See Mr. Napper, "Is Cambridge Camborico?" *East Anglian Notes and Queries*, vol. viii., third series, p. 84.)

The Ninth *Iter.* starting from Venta Icenorum, identified with Caistor, near Norwich, and passing to London, gives the stations as follows. In the parallel column are the sites now generally accepted for them:—

---

[1] See *East Anglian Notes and Queries*, July, 1894, p. 287, for Mr. Beaumont's Great Chesterford-Camulodunum theory. This places the stations between London and Camulodunum along the Ermine Street to Royston, and thence to Great Chesterford along the Icknield Way. A modification of the theory would be to travel from the Ermine Street at Braughing, along the recently re-established straight road to Great Chesterford. Exact correspondence of the distances is the basis of this theory.

See also the late Mr. I. C. Gould's pamphlet in reply to above, *The Site of Camulodunum*, containing summary of arguments for Colchester, and statements of original authorities. Also Mr. Napper's paper, *East Anglian Notes and Queries*, vol. vi., N.S., p. 161, for his theory that Camulodunum was at Heybridge-on-Crouch, and that Colonia was re-established after the sack by the Iceni, not on the same site, but at Colchester, Camulodunum and the Colonia of the Itineraries thus being separate places. The evidence of the British occupation of Heybridge is very slight compared to that of Colchester. (See *ante*.)

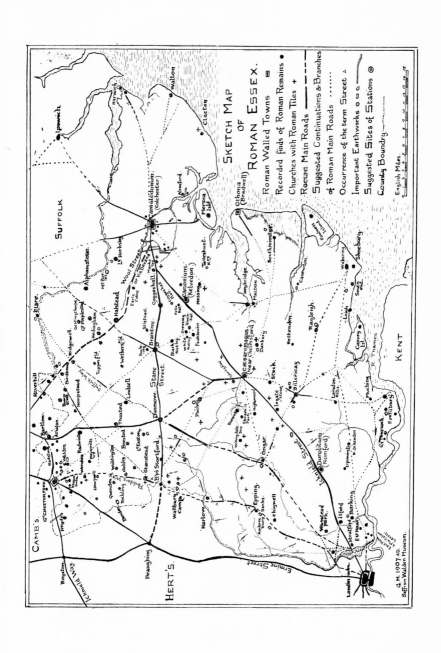

SKETCH MAP
OF
ROMAN ESSEX.

Roman Walled Towns ▣
Recorded finds of Roman Remains ●
Churches with Roman Tiles +
Roman Main Roads ▬
Suggested Continuations & Branches
of Roman Main Roads ┈┈┈
Occurrence of the term Street ∴
Important Earthworks ○○○
Suggested Sites of Stations ◎
County Boundry ▬▬▬

English Miles.

G. M. 1907 A.D.
Saffron Walden Museum.

A Venta Icenorum		From Caistor to			
Sitomagus M.P.+	XXXII	Thetford	32 miles		
Combretin	XXII	Brettenham ...	22 ,,		
Ad Ansam	XV	Stratford S. Mary	15 ,,		
Camulodunum	VI	Colchester... ...	6 ,,		
Canonium	VIIII	Kelvedon	9 ,,		In Essex.
Cæsaromagus	XII	Near Chelmsford (Widford?)	12 ,,		
Durolitum	XVI	Romford	16 ,,		
Londinium	XV	London	15 ,,		

M.P.+ = M.P.M.?

Millia plus minus = miles, more or less, approximate distances.

Too much importance must not be placed upon this series of names, as, except Camulodunum, some may have been only small posting stations, or examining posts connected with the Inland Revenue. Besides the five stations, there must have been a multitude of settlements of whose name no trace remains, but of which evidence exists in the many sites upon which Roman objects are discovered. Reference to the map which accompanies this article will help the reader to appreciate the widespread character of the Roman remains which have been found in Essex, more detailed reference to which is impossible in the space at our command. The sites marked are probably incomplete, but they serve to show the general distribution of the population. Among notable Roman "finds" we may mention one made at Terling, near Witham, which revealed a deposit of gold and silver Roman coins, with two gold rings. To the south-east of Icknield Street is Mersea Island, connected with Colchester by a Roman road, and this island has yielded tesselated pavements, urn burials, and Roman coins. Billericay was evidently a populous site, and there many urn burials have been revealed, and much broken pottery and coins. Along the Essex shore of the Thames estuary Roman sites are numerous. The foreshore near Tilbury is in places lined with broken Roman earthenware. At Gray's Thurrock a

broken bronze bust of Jupiter was unearthed, and a Roman
pavement ; at East Tilbury, a Roman causeway ; at West
Tilbury, pottery ; at Low Street Manor Way, Roman urn
burials and Samian pottery. Similar deposits were
found at Mucking Creek, and the eastern spit of Canvey
Island has yielded Roman pottery, while a Roman amphora
was dredged up off Leigh. At Bradwell, of course, there
is the site of a walled fortress (Othona ?). Records of
these and many other traces show that the coast-line was
well occupied in Roman times, particularly where the low
shore was, perhaps, not so submerged as it now is. Indeed,
Mr. Spurrel came to the conclusion that the low shores
were thickly populated for a long period and then
abandoned, and that when re-populated in Saxon times
submergence had reduced the available area.

The north-west section of the county seems to have
been a thickly populated area, and has yielded perhaps a
larger quantity of Roman remains than any other district
of Essex, except the immediate vicinity of Colchester and
London. Great Chesterford, on the north boundary of the
county, although not so large a Roman town as Colchester,
was certainly a place of importance. All trace of its
defences has vanished ; but we know that it was a walled
town from the notes of Dr. Stukeley, who described the
foundations in the eighteenth century. The wall was built
of flints and banded with Roman tiles, and enclosed
about fifty acres. Notes by eighteenth century writers
point to some of the suburbs outside the main walls having
also been defended by walls or ramparts. Dr. Stukeley
saw a bare place in the corn, caused by buried foundations,
which he thought probably those of a temple.[1] He states
that numerous Roman pavements then existed within the
walls, and that vast quantities of Roman coins were found
there. Dr. Foote Gower also mentions a network of
Roman roads in the vicinity, and states that the lines of

---

[1] Stukeley, *Itinerarium Curiosum*, 1776. Also letter to Roger Gale,
1719.

the streets within the station could still be traced.[1] Between
1848 and 1860-1, the Hon. R. C. Neville, afterwards
fourth Baron Braybrooke, thoroughly excavated the site.
The foundations noticed by Stukeley proved to be those
of a building 105 feet long, consisting of two end blocks
forty-nine feet wide, joined by a central range forty feet
in length. The end blocks each contained two rooms
about twenty feet square, one of which had a hypocaust,
or heating vault, sunk into the ground beneath the room.
The floor was supported by massive columns of flint. In
one room traces of a plain red tesselated pavement were
found. The central range contained four rooms opening
out of a corridor on the south-west side of the house.
The heating furnace was outside the house wall, and the
hot air passing into the vault or hypocaust was carried by
two lines of hollow flue tiles the length of the house,
warming both central rooms and corridor. The main
walls, about two feet eight inches thick, were of chalk
blocks, alternating with courses of flint. The angles were
turned with well-burnt tiles. The rooms had been
decorated with brilliant and well-executed paintings on
the wall plaster, fragments of which were found, showing
among the designs red roses and other flowers arranged
on a trellis work, and also draped figures dancing. The
building occupied a central position at the west end
of the town, and probably was the residence of some
important official or wealthy townsman.[2] Like all others
excavated in the county, it was probably a single-story
building. In the parish of Ickleton also, rather less than
three furlongs distant from the above site, and just across
the county border line, the investigators uncovered the
foundations of two important Roman buildings—one a

---

[1] *Journal British Archæological Association*, vol. v., giving list and
direction of Roman roads around Great Chesterford.
[2] Plans and details of buildings and finds, *Journal Royal
Archæological Institute*, vol. vi., p. 14. *Ibid*., p. 181. Also Roach
Smith and Neville's Report, with plans and cuts, *Journal British
Archæological Association*, vol. iv.

villa over 100 feet long, with end wings 70 feet in
length. There were more rooms than in the station villa,
and there were two hypocausts. The other, a hall 78 feet
by 36 feet, was evidently a public edifice of some kind.
For plans, with plates of " finds " and a valuable article,
see *Journal Royal Archæological Institute*, vol. xvii,
pages 117 and 158. In these buildings were found
the remains of very young children, buried close to
the walls, a circumstance explained by the statements of
Juvenal and others, " that infants were interred without
cremation under the eaves of their parents' dwellings."
In several cases miniature earthen vessels[1] were found
with the bones, apparently copies of the larger vessels
buried with adult persons. It was evident that the houses
had stood thickly outside the town walls, for not only
was the soil in some places literally sown with small
bronze coins and broken pottery, but numerous wells and
filled-up rubbish pits[2] were cleared out, and found
to contain enormous quantities of broken Roman
earthenware and glass, and also some bronze articles,
remains of the ox, horse, sheep, red deer, pig and domestic
fowl, shells of oyster, whelk, and mussel, clear evidence
of the food of the population.

Near the church was found a large square excavation
in which was carefully buried a remarkable series of iron
articles—chariot wheel tyres, many iron axle, yoke pole,
and other carriage fittings; plough coulters, scythes, turf
cutters, hammers and anvils, locks and keys, iron wall
hooks—perhaps for harness—and a quantity of
elaborate and splendidly worked cabled chain.[3] A terrible
six-tailed scourge, formed of plummets and linked rings

---

[1] For plate and details see *Journal Royal Archæological Institute*,
vol. x., p. 21 ; also vol. vi., p. 21.

[2] *Journal Royal Archæological Institute*, vol. xii., p. 109, for list of
pits and finds (plates).

[3] See Memoir of this find, *Journal Royal Archæological Institute*,
vol. xiii.

of bronze wire, was discovered in foundation diggings, with a coin of Theodosius the Great. Five cemeteries,[1] yielding many urn burials, were discovered by Mr. Neville, and in the Saffron Walden Museum is a small plain Roman coffin of lead, also found here. The remains of a pottery kiln were found near the river,[2] and some of the pottery may have been locally made, but specimens of Caistor, Upchurch, and Samian wares were numerous. Stukeley thought that he detected the circular track of an amphitheatre in one of the cornfields. In the British Museum is a stone trough, with relief busts of Mars, Venus, Mercury, and Jupiter, found here.

About a mile east from Great Chesterford the foundations of a small Roman building, forty feet square, were uncovered by Mr. Neville in 1847.[3] It comprised one square room, surrounded by a corridor, which may have been divided into separate rooms. In the outer corridor was part of a fine mosaic pavement in five colours, with an interlaced scroll pattern border. The central apartment also contained a square decorated pavement, with a rayed sun for centre, enclosed within a blue and white border. Four miles north-east from Great Chesterford a remarkable series of Roman buildings was explored by Mr. Neville. In the parish of Hadstock, where a mosaic pavement had already been found, he excavated the ruins of a villa, which must originally have been of great extent—possibly one of the larger courtyard type of Romano-British houses. The remaining portion was over eighty feet long, and, from the area of the broken ground from which the foundations had been dug for road-mending, it had evidently been of great extent. The rooms had plain tesselated floors ; there was a large

---

1 *Journal Royal Archæological Institute*, vols. xiii., xiv., xvii.
2 For notes by Neville on Roman pottery found in this district see *Journal Royal Archæological Institute*, vol. x., p. 224—plates and list of Samian potters' marks.
3 *Royal Archæological Association Journal*, vol. iii.

E

hypocaust, and two large baths. The painted wall decorations also were of a very superior class.[1]

In full view of several undoubtedly Roman sites in the parish of Ashdon stands perhaps the most remarkable group of Romano-British burial mounds in the Eastern Counties—the Bartlow Hills, an old drawing of which forms the frontispiece to this volume. Agriculture and the Great Eastern Railway have sadly disfigured the mounds and their surroundings, but the records of careful investigations by Lord Maynard, Lord Braybrooke, and other competent archæologists between 1832 and 1840 enable us to realize the importance and extent of this unique burial-ground.[2] Originally it comprised a row of four large circular mounds, the largest forty-two feet in height, and the others a few feet less. Parallel with these was a row of much smaller mounds, four, or perhaps more, in number. For centuries tradition had indicated these tumuli as the resting-place of those slain in the great battle of Assingdune, between Edmond Ironsides and Canute the Dane, in 1016. When excavated the mounds in every case yielded Romano-British burial deposits of great importance, and they may be accepted as the tombs of persons of great wealth and rank.

On the ground level, in the centre of the largest barrow, was found a small chamber, originally lined with timber, and containing the funeral deposit. There were glass vases, bottles, and phials, containing traces of unguents; two bronze strigils—articles of the bath equipment used to remove moisture from the limbs; a bronze hand lamp, with a magnificently worked acanthus leaf for hand guard; a fine bronze patera with fluted handle, terminating in a ram's head; a graceful bronze pitcher, inlaid with bands of silver line ornament; the bronze frame of a folding chair or seat; a globular bronze

---

1 Plans and details, *Journal Royal Archæological Institute*, vol. viii., p. 27; also vol. x., pp. 9 and 22.

2 See Reports with plans, plates, etc., in *Archæologia*, vols. xxv. 1-23, xxvi. 300-17 and 462-3, xxviii. 1-6, xxix. 1-4.

vessel, ornamented with red, blue, and green enamels, and having a square gilded handle, certainly one of the finest enamelled objects known from the Roman period. The cremated bones of the occupant of the tomb were contained in a large glass bottle fifteen and a half inches high, seven and a quarter inches square, and five inches diameter of mouth. With this there were also a few earthenware vessels. The remaining three large hills yielded surprisingly similar rich deposits, as did also the row of smaller mounds. The end barrow of the lesser row contained a sarcophagus built of Roman tiles; and here also the cremated remains were found in a large glass bottle. They were immersed in a yellow liquid, and accompanied by a second brass coin of Hadrian (A.D. 117-138) and a gold ring with an intaglio bearing the design of two bearded ears of wheat—a symbol found on some of the coins of Cunobelin and Tascovanus.[1]

In 1815, Sir Busick Harwood had opened the most northerly of the four large mounds, and discovered a quantity of pottery, a bronze paten, an iron lamp, and a small sickle-shaped iron knife. Most of the pottery was dispersed, but the metal objects and one small earthenware vase eventually came to the Saffron Walden Museum, where they remain. The valuable collection obtained by Lord Maynard from the other hills was most unfortunately destroyed by fire at Easton Lodge in 1847. The wreck of the unique enamelled vase is exhibited with a restored model in the British Museum. Models and a complete series of full-size drawings of the " finds," together with a large view of the " Hills " in their untouched condition (which forms the frontispiece of this volume), are exhibited in the Saffron Walden Museum.

---

[1] For account of Rings found in these Roman villas, etc., see article by Lord Braybrooke, *Essex Archæological Society's Transactions*, vol. ii., Old Series.

A long stretch of earthwork exists between the hills
and the adjacent stream, which forms the county
boundary. Possibly the tumuli were originally surrounded
by an entrenched enclosure.[1] Within one hundred yards
of the north-east base of the mounds in Church Field
Lord Braybrooke excavated the foundations of a Roman
building[2] about forty-five feet long, with a hypocaust,
cemented floors, decorated wall plaster, and moulded wall
skirtings; skeletons with coins of the later Emperors were
discovered, and Roman pottery and coins are still found
near the site.

The records of Lord Braybrooke and others show that
almost every Essex parish north of the Stane Street has
produced some vestiges of Roman occupation. The Colne
Valley has many Roman sites on or near the Via Devana.
Sible and Castle Hedingham produced a Roman mirror
of silver on bronze, and other remains. Great Maplestead
has a Roman cemetery,[3] and Roman urn burials are found
at Alphamstone and Great Horkesley. Bronze fibulæ
and other Roman objects have been discovered at Marks
Tey.[4] The central and western parishes of this large
area also provide many Roman records.

On the north-west border of the county Lord
Braybrooke excavated a chamber[5] sunk into a hill-top
at Heydon, and which contained a chalk-built altar and
much broken Roman pottery, bullock bones, etc. At
Elmdon and Strethall Roman coins and pottery have
turned up; and a barrow in Langley parish contained
fragments of Roman glass. At Arkesden was found a

---

1 See *Essex Archæological Society's Transactions*, vol. vii., New Series,
p. 349 (Goddard).
2 *Journal Royal Archæological Institute*, vol. x., plans, etc., p. 19;
also p. 357.
3 *Essex Archæological Society's Transactions*, vol. v., New Series,
p. 69.
4 Plates in vol. xi., *Essex Archæological Society's Transactions*, Old Series.
5 Plans by J. Clarke, *Journal British Archæological Association*,
vol. iv.   Report by Neville, *British Archæological Association Journal*,
vol. v.

terra-cotta figure of a woman with two infants, emblematic of fruitfulness; and Romano-British and Samian pottery. At Ring Hill, the British camp opposite Audley End Mansion, a gold coin of Claudius and a silver patera were found. Grymes Dyke Wood entrenchment, near Saffron Walden, recently surveyed, but as yet unexplored, may quite possibly be the site of a British or Romano-British village; Lord Braybrooke records Roman pottery from the farm on which it is situated. At Little Walden, and quite near to this site, was found a Roman burial deposit, comprising a very fine embossed or pineapple pattern vase of thin white glass, an iron lamp, iron spear-heads, and a number of well-executed bronze lion-headed studs, probably belt or shield mountings; a set of corroded iron hinges showed that the objects had been enclosed in a wooden box.

Besides the foregoing and other authenticated " finds," much valuable evidence has been wantonly destroyed in the past; but enough remains to show how widespread and complex was the population of Romanized Essex. And when one looks out from the crest of the chalk range across the Cambridgeshire border, the tale is still the same. At the foot of the hills runs the Icknield Way,[1] once lined with British burial mounds. Eight miles away across the level edge of the fen country looms up the Gog-Magos, crowned by the great double-ditched British Camp of Wandlebury; and far over the lowland to the north, where on the clearest days one may see the towers of Ely dimly against the flat horizon, the eye rests upon a country seamed with Roman roads, and upon numerous spots which have yielded evidence of British and Roman occupation.

The foregoing evidence proves that there was a considerable civilized population, not only on the

---

1 See Mr. Beldham's article on " Icenhilde, or Iknield Way," vol. xxiv., *Journal Royal Archæological Institute;* also Codrington's *Roman Roads in Britain.*

north-west border of the county, where the chalk hills
rise clear of the heavily wooded clay deposits of the south,
but also along the main road lines, where the present open
country probably originated in chains of British forest
clearings, and many of the present towns in British or
Roman settlements. The coast also was well occupied,
and where the roads converge upon London and Colchester
we may assume a thickening of the population. We may
picture the settled districts as studded with low-built but
substantial villas, which were furnished and decorated
with the essentials of comfort and art demanded by
Roman taste. It is noticeable that the Essex " villas,"
although in several cases of considerable size, cannot vie
with those of the south and west of Britain; no traces of
such magnificent residences as the villas excavated at
Woodchesters or Bignor having been found in our county.
Perhaps its exposed position on the pirate-haunted East
Coast may have been responsible. Those decorated
mosaic pavements discovered, while usually well designed
and executed, are also not of the highest order. Except at
Wansted Park, we meet with no classical or mythological
subjects, such as Orpheus and the beasts, which have been
found elsewhere, and the Essex pavement-makers seem to
have limited themselves to conventional geometric designs.
The occupants of the villas were probably wealthy
landholders, seated in the midst of their farms or estates,
and busily engaged in corn-growing and cattle-raising.
The red deer and the wild boar of the woods gave them
sport and provender. They had shell-fish fresh from the
coast. Their wants in clothes, ornaments, and utensils
were supplied by the traders and craftsmen of their local
town; or, at the worst, it was only a ride of a few
hours over good roads to Verulam or Camulodunum, or
Londinium itself. These landholders were probably in
most cases the descendants of the earlier settlers who were
poured into the island. Some natives of Italy, many,
however, from distant provinces, were Roman in nothing

but their citizenship; an extremely mixed population thus tended to arise, complex not only in blood, but in worship. Often the Romanized Briton identified the classical divinities with his own tribal deities; thus we get " Mars-Camulos," a joint Romano-British war-god. After A.D. 312 the population was probably Christian in name at least, but Christianity was not the only faith which came to Britain from the East, for Mithra and Isis are known to have found worshippers here, and the strange subterranean altar at Heydon was far more probably devoted to an Eastern than a classic worship. In every district there were sure to be a few true Romans in the magisterial, revenue, and military conscription service, who formed the exclusive set, and within whose villas was to be found what culture the district possessed, and who were more or less in touch with the contemporary life of Rome. Beside the farming class we must assume the existence of traders and artizans, provision dealers, smiths, builders, painters and decorators, leather workers, weavers, and potters, who made up the town populations; while all centres of any size probably had their bands of public guardians, police, night watchmen, and firemen, under some form of military organization.

The Bartlow Hills seem to indicate that as late as the reign of Hadrian there were wealthy native families in the district. It is improbable that Romans of sufficient wealth and culture to demand such elaborate funeral deposits would have chosen to be buried under these enormous mounds of earth without a line of durable inscription to preserve their name and rank, rather than in an inscribed stone sarcophagus or beneath a graven memorial pillar, after the orthodox Roman manner. On the other hand, it is far more probable that the wealthy British families who survived the conquest rapidly acquired the Roman fashions in household furniture and possessed themselves of the rich vessels which were buried with them in tombs of their own ancestral type. It has been suggested that the difference in size between the two rows of mounds marks two periods in the history of the family buried there—an earlier and very important period, and a later time when the British magnates had sunk to social obscurity. The uniform nature of the deposits, however, does not seem to support this.

The subdued British tribesmen, of whose frail dwellings no trace remains, formed the lower strata of the population. We may assume that the tribal sub-divisions were adopted by the Roman governors for local administration and taxation purposes, and to some degree survived the Roman occupation. But there was inevitably a vast gulf between the cultured British aristocrat who had embraced the learning and life of Rome, and the sullen cultivators of the fields, who stubbornly clung to their old faiths, and who, off the main road lines, lost little of their racial purity, and were to the last regarded with contempt by their masters and the Romanized townsmen.

Quiet as was the average life of Roman Essex, we must not assume that its roads never rang to the shrill music of the clarions, or the tramp of a marching legion. There was always the disturbing possibility at the back of men's minds that the intermittent struggle with the northern tribes might at last endanger the very existence of the civilized society of the south. Seldom a generation passed without a series of frontier disasters, which occasionally culminated in such disorder and raiding of the northern districts and alarm in the south that some great general or the Emperor landed with an army to quell the disturbance and re-garrison the frontier works, and then peace would ensue for a few decades. There was also a nearer danger. With any eastward shift of the wind the sea line might be crowded by the black sails of the Saxon pirates. The revolt of Carausius, admiral of the fleet maintained in the Channel to keep these raiders in check, showed the danger of entrusting the security of Eastern Britain to a navy manned by allies, and thus, after the re-establishment of the authority of the Emperors in Britain, Constantius Chlorus, representative of Diocletian, erected a chain of forts along the south-east coast from the Wash to the shores of Surrey. The chief of these works appears to have been the walled fortress of Othona, confidently identified with the Roman site at Bradwell,[1] in Essex, where three sides of the defences can still be traced, and where many Roman remains are found. These eastern defences and their garrisons were commanded by a " Comes Littoris Saxonici," or Count of the Saxon Shore, who was probably also entrusted with revenue duties, as he had two " Numerarii," or revenue officers, and many officials on his staff. He was under the general orders of the Comes Britanniarum, or Count of the Britons, *i.e.*, the commander of the field army, who was responsible to the general commanding the forces in the western part of the empire (Master of Foot in the West).

Indirect and scattered references to South-east Britain proves that the fourth century was anything but a period of unruffled calm. We read of highway robberies, armies unpaid, and soldiers deserting. Again and again the Picts and Scots broke across the heavily garrisoned frontier, and as the century closed disaster followed disaster. There had been heavy but successful fighting in the north in A.D. 360; but in 367 the northern tribes came across the Wall of Hadrian in such numbers that they penetrated to the gates of London itself. The Duke of the Britons (commanding the northern frontier force) and the Count of the Saxon Shore were slain, the sea rovers were busy on the coast, and there was very heavy fighting in the south before Theodosius, who came with two legions and a horde of

---

1 *Journal Royal Archæological Institute*, vol. xxiii. ; also *Essex Archæological Society's Transactions*, vol. vi., for " Othona and rank, duties and staff of Count of Saxon Shore." See also Roach Smith on Othona, with sketch at base of wall, and other forts of the series. *Collectanea Antiqua*, vol. vii., pp. 152-69.

auxiliaries, was able to sweep out the raiders.[1] It looks as if some of the Britons themselves may have sided with the invaders in this crisis. Following this, the policy of garrisoning the eastern coasts with German mercenaries was tried, for a time with success. At the first opportunity, however, Pict, Scot, and Saxon swooped down again, and at the close of the century the great Stilicho was obliged to send a legion to the rescue of the Province. But the tide of misfortune was only checked. The Roman authority in Western Europe was gradually disappearing. Not Britain alone, but every other Province of the Empire was ravaged by the northern barbarians. Britain itself was the battle-ground of rival pretenders to the imperial power. There were fierce dissensions between the Romanized townsmen and the more primitive country people when the Roman army of Britain was withdrawn to the defence of Italy; and when, after Rome had yielded to the Goths, some semblance of order returned, Britain, like Gaul and Spain, was practically severed from the Empire. Essex was one of the areas to receive the first fury of the barbarian onslaught in that dark period of which so few facts and so many theories exist. Although the district officials were no longer sent from or appointed by Rome after 409, yet the upper classes of the population spoke Latin and called themselves by Roman or Romanized names, and tried from their own circles to keep the machinery of local government in motion ; and probably it is due to the defences and organizations left by Rome that the extinction of civilization in Eastern Britain was a matter of many years and not of months.

One fact seems clear—there was no parleying, no treaties, no mutual arrangement such as was reached between the Teutonic invaders and the Britons of the west

---

[1] *Ammianus Marcellinus*, quoted by T. Hinde : " Having scattered and put to flight the invaders, Theodosius restored in their integrity the cities and forts which had suffered great damage, but which were constructed for permanent defence."

in later years, when Christianity had formed a bond of understanding between the two races. In Essex, if anywhere, the theory of the total destruction of the Roman and all his works holds good. We do not know when it was that the Saxon keels drew up-stream to the walls of Colchester, or when the smoke of burning homesteads marked the progress of the war bands through the valleys of North Essex; but the violent end of those Roman buildings which have been excavated is unmistakable. The smashed-up mosaic pavement, the broken and buried wall paintings, the torn-down walls and filled-up well are significant of the last chapter in the story of Roman Essex.

The precise degree in which the lower orders of the Romano-British population were expelled, slaughtered, or enslaved is very uncertain. Probably from the first there was a considerable Romano-British element in the new population. One can only accept the broad fact that the Roman social organization was destroyed, and that, within a century, large areas, well cultivated in the security of the peace of Rome, had reverted to waste and forest; and that the only remains of the Roman rule in Essex were the neglected roads, the ruined country mansions, and the slowly decaying walls of the deserted towns, to which, in a few cases, some memory of the past clung in their Saxon names, as in Colonia Ceaster (transformed later to Colneceaster and Colchester), and Ythanceaster, the Saxon version of Othona. But usually all trace of the Roman name was lost, as at Chesterford, where the ruins which frowned upon the Saxon horseman as he splashed through the shallow waters of the Granta became simply " the Ceaster by the ford."

THE FOREST RECORDS OF ESSEX

By Rev. J. Charles Cox, LL.D., F.S.A.

IT will surprise all, save students of forest law, to learn that at one time, within historic days, the whole of the county of Essex was forest, and known as the Forest of Essex. Such a term, however, by no means implies that the whole of Essex was continuously wooded. The word "forest" had originally no connection with woods, but simply implied a waste place. In the later Saxon days a forest signified a considerable tract of country, reserved for the king's hunting, and subject to special laws. Such tracts always included a considerable amount of open or moor land, which was as necessary for the due sustenance of the deer as were the coverts or woods for their shelter. In some of these royal forests the woodland was extensive, as was the case in the New Forest and Sherwood. In others, such as Dartmoor, Exmoor, and the High Peak, there were but fringes of woodland on the outskirts or in the deeper dales.

If we desire to know, after a rough fashion, the amount of woodland of any county in early historic days, two sources of information are open to us, both of which are fairly infallible, namely, local nomenclature and the Domesday Survey. With regard to the first of these, it will be noticed, on looking at an ordinary map of the county, that the terminal "field" occurs to the left hand, or west, of a line drawn from the north of the county through Halstead, Coggeshall, and Maldon, and thence in a sloping line to the west to Tilbury in the south. This term, it is hardly necessary to explain, always implies former woodland; the Anglo-Saxon *feld* was a forest clearing where the trees had been felled. The following places occur to the left of the line just named: Bardfield, Broomfield, Canfield, Finchingfield, Fyfield, Gosfield, Hanningfield, Hatfield, Panfield, Shenfield, Springfield, Toppesfield, and Wethersfield. This list might be considerably extended if the names of farmsteads and closes on parish maps were studied. There is one exception in the position of these names, for there is a Bradfield on the estuary of the Stour. It is, too, in the western half of the county that such names as Ashdon, Birchanger, Brentwood, Buckhurst, Broadoak, Elmdon, Hainhault (originally Hainholt), High Beech, Maplestead, Theydon Bois, Woodford, and Woodham occur.

The Domesday Survey is always of much assistance with regard to the distribution of woodland in the days of the Confessor and the Conqueror, because the Commissioners seem to have invariably entered the number of swine that fed in the woodlands on the different manors. Judged by this standard, the south-west of the county was a heavily wooded district in the eleventh century. Waltham, Loughton, the three Theydons, Woodford, Leyton, and Navestock had a great abundance of acorns and beech-mast, on which the swine fed. The two Ongars, Norton Mandeville, Greenstead, Thorndon, Blackmoor, and adjacent manors also offered abundance of woodland for the sustenance of the pigs. North of these places we come to what was then the most densely wooded district of all Essex, lying to the west of the county between Bishops Stortford and Dunmow, with Hatfield Broad Oak on the south and Saffron Walden to the north. Thus Takeley and Elsenham fed between them 3,500 swine, Stanstead 1,200, Little Easton 800, and Hatfield Broad Oak 820.

Mr. Round, in discussing at length this question of the early woodlands of Essex in vol. i. of the *Victoria County History*, says: "Broadly speaking, if we draw a line north and south through the county from Haverhill to Tilbury-on-Thames, we shall find that the great bulk of the woodland lies to the west of it." This result is very similar to that which we have already drawn from a study of the place-names.

Domesday Survey contains no reference to the Forest of Essex, save in mentioning the promotion of a swineherd of the manor of Writtle to the position of forester of the King's Woods. There can be no doubt that a great deal of the county was royal forest under the later Saxon kings. There is a curious rhymed charter, of which there is a copy, *temp.* Henry VIII., in the British Museum, purporting to be a grant by Edward the Confessor of the office of keeper of part of this forest to Randolph Peperking and his family. Morant, the historian of Essex, long ago pronounced this charter to be a forgery, as the language is that of the fourteenth century. It is, however, quite possible that this rhymed rendering is a free translation, in the vernacular of that period, of a genuine Anglo-Saxon grant. The Conqueror and his immediate successors brought the whole county under the extreme severity of forest-law, save perhaps a small portion to the north, beyond the great Roman road. The pressure of public opinion, even in those rough days, brought about the disafforesting of certain parts, both by Henry II. and John.

The Forest Charter of 1217, granted by the council of the boy-king Henry III. in return for special privileges, brought about the disafforesting of all that had been added to the royal forests after the coronation of Henry II. in 1154. The perambulation of Essex was not completed until 1225, with the result that about three-fourths of the county was ruled to be outside forest jurisdiction, leaving only the district of Havering, which had been demesne land of the Crown from the earliest known days, and the districts of Romford and Waltham, as forest proper. However, Henry III., with great audacity, upset this scheme in 1228, alleging that the perambulating knights had blundered in several particulars. It was claimed that much of the disafforested parts had been old forest in the time of Henry I., which had lost its rights during the civil upheavals of the reign of Stephen, and had merely been restored to the position of royal hunting grounds by Henry II. In 1250 the king had foresters, verderers, regarders, and woodwards in the Hundred of Tendring in the extreme north-east, as well as throughout the whole of the centre and south-east of the county. Right through this long reign, and the greater part of that of Edward I., these boundaries were maintained; but in 1301 Edward I. consented to another formal perambulation of the county, with the result that Essex was once more freed from the burden of forest laws, save in the south-west corner, after much the same fashion as the original decision in 1225. Certain parts of the ancient demesne of the Crown which were separate from the forest of Waltham— such as Hatfield Regis, Writtle, and Colchester—were declared, by the decision of 1301, to be only royal chases and warrens, and therefore merely subject to the common law of the land.

The forest of Essex, from the beginning of the fourteenth century, was known as the forest of Waltham; it is only in our own days, now that the area is so much more restricted, that it has taken its name from the little town of Epping. It was the confusing custom, in this county as elsewhere, during the Plantagenet and Tudor times, to occasionally use the names of certain outlying parts, or even integral portions, of a main forest district as if they were complete in themselves and under independent jurisdiction. Thus we find mention, in different forest proceedings, of the forests of Chingford,

Hainhault, Havering, Kingswood, Loughton, and Theydon; but each of these was in reality a part of Waltham Forest, and administered by the same chief officers.

The Forest Courts were of two kinds. In the first place there was the Forest Eyre, or Court of Forest Pleas. This was a court called into being by the King's Letters Patent, by which justices were appointed to hear and determine pleas of the forest in a particular county or other special area. Shortly before the Eyre was held, Letters Close were directed to the sheriff as to its business; he was ordered to summon (1) all dignitaries and other freed tenants who had holdings within the meets of the forest; (2) the reeve and four men from every township within the meets; (3) all foresters and verderers, both those then in office or those (and their heirs) who had held such office since the last Pleas; (4) all those persons who had been " attached " since the last Pleas; (5) all the regarders; and (6) all the agisters.

The proper interval between these forest courts is supposed to have been seven years; but in practice the intervals were usually much longer, and very capricious. The amount of business transacted at these Eyres was very considerable, and usually involved many adjournments. The proceedings were, roughly speaking, divided into two parts, namely, the pleas of venison and of vert. In both cases the chief object of the proceedings was the collection of fines for breaches of the forest law. The old Norman severity of forest punishments disappeared under the Forest Charter of 1217. Under that charter a man might be imprisoned for a year and a day; but in practice any offender caught by the foresters and imprisoned was speedily released on bail, and bound over to appear at the next Eyre. It was very rarely that the justices in Eyre imposed any term of imprisonment. The fines were

imposed in accordance with the position of the offender,
varying from very heavy penalties laid on noblemen,
gentlemen, or holders of benefices, to mere trifling sums
from the yeoman or labouring classes. In not a few
cases the justices of these courts forgave the offender
all fines on the score of poverty. In case of
non-appearance at the Eyre, the delinquent was eventually
outlawed by the Coroner, after the due preliminaries had
been fulfilled.

The "Swaynmote," or Attachment Court, was one
of local administration, which, if regularly kept, as
ordered by the forest charter, had to meet every
forty-two days in each of the several bailiwicks or
wards (afterwards termed walks) into which a forest
was divided. The object of the court was to receive
the attachments or presentments of the foresters and
woodwards, and to enter them on the verderers' roll.
As to the forest officials by whom these local courts
were administered, the chief local authority was the
master-forester, keeper, or warden, who was generally
known by the last of these names in Essex. The warden
or his deputy usually presided over the Swaynmote, and
he had considerable perquisites and privileges. The
verderers were forest officers directly responsible to the
Crown, by whom they could be removed for inefficiency;
but, like coroners, they were elected by freeholders in
the County Court. They were always men of some local
position, and frequently knights. They had no salary,
but usually certain perquisites; in Essex, each verderer
received a buck in the summer and a doe in the winter.
It was their duty to sit as judges at the various local
courts. There were naturally many verderers when the
forest of Essex was almost coterminous with the
county. In 1250 the Essex verderers numbered eighteen,
namely, two for most of the hundreds, and three in
one or two cases. In 1285 they numbered fifteen. After
the limitation of the forest area in the beginning of

F

the fourteenth century, the number of the verderers was reduced to four. In the Swaynmote Court the verderers were judges in all vert cases of the value of 2d. or under—a sum which was afterwards raised to 4d.

The foresters were usually appointed by the chief forester or warden. They were sworn to preserve the vert and venison in their own divisions, and they had to attach offenders and present them at the forest courts. Anyone found by them in the forest with bows and arrows, snares or dogs, was to be arrested, even if he had not been actually seen to hunt or kill the deer. The grant of the wardenship of Essex forest to Richard de Montfichet in 1252 included the right to appoint and remove all foresters. Besides these ordinary foresters, who were usually paid at the rate of 2d. a day, there were in many districts foresters-in-fee, who held hereditary office, and had the charge of certain bailiwicks or divisions. In the thirteenth century there were three of these hereditary foresters, usually termed riding foresters, who had considerable perquisites in the way of wind-fallen wood and other payments in kind.

Another set of forest officials were the regarders. The regard, or view, of the forest had to be taken every three years by twelve or more local knights, who had to draw up answers to a long set of interrogatories which covered almost every possible particular as to the condition of the forest demesnes. They were bound to draw up complete rolls of the *assarts*, or unlicensed enclosures, of waste, as well as of purprestures, or encroachments made by the building of houses or the like. These officials were revived during the irritating procedures of 1630, when the regarders actually made more than four hundred presentments, including such matters as the building and digging pits on the waste, and leaving lanes encumbered with woods and bushes, so that the king would be hindered if he came a-hunting.

The earlier forest records show that there were roe-deer in this county, as well as red and fallow. The elegant little roe-deer never seems to have been abundant, but the mention of them occurs on a few rolls of the thirteenth, fourteenth, and fifteenth centuries. Some remains were found when digging the reservoirs of the East London waterworks at Walthamstow. Their antlers and bones also came to light in excavating the remains of a Roman villa in West Mersea in 1897. The roe had apparently disappeared from the county before Norden wrote his *Description of Essex* in 1594. It was successfully re-introduced into Epping Forest by Mr. E. M. Buxton, from Dorsetshire, and there is now a small herd.

The fallow deer, which, according to the best writers, was introduced into Britain by the Romans, may fairly claim to have been a continuous native of the county for at least sixteen centuries. When the Corporation of London took over the charge of Epping Forest in 1871, the fallow deer of the forest had dwindled down to five or six brace of deer and a single buck. It is said that they now number about two hundred. In 1495 the fallow deer of the open forest numbered only forty, but in earlier times they were far more numerous. The wild fallow deer of Essex are comparatively small in size, and are of a uniform dark-brown or almost black colour; they have also very attenuated antlers, and all these points are said to be marks of the antiquity of the stock.

The hardier red deer, undoubtedly indigenous to England from the earliest days, bred freely in the Essex forests, but their numbers considerably decreased towards the end of the fifteenth century and onwards. The last of the wild red deer were removed from Epping Forest to Windsor in 1827. An effort was made about 1880 to restore red deer to Essex by bringing back some from Windsor; the effort was not, however, successful, for they did such damage to the crops on the adjacent farms that they soon had to be destroyed.

Interesting records have lately been brought to light showing the damage done to sheep, and even to a colt, by wolves in Derbyshire forests during the thirteenth century, and in Cannock Forest, Staffordshire, as late as 1281. It is supposed that they did not actually die out in England until the time of Henry VII. The last wolf was killed in Scotland in 1743, and in Ireland in 1770. No entries have hitherto been found concerning the wolf in any records of the forests of Essex; but that it was once fairly common in the densely-wooded districts is shown by the discovery of its remains during the construction of the Walthamstow reservoirs. There is also other evidence of the presence of wolves in the county in the charter of lands granted by the Confessor in 1062 to Waltham Abbey. Mention is made of a wolf-pit in giving the boundaries of land in Weald, and of a wolf-leap in the boundaries of Elverton. The name of the manor of Wolfhampston, Barking, has obvious reference to the animal, and in a forest roll of 1277 there is presentment for wasting a wood called Wolvesgrave. Search among the field-names of Essex has resulted in the discovery of about a dozen names in the west of the county which are obviously associated with this former wild beast.

The wild boar, as distinct from the semi-domesticated swine—turned out in certain seasons in such large numbers to feed in the Essex forests—existed in Essex until at least the sixteenth century, and possibly somewhat later. References to the hunting of the wild boar in the times of John and Henry III. are fairly frequent. Its remains are abundant in the peat at Walthamstow. There is an interesting entry in the muniments of Colne Priory, quoted in the *Essex Note Book* of 1885, to the following effect:—

" The survey of the lordshipps and manors of Earls Colne and Colne
Priory, parcels of the possession of Richard Harlackenden, made in *anno
domini* 1591 by Israel Amyse Esq.—Chalkney Wood—this wood in tymes
past was impaled and the Erls of Oxenforde in former times for their
pleasure bredde and maintayned wilde swyne in the same untill the reigne
of King Henry the Eight.   About which time they were destroied by then
Erle of Oxenford, for that he understode that the inhabitants thereabout
sustained by them very great loss and damage."

Although the hunting of the deer was most strictly
reserved to the Crown and the forest ministers, royal
licenses were not infrequently granted within forest
areas for hunting the inferior game, such as the fox,
hare, and wild cat.   The Close Rolls and Charters cited
at the Forest Pleas of the thirteenth and fourteenth
centuries give much information on this subject.   King
John in 1200 granted to Richard Gosfield and his heirs
the right to hunt the fox, hare, and wild cat within
Essex Forest, but to limit the number of his hounds
to eight braches, or brackets (which was the general term
for dogs which hunted by scent), and to two harriers.
In 1212 the same king granted leave to the son of
the Earl of Arundel to hunt hares in Essex; whilst three
years later there was a grant to the steward of Waltham
Abbey to hunt hares and foxes.   Waltham Abbey had
been empowered by Richard I. as early as March 14th,
1190, to hunt fox, hare, and cat; this hunting charter
was successfully maintained by the abbot and canons
to the end of their days, and afterwards by the successive
owners of their lands, as late as the days of Charles II.

The Abbess of Barking held an ancient prescriptive
right of pre-Conquest date to hunt the same animals
in the adjacent forest.   Both the Bishop of London and
the Dean and Chapter of St. Paul's claimed rights to
like hunting when passing through the forest.   Among
other claims that were also made good at the Forest
Pleas of 1292 were those of Thomas Huntercombe of
a right of free chase through the whole forest with two
greyhounds and four brackets; and of George Rodney,

as lord of Walthamstow Toney, to hunt with eight
harriers and twenty brackets. The first of these cases
was limited to the fox, hare, and cat, and to these in
the latter case was added the badger.

So far as the deer were concerned, royalty was
usually fairly generous in the making grants of forest
venison. Occasionally the religious orders had special
grants of deer to be taken yearly, as in the well-known
case of Westminster Abbey, where the abbot received
eight deer yearly from the forest of Windsor on the
vigil of St. Peter ad Vincula. King John in 1199
granted to the Knights Templars the right of taking
three harts yearly from the forest of Essex, by view
of the foresters. A yearly grant of three bucks in the
winter and three does in the summer was made to the
Abbot of Waltham by Richard II. Edward IV. granted
to the Abbot of St. Mary's, Stratford, two bucks and
two does yearly within the forest of Waltham, but only
for his lifetime.

Among the occasional grants of venison from this
forest there are instances in which permission was given
to take live deer for the stocking of private parks.
The largest of such recorded grants from Essex occurred
in the time of John, when the king granted forty live
deer to Roger de Bigod; about the same time there
was a grant of twenty-two live deer to William, Bishop
of London. The Bishop of Ely had license from
Henry III. in 1225 to take twelve live deer from the
forest of Essex; but it would seem that the deer were
already getting comparatively scarce in this county, for
the bishop was told that if he could not obtain them
in Essex, he might secure them from the forest of
Rockingham, in Northamptonshire. There was another
grant from the Crown in the same year to Thomas de
Multon of ten does and one buck, to place in his park
at Kelvedon.

The last direct royal gifts of Essex venison were those of Charles I. In 1639, when the king issued orders for distribution of fat venison to the foreign ambassadors, the French Ambassador received a buck from Woodford Walk; the Venetian Ambassador one from Epping Walk; the States Ambassador one from Chingford Walk; one from Walthamstow Walk for the Duke of Florence's agent; two for the King of Spain's agent from West Henalt and Chappell Henalt Walks; and two for the Queen and Crown of Sweden's agent from Loughton Walk and New Lodge Walk, which were all sub-divisions of Essex Forest. In the following year, in the schedule of Christmas venison supplied to Charles I. at Whitehall, occurs the mention of a hind from Loughton Walk, showing that there were then a certain amount of forest red deer in the county.

The deer of Essex, as well as those of other royal forests throughout the country, naturally suffered much during the Commonwealth disturbances. On the re-establishment of the monarchy, various measures were taken to re-stock several of the royal forests. In addition to presents and purchases of foreign deer from over the seas, several English noblemen and country gentlemen united in presenting the king with three hundred head of deer, which were distributed among the parks of Windsor, the chase of Enfield, and the forest of Waltham.

Next in importance to the venison rights of a royal forest came the vert rights, which included everything relative to the woods and the pasturage. In every royal forest there were a certain amount of woods, or plantations and parks, which were in the hands of private owners, but under considerable restrictions. The fences, as a rule, although high enough to restrain cattle, were to be made in such a manner as would permit the free egress and ingress of the deer. Nor might the owner

do anything, save under license, which might be held
to annoy or disturb the deer. Thus unlicensed felling
of timber was forbidden, as well as any clearing away
of undergrowth for sale, the burning of charcoal, or the
erection of furnaces for smelting.

The owners of woods were bound to provide an official,
termed a "woodward," whose duties were somewhat
similar to those of a forester, for he had power to
attach or apprehend any venison and vert trespasser, and
had to take an oath of obedience to the forest officials
at the time of his appointment. In Essex, the Abbess
of Barking was bound to provide five woodwards, sworn
to the king, of the five great woods of Alfrefen,
Hyneholt, Gaysham, Alesereth, and Henylegh, which
were declared at the Forest Pleas of 1292 to belong to
her house and manors. If woodwards were not
appointed, or neglected their duties, the woods were
seized into the king's hands. Several of the Essex woods
were thus seized in the thirteenth or fourteenth centuries;
they could only be recovered on payment of a fine. In
the Essex Forest there was also a king's woodward, with
two assistants; these offices continued to exist so long as
any forest courts were held. Their chief duty consisted
in superintending the exercise of the various rights
possessed by the forest tenants of lopping the trees,
etc. Such rights of a general nature were far more
extensive in Essex than in other forest districts, and
hence the necessity for special officials, which are but
rarely found elsewhere. The Essex Crown woodwards
had also to mark with the broad arrow the "spear"
trees (*i.e.*, the standard trees left when a coppice was
felled for future growth), which were not to be
pollarded; and to cut timber or trunks of dead pollards
for the repair of footbridges, gates, and fences. In
later times they were employed in lopping the trees,
particularly the hollies, to provide food for the deer
during severe weather.

The vert of the forest, sometimes called by the old English word "greenhue," included every kind of tree, even such underwood as blackthorn, whitethorn, or hazel. The cutting of any kind of timber or undergrowth without license was an offence; the fines for such trespass were but small, unless the wood was cut for sale. The claims, however, of special grant by charter, or long established custom, to lop and cut trees for burning on their own hearths, or for mending their hedges and enclosures, as well as their houses, were commonly claimed in most of the old forest manors of Essex by the freeholders and general inhabitants. The law-suits as to these claims throughout the seventeenth and eighteenth centuries, when most of the old forest legislation had become a dead letter, were endless. This was particularly the case throughout the extensive manor of Loughton.

Apart from the beasts of the forest and chase, every forest district had its quota of domestic animals feeding, regularly or occasionally, within its bounds. Such animals were the property of the tenants of the forest or its purlieus, and were, as a rule, subject to the oversight and direction of special officials termed the "agisters." Swine were only allowed to roam in forests during the season called "the time of pannage," when they fed upon the acorns and beech-mast which had then fallen. The mast season, strictly speaking, lasted from 14th September to the 18th of November; but it varied somewhat in different forests. The usual agistment fee was a penny for each pig above a year old, and a half-penny for every pig above half-a-year old.

The agistment of a limited number of horses, more particularly of mares with colts, was common throughout England; but this custom was strictly limited, and under a comparatively high fee. Sheep were, as a rule, severely restricted within forests, as the deer—especially the red deer—refused pasturage where sheep had fed. Flocks of sheep were, however, suffered to feed in certain

clearly defined parts of Essex or Waltham Forest,
subsequent to the limitation of its bounds in 1301. The
turning out of goats to pasture upon forest wastes was
considered a dire offence, because by tainting the pasture
they effectually drove away the deer. If found by the
forest ministers, they were liable to be seized, without
redress, in addition to the fining of the owner.
Nevertheless, there were frequently found within the
wide forest areas those who attempted to set this
regulation at defiance. At the Essex Justice Seat of
1323-4 there were divers presentments for the keeping
of goats (fifty-six in all) on the forest contrary to the
assize.

The cattle belonging to the various forest parishes
of Essex were entitled to feed upon the wastes; but
in order to duly restrict their numbers in proportion
to the tenancy, and to ensure their only feeding upon
wastes specially assigned to particular parishes, no cattle
could be turned out unless duly marked with the parish
brand. Several of these old branding irons are still
extant, and some of them are reproduced in our
illustration. In every forest the " fence month " (in
Latin, *mensis vetitus*) was observed. It lasted from
fifteen days before Midsummer to fifteen days after,
and was the special time when the deer required quiet
and protection, as it was the usual time for fawning.
During this month every kind of agistment was, as a
rule, forbidden, or, if permitted, at least a double fee
was levied to restrict the numbers. Double fees (*i.e.*, of
two shillings) were charged throughout Waltham Forest
for impounding cattle in the fence month. The charge
during the time they were in the manor pound was a
shilling a day, and after seven days they were cried,
at a further charge, in the three market towns of
Romford, Waltham Abbey, and Epping. If not then
owned, they were sold by auction.

A- *Waltham Holy Cross*

E - *Epping*

C - *Chingford*

K - *Barking*
(*Maypole*).

K - *Barking*
(*Crooked Billet*).

H - *Chigwell*

L - *Dagenham*

O - *Walthamstowe*

Q - *Wanstead*

ESSEX FOREST CATTLE BRANDS.

In several forests, notably that of Essex, there was also a regular winter interval, somewhat variable in duration, when all agistment was prohibited for the purpose of preserving the food for the deer; this was called the "Winter Heyning."

Among the various restrictions with which residents in a forest area had to comply, was the old custom of lawing of dogs. The Forest Charter of 1217 provided that an inquisition of the lawing of dogs was to be held every third year, and he whose dog was then found unlawed was to be fined in the heavy sum of three shillings. The charter provided that this mutilation of dogs, to prevent them chasing the game, was to consist in cutting off the three claws of the four feet without the ball. The right to have unlawed dogs was occasionally granted by the Crown to persons of position and influence. Thus the canons of Waltham had this exemption granted them by Richard I., so far as house-dogs were concerned; they successfully supported this claim by showing their charter at the Forest Pleas of 1323-4. At the same time, Stephen, Bishop of London, and the Dean and Chapter of St. Paul's, successfully maintained a like privilege by showing a charter of John.

In some forests it was maintained that this lawing was only intended to apply to mastiffs; but the officials of Waltham Forest always reported to the courts every kind of unlawed dogs. Out of one hundred and forty-seven presented as late as 1630, eighty-five were "mongerels," forty-one mastiffs, nine greyhounds, six spaniels, three hounds, and three "stucklecurrs."

When the advisors of Charles I. were foolish enough to attempt to raise money by reviving the obsolete jurisdiction of forest courts, the boundaries of the Essex or Waltham Forest were again perambulated, and declared to be practically the same as those of 1301. Four years later the Crown officials excited much indignation by attempting to extend the forest area for the purpose of raising more money. Failing in this, an attempt was made, which was also defeated, to secure its disafforestation and sale. In the first session of the Long Parliament an Act was passed to fix the boundaries, and a perambulation showed that Waltham Forest comprised about 60,000 acres.

The machinery of the forest laws, so far as the local courts were concerned, was maintained, with some degree of strictness, far later in Essex than in any other part of the kingdom. It was in active operation until about the close of the eighteenth century, and certainly had the good result of preventing encroachments either by lords of the manor or far humbler folk.

Mr. Wellesley Pole (afterwards Lord Mornington) became hereditary Lord Warden in 1812 in right of his wife. This gentleman, as Mr. Buxton, the present verderer, puts it, "saw that more profit was to be made in breaking his trust than keeping it." He refused to support the authority of the verderers, and did everything he could to bring the forest laws and customs into contempt. Eventually he sold the very rights he had been appointed to guard.

In the middle of the nineteenth century wholesale enclosures began, which resulted in the complete destruction of the ancient woodlands of Hainhault, and their conversion into arable land. Steam ploughs were actually attached to the roots of the old oaks, including the "Fairlop Oak" of ancient memory, in order to effect a complete clearing. This ruthless conduct brought about a reaction, and after a legal contest extending over fifteen years, in which the Corporation of the City of London played a prominent part, the preservation of 5,500 acres of Epping Forest—as it is now termed—was secured for the enjoyment of the public. Certain local rights were also re-established. By this victory, which was won in 1874, the management of the forest was vested in a committee consisting of twelve members of the Court of Common Council and four verderers. The latter have to be resident within the forest, and are elected by the commoners.

Essex has the distinction of being the only county which has a good monograph on its forest history. A quarto volume, entitled *The Forest of Essex*, was produced by Mr. W. R. Fisher in 1887. This scholarly work was chiefly based upon investigations undertaken by Mr. Fisher as a barrister whose advice was sought by the Corporation of London in their long litigation. It is now rarely to be met with, and has long since been out of print. Since that time further attention has been given to ancient forest procedure, and those who are interested in the question will find Mr. Turner's work, *Select Pleas of the Forest*, printed by the Selden Society in 1902, of great value and interest. The writer of this article may perhaps also be permitted to refer to his briefer but more general work, *The Royal Forests of England*, published in 1905.

ANCIENT CHURCHES OF ESSEX

By T. M. Grose Lloyd

THE mediæval churches of Essex are not of a universal type, but in many districts there are groups of churches that have a general resemblance, especially in details. This resemblance is very generally due to their environment— viz., the local requirements, resources, materials, and workmen employed. Facility of carriage of materials was an important factor in the task of building our ancient churches. Many fine churches owe their existence to wealthy patrons, as Thaxted to the Clares and Mortimers, and Dedham to the Webbs. Speaking generally, we may note that churches away from the highways and routes of commerce, or in outlying and rural districts, are mostly small and plain, as in the Rodings. Several of the churches in the Stour Valley are influenced by, and partake of, the Suffolk type, and some in the north-west district resemble those in the adjacent counties of Cambridgeshire and Hertfordshire.

As no building stone is quarried in the county, this has to be imported; hence the general meagreness of the masonry, which is only used for windows, doorways, columns, arches, quoins, etc. The walling is largely of flints, rubble, conglomerate or "pudding stone," tiles, or bricks. Flints are wrought into voussoirs, or arch stones, at Little Bardfield; conglomerate is wrought into voussoirs at Inworth. Red brick is a distinct characteristic of Essex churches; indeed, there are not

Greenstead Church.

many churches in the county which do not contain brick or tile in their construction. Moreover, it occurs at all periods—*e.g.*, in Saxon at Holy Trinity, Colchester; in Norman at St. Botolph's Priory, Colchester; in Early English at Little Coggeshall; in Decorated at Pebmarsh; and in Perpendicular at St. Osyth's. Brick window-tracery is frequently used, and terra-cotta window-tracery occurs at Elmstead and Little Totham.

The red-brick towers are a unique characteristic of Essex; there is not such a fine group elsewhere. There are a few brick porches in the adjacent counties, evidently copied from Essex examples. The porch of Feering is vaulted in brick; the tower of Sandon is domed over in brick; and Chignal Smealy is built entirely of brick, even to the font. There are several brick nave arcades, parapets, niches, etc. In fact, it may be said of Essex that the timber towers and turrets, and the brick towers, are the most characteristic features of its churches. As a rule, the roofs are covered with lead or tiles (the use of slates is, of course, modern); doubtless many were thatched, as some still are in East Anglia. The wood towers and turrets are often covered with shingles—*i.e.*, tiles of cleft oak. About half the churches in the county were built without aisles, and to-day there are more north than south aisles. Several aisles have fallen, and the arches are now blocked up, as at North Shoebury. A few churches end in an apse. Langford is the only church in England having an apsidal west end. The east apse has been demolished. Some churches originally had no chancel arch, and modern ones have been added. There was sometimes a tympanum as well as a screen to mark the division between nave and chancel. None of these tympana remain, but there are evidences of their having existed, as at Asheldham.

Only a few of the cruciform churches have central towers. The towers are nearly always at the west end, and project from the nave. The irregular towers are

Eastwood, which is at the west end of the south aisle; Elmstead, on the south side of the nave at the west end; and Stisted, which is at the east end of the south aisle. Some churches have lost their towers, as at Hempstead.

Although there are some magnificent Essex churches, the majority are small; but if wanting in architectural effect, they are enjoyable to the antiquary, and intensely fascinating to the ecclesiologist. There is hardly a church without some interest. Six churches have their round towers remaining, and several towers of this kind have been destroyed. Little Maplestead is the smallest, and latest in date, of the five remaining circular churches in England.

Having said so much by way of general introduction, we may now note, in some detail, architectural work of the various periods still to be discovered in our Essex churches, beginning with examples from Saxon days. In this connection reference may be made to the series of volumes on Essex churches which was projected by that earnest and careful student, the late Mr. Ernest Godman, whose early and lamented death prevented the completion of his admirable effort. His books on Norman and Mediæval Architecture remain to show how rich the county is in examples of those periods. It is to be hoped that the series so well begun may yet be completed on the lines Mr. Godman laid down. Our own notes, in the limits of a comparatively short article, must necessarily be of the briefest character.

With Christianity possessing some hold over the Essex people during the latter part of the Roman occupation, and, later, the splendid missionary labours of St. Cedd, brother of St. Chad, and Bishop of the East Saxons, the story of the Church in Essex goes back to very early days, isolated memorials of which are still visible here and there in our most ancient churches.

ASHINGDON CHURCH: SAXON TOWER.

SOUTH OCKENDEN CHURCH: ROUND TOWER.

First of all, as to the Saxon work, or work of Saxon type, of which several remains exist, and more may yet be discovered. Greenstead-juxta-Ongar is the only remaining wooden-walled nave in England of this period. The walls are of half-round trunks of oak, set upright, like a palisade, with the round part outside. As the tops and bottoms of these logs, which vary from 8 in. by 6 in. to 18 in. by 9 in., were decayed, sills and heads were added to them in 1849. This nave is about thirty by fifteen feet, and the walls about seven feet high. The body of King Edmund of East Anglia rested in this church on its return to Bury St. Edmunds in 1013 (*vide* Dugdale's *Monasticon*). The lower part of the tower of Holy Trinity, Colchester, with the semi-circular tower arch and triangular-headed west doorway, is Saxon, constructed of Roman brick. The nave of Tollesbury is Saxon, and is built of flint, rubble, and tiles. The walls of Hadstock and Chickney are probably Saxon. Great Hallingbury has a Saxon brick chancel arch; Strethall has a stone chancel arch, and the nave has the characteristic " long and short " quoins The tower arch of West Mersea is also Saxon.

The Norman period—which may be reckoned as the time extending from the Conquest to the end of the reign of Henry II.—is very richly perpetuated in our county. Indeed, the number of Essex churches that were either built or rebuilt at the end of the eleventh and during the twelfth centuries is extraordinary; probably one half of the churches in the county contain some sort of Norman work, although very little that is elaborate or of special interest. Waltham Abbey is, of course, far and away the finest example of this period that we now have in the county. The nave columns are ornamented with chevron and spiral grooves, doubtless copied from Durham Cathedral. The vaulting of the aisles has been removed, as also have the sub-arches of the triforium (this is the only triforium in the county). The clerestory

G

appears intact, but the transepts and chancel have been
destroyed. Rainham is the most complete church of
this period. The east end of its chancel has been
carefully restored, and the chancel arch has the chevron
ornament. The north and south aisles are divided from

WALTHAM ABBEY: DETAIL OF ARCHES AND PIERS.

the nave by massive piers, of three bays, with scalloped
capitals and banded angle shafts. The curious vesica
piscis-shaped clerestory windows are unique, and the
priests' doorway is very fine.

Among the best specimens of this style, the following
churches are worthy of inspection: Belchamp Otten, the

south doorway of which has spirally worked shafts; the north and south doorways of Great Bentley; and Blackmore, the west bays of which have angle shafts to the piers. Great Canfield is a small, fine, and almost perfect church. There is a recess containing a good fresco of the Virgin and Child between the windows in the east end of the chancel. The massive chancel arch has a billeted hood mould. On the west jamb of the south doorway are carved five Fylfot crosses. Faces are carved on the capitals, and the tympanum has concentric rows of zigzags. The priests' doorway of Castle Hedingham is the largest and richest of its class. Great Clacton has a wide aisleless nave, with springers for transverse arches; the chancel has been altered, but the north doorway is unrestored. Copford has springers for transverse arches on the north side of the nave (the south aisle is of the Decorated period); but the point of greatest interest in this church is the very fine frescoes which cover the entire apse and walls. In a buttress on the north side is a tile measuring 23 in. by 22 in. Corringham has a good, sturdy west tower.

St. Botolph's Priory Church, Colchester, was ruined in 1648, but part of the west front, with its fine recessed doorways, above which are two arcades of interlacing arches, still remains. The nave arcades exist in a ruinous condition; all is of Roman brick. Elsenham chancel arch has chevron and other carvings on it. The south doorway has shafts spirally ornamented. The lintel of the tympanum is on a level with the necking of the capitals—an unusual arrangement, which causes a heavy effect; the tympanum is carved with the star ornament. The lintel inside is formed of a coped stone coffin lid.

Of all our Essex churches, that of Finchingfield has the richest west doorway (an illustration of it is given herewith). The tympanum has been removed and the space is now a fanlight. The three richly-carved recessed arches are shafted, the cushion

capitals being ornamented. On the north jamb is a
representation similar to a Lacy knot. The lower part
of the tower, too, is good, the north-west angle being
worked into a spiral angle shaft. The jamb of the
internal west arch has interesting fragments of Norman
carving built into it; but the chief features are the arched
recesses, with carved capitals to the dividing columns
on the east, south, and north sides inside the tower.
The east recesses probably contained altars.

Hadleigh has an apsidal chancel, and the chancel
arch is flanked on the north and south sides with recesses
for altars. This arrangement is frequently met with in
churches of this period, as at South Shoebury, Inworth,
and other places in the county.

At Hadstock the impost of the south transept and
the north doorway have large, yet shallow, ornament of
uncommon design. This north door once had a human
skin stretched on it, a fragment of which is now in
Saffron Walden Museum. The proportions and technique
of the nave walls are of Saxon type. The doors at
Copford and Castle Hedingham once had human skins
on them. East Ham has an apsidal chancel, and there
is a chevroned interlacing arcade in stone on the north
side of the choir. The west doorway is boldly but
plainly moulded. Heybridge has diapered tympana
above the north and south doorway, and the latter has
the remains of rich " C " iron hinges; the handle plate
is very good. The chancel arch of Inworth is plain,
and is flanked on the north and south with altar
recesses; but these are now pierced, and form squints
to the altar. At Great Leighs the round tower of the
church has a circular-headed doorway. This is a rare
occurrence, although circular-headed windows in round
towers sometimes occur.

The north doorway of South Ockenden Church is
the most embellished specimen of its kind in the county.
The shafts are spirally carved and banded, and there is

Norman Doorway, Finchingfield.

also some conventional foliage on the capitals and impost. The arch has various kinds of chevrons or zigzags. This doorway is familiar to readers of the *Essex Review*, as an illustration of it adorns the cover of that journal. Another doorway of interest is found at High Ongar, where the south door is surmounted by a stilted arch, with chevron, billet and star ornaments. The lintel also is arched, and has chevroned carvings, whilst the tympanum has a diaper of circular eight-rayed stars. Pentlow, again, has a west doorway which contains a unique feature in Essex, though familiar in some other districts, namely, a carved corbel of a horse's head over the arch. Without propounding any theory, we may say that our Scandinavian progenitors regarded the horse's head as a symbol of strength and vitality ; they certainly enjoyed eating horse-flesh. The south doorway of Margaret Roding Church is a finely restored specimen, with a diapered tympanum over an arched lintel. Southchurch, too, has good north and south doorways. The north doorway of Stanstead Montfitchet is the largest in the county. With its deeply-recessed horseshoe-shaped arches, richly embellished, its diapered tympanum and shafted jambs, this forms a magnificent piece of work. Tillingham, Orsett, and South Weald, too, have interesting doorways.

The only really good central Norman tower in Essex is found at Great Tey, where, unfortunately, the splendid nave was ruthlessly destroyed about 1829. There are, unfortunately, no ornate Norman sedilia in our churches, though there are several piscinas of this period, some of which are on pillars, as at Great Horkesley. Castle Hedingham possesses the richest holy water stoup of Norman date.

The county contains many Norman fonts of Purbeck marble. They are generally square or octagonal in plan, the sides ornamented with shallow, incised, semi-circular arcades. Perhaps the finest " tub-shaped " font is at

Eastwood. The font at Tillingham is said to be made from a stone of the quay wall of Orthano; it is adorned with late Norman carving. At Little Maplestead the square font has had its corners cut off, but the relief carving on the sides is unique, and said (without authority) to be Saxon. There are many fonts which may be of Norman date, but there is no ornament to

NORMAN FONT IN HOCKLEY CHURCH.

so designate them. Frequently the font is the oldest thing about a church, and may be a token of early establishment; but there are several instances of old fonts being moved into churches of later date. New fonts, carved in imitation of old ones, are not unknown, Heybridge affording an example. At Corringham, where portions, at any rate, of the font are believed to be of Norman date, nineteenth-century painting has been

NORMAN FONT, EASTWOOD.

permitted to obscure the outer surface of the ancient stone.

Leaving the Norman period and passing to the Transitional, we do not find many good examples in the county. The nave arcade on the north side of Little Dunmow, which was the south aisle of the Priory Church, is a splendid specimen. The richly moulded pointed arches rest on large circular abaci of grouped capitals, enriched with carving, on bold shafted pillars. The south doorway at Littlebury has a semi-circular arch, and the square abaci have caps with reversed volutes. At Hadstock the south doorway has a pointed arch, with square abaci to the foliaged capitals. The north and south arcades of Castle Hedingham have square abaci, with foliaged capitals to pillars, alternately round and octagonal. There are a few mutilated Transitional piscina bowls, as at Rainham, Writtle, etc. There are several fonts of this period. The group of Fryerning, Little Laver, and Abbess Roding provide unique examples. Shobden font is boldly carved in arcades, and Belchamp Walter font is very fine, whilst the Pentlow carving is a curious jumble. Probably the fine ironwork on the doors at Eastwood is of this period, as may be some other plain strap hinges.

Although the county is by no means destitute of Early English work, it is mostly rather plain in character, the capitals and corbels at Kelvedon being about the richest examples, but these have been mutilated, unfortunately. The capitals at Thundersley are good, and Horndon-on-the-Hill has some curious and unusual work of this period. The south doorways of Doddinghurst and Little Leighs are good. Navestock has some moulded capitals, and Rettendon has a good east window, piscina, and sedilia. At Mucking almost the only antiquity is a capital, with a bridled woman's head amongst the foliage. There is a similar head, but mutilated, at Mountnessing. There are some moulded

capitals at Newport, and at Sheering is a restored triple
chancel arch late in this style. The fine double piscina
at Barnstone, in which the arches are interlaced, is the
only one of its type in the county; whilst Elsenham
has a good double piscina, enriched with dog tooth.
Springfield has the most ornate square font of this
period.   Stanford-le-Hope has a mutilated Purbeck
font, octafoil in plan, which once was undoubtedly very
fine ; and Coggeshall has a circular font with arcaded
sides.

There are some doors with ornamental " C " and
strap hinges, and on the disused south door of St. Peter's,
Colchester, are fine scroll hinges, which were made by
Thomas, of Leighton Buzzard, late in the thirteenth
century. It is a pity such rare and beautiful ironwork
is not better preserved. Thomas de Leighton made the
most beautiful ironwork of his time, his grille to Queen
Eleanor's tomb in Westminster Abbey being his best-
known example.

The work of the Decorated period in Essex is not
very ornate. The restored chancel at Lawford forms
the richest example. The inside jambs of the windows
of this church have birds, animals, and grotesques carved
on them; the spandrils above the foiled ogee heads of
piscina, triple sedilia, and priests' doorway are richly
carved with figures and foliage, but they are mutilated.
The chancel of Great Sampford has a splendid east
window of geometrical tracery. The windows on the
north and south sides are also good. In addition to
the piscina and triple sedilia, the chancel has a fine
arcading all around of richly moulded and foiled arches
on deep moulded capitals and shafts. The other
capitals are deeply carved with figures and foliage. The
arched recesses in the south transept were very good
once. Altogether, this fine church well repays a visit.
The chancel of Great Dunmow is very spacious, and
the east window is good. The south wall of the chapel

of the Guild of the Holy Trinity in All Saints', Maldon, is a rich but mutilated example of wall arcading of this period. At Little Maplestead the hexagonal nave has a peristyle of six elegant clustered pillars, with well moulded arches and transverse arches to the circumscribing aisle wall. Thaxted has the finest Decorated nave arcade in the county. Radwinter is similar, but later. The north arcade at Finchingfield is good, and Pebmarsh has some interesting work. The chancel arch and south arcade of Rickling are interesting. The arch on the south side of the chancel of Saffron Walden, and the carved arcading against the wall in the north aisle, are good. The east window of Tilty is the finest in Essex, and the window on the north side of the chancel is good; the piscina and sedilia are very choice. The double piscina and triple sedilia at Bulmer, and the piscina and triple-stepped sedilia at Alphamstone, are both excellent and similar. The sedilia at Fyfield, Little Thurrock, and Shalford are all handsome. There are not many ornate fonts of this period, but Great Sampford is about the best. West Hanningfield has a mutilated font, upon which is one of the only instances of ball-flower ornament in the county.

There are a few plain roofs and doors of this period, and there are wood chancel screens of late type at Rickling, Wimbish, etc. Some of the wood porches have good pierced tracery, as at Lawford, Little Hallingbury, and Bradwell. There is a large Decorated stone semi-circular entrance arch at St. Osyth Priory.

The great glory of Stebbing is the restored stone triple arch, the heads containing tracery which fills the chancel arch as a screen. The nave arcades are very fine, and the aisle windows contain good reticulated and flowing tracery. The rood-stair is in the south aisle wall, opposite the first pillar. This church is well worth visiting.

By far the finest architectural work in the county belongs to the Perpendicular period, as at Thaxted and Saffron Walden. Indeed, the nave arcades of the latter church are magnificent, and must be seen in order to be fully appreciated. The aisles also are very good. The spandrils have quatrefoil circles, while the spandrils of the lofty chancel arch have beautiful tracery in them. Altogether, this is a very grand church. The chancel arcades of Thaxted are unique in having in the spandrils pierced quatrefoils. The clerestory above is poor, but the nave clerestory is very fine, as are also the aisles. The chancel aisle windows occupy the entire space between the buttresses, and they retain some of the old glass. The north transept retains a very beautiful reredos of Clunch stone. The south porch is unique in having doorways on the east and west sides, as well as in front. The north porch has a magnificent front. Above the doorway are two large panels with the royal shields of arms of Edward IV., and above the panels are two large windows to the room over the porch. There is a bold projecting staircase at the south-west angle. This porch was to have had an elaborate groined vault. The lofty west arch is richly moulded, and the tower vault is the best in the county. The restored west doorway forms a handsome entrance, above which rises the noble tower, flanked with stately buttresses. A graceful spire rises from within the parapet—the only mediæval stone spire in the county. The gables of the east end and north porch retain the original crucifixes— a feature which is very rare. The numerous carvings that ornament this church are fine, especially the fearfully grotesque gargoyles. This delightful church well repays a visit.

Great Bardfield has a stone screen in the chancel arch, similar to that of Stebbing; the nave arcade is a good specimen of this period. At Newport the massive tower has turrets at the corners. The

St. John the Baptist, Thaxted (North Side).

imposing south porch has a room over it, in which is a celebrated mediæval painted oak chest. The piscina bowl in the chancel, fourteen inches in diameter, is perhaps the largest in the county. Clavering is a spacious church, with graceful arcades to north and south aisles. The interior is well lighted by large windows, which have tracery typical of the district. Bocking is another imposing church, having a massive west tower, the doorway of which is particularly good. Brightlingsea occupies a lofty situation, and the tower is visible for a long distance, especially seaward. This west tower is remarkably fine, having large buttresses and a handsome west window over a good doorway. The nave arcades are good, and the pillars contain several small niches. Amongst other churches containing interesting work are Great Dunmow, Earls Colne, Canewdon, Great Yeldham, Great Chishall, Dedham, Chelmsford, Great Bromley, Ardleigh, and Fingringhoe. The four latter have handsome stone and flint porches. Dedham has a carriage-way under the west tower, having a richly panelled stone vault, ornamented with Tudor roses and portcullises. Mention of Chelmsford reminds us of the very special interest which will henceforth be attached to that ancient and beautiful edifice, now destined to be the Cathedral Church of the county. Dedicated to the Blessed Virgin, the building has passed through various vicissitudes since its erection in the fifteenth century on the site of a still older church. The whole of the nave and part of the chancel fell in 1800. The tower is within the church, at the west end, and has bold and lofty arches. This handsome tower has been recently restored. There are badges of the De Veres and Bourchiers over the west doorway. With its possibilities of enlargement eastward, Chelmsford church forms no unworthy seat for the newly created bishopric, and one, moreover, that is rich in historic and antiquarian interest.

Amongst the best of the brick porches are Feering, which is vaulted, and Pebmarsh. Ingatestone has the most massive brick tower. Fryerning has a very effective parapet and pinnacles to its tower; and Colne Engaine has a good tower. The red bricks which are used in these towers, etc., have a genial aspect; they are not aggressive in appearance as are many modern red bricks. Large wall spaces often have a trellis of black bricks built in with them for effect. The spacious north porch of Southminster has three large niches on the front. This porch has a good vault, the central boss of which has carved on it a representation of the Almighty holding a cross, on which is our Lord Jesus Christ, whilst the Dove is seated on an arm of the cross; in the background are censing angels. This is the only occurrence of this carving in the county. There is a room over this porch, from which there may have been a squint to the altar. Among wooden porches, Aldham, Terling, South Benfleet, Margaretting, and Doddinghurst are worthy of mention. There are several good barge boards on stone porches. No original lych-gates remain. Great Stambridge is unique in having a priests' room over the only mediæval west porch in the county. Several churches retain their priests' room.

There are several fine fonts of this period. Most of them are octagonal in plan, the sides having foliated sinkings. Finchingfield, Henham-on-the-Hill, Halstead, etc., have shields of arms on each panel. At Little Bromley are the emblems of the Four Evangelists on the alternate faces of the bowl, while Mountnessing has the masonic globe above the pyramid, with square and compasses, on one of the panels. Some fonts are entirely enclosed in a wood casing, which is carried up to form a tall cover, in which some of the panels are hinged to give access to the bowl, as Thaxted and

CATHEDRAL CHURCH OF ST. MARY THE VIRGIN, CHELMSFORD.

Littlebury. Marks Tey has a richly carved wood font of the Suffolk type. There were wooden fonts at several churches until recent years. Many fonts have elaborate wood covers, the best of which are Fingringhoe, Takeley, Great and Little Horkesley. There are several fine piscinas and sedilias of this period.

Great Bromley has the grandest double-hammer beam roof over the nave, whilst Castle Hedingham has the richest double-hammer beam curb roof over the nave. Many of the fine panelled roofs have bosses carved with foliage, armorial bearings, and grotesques, as at Thaxted, Saffron Walden, and Bocking. There are several magnificent chancel screens, as at Castle Hedingham, Finchingfield, Henham-on-the-Hill, and Newport Clavering. Only the lower part of Thaxted screen remains; it is richly carved with grotesque animals and foliage. No rood-lofts exist, but many stairs to them remain, and evidence of several more. Some of them are open; that is, they were formed in a chase in the wall. Probably numerous wood rood-stairs existed.

There are stalls with *miserere* at Castle Hedingham and Belchamp St. Paul. The finest poppy-heads are at Rettendon; they consist of large well-carved representations of the eagle and child, a badge of the Derbys; the bear and ragged staff, a badge of the Warwicks; dogs, lion, etc. There are many good bench ends of the Suffolk type, whilst the Essex type is a framed panel, with buttresses against the styles.

The wood towers sometimes project from the west end, as at Blackmore, Margaretting, and Stock. They consist of massive oak uprights, braced together and carried up sufficiently high to form the bell cage, above which is the framing of the spire, which is generally shingled. Sometimes this framing is inside at the west end of the nave, as at Mountnessing and Horndon-on-the-Hill. Occasionally the spire or turret is carried on huge tie-beams, as at Norton Mandeville. There are several splendid Perpendicular wood pulpits—Sandon, Wendens Ambo, and Leaden Roding may be instanced; and there are a number of Jacobean wood pulpits, some of which have sounding boards, as at Great Baddow (dated 1639). Canewdon has a pulpit of the Grinling Gibbons type, and Thaxted has a fine Georgian pulpit with sounding board. Iron-bound chests remain at Copford and elsewhere.

Hagioscopes, or squints, are not common, but examples are at Eastwood, Latton, etc. There are about sixty low side windows, or windows suitable for their purpose, in Essex churches. Several holy water stoups remain. They are generally east of the doorway inside the porch, or, if there is no porch, east of the doorway inside. There are not many Sanctus cots in the county. Before the Dissolution, Hatfield Broad Oak had a Lady Chapel east of the high altar; now Waltham Abbey only has a Lady Chapel.

The monumental brasses of Essex are treated of elsewhere in this volume, but other sepulchral memorials are to be found of interest, including several oak effigies. Those at Danbury are probably the oldest; one is represented in entire chain mail. At Little Horkesley are wooden effigies to two knights and a lady. Ten wooden effigies in all remain in the county. At Hatfield Broad Oak is a stone effigy to Robert de Vere, third Earl of Oxford (*circa* 1221). There are several later effigies to the De Veres at Earls Colne. There are mutilated effigies of crossed-legged knights at Stanstead Montfitchet, Clavering, etc., and monuments to Knights of the Garter at Earls Colne, Castle Hedingham, Little Easton, Saffron Walden, Layer Marney, St. Osyth, and (to three) at Boreham; good alabaster effigies on altar tombs remain at Little Dunmow, Layer Marney, and elsewhere; elaborate arched wall tombs remain at

Shalford, Great and Little Leighs; and "sideboard" tombs still exist, as at Dedham. The canopied terra-cotta altar tomb to Lord Marney (1523) at Layer Marney is unique. At Waltham Abbey are the royal arms of Queen Mary; at Messing are the royal arms of James I. and the feathers of Prince Charles. The Georgian shields of arms are common in Essex churches.

THE MONASTIC HOUSES OF ESSEX

By the Editor

TO the chequered history of Monasticism in England the county of Essex has contributed many interesting pages. This is hardly to be wondered at when we recollect how rich the county was in those religious houses wherein men and women sought to yield themselves up to the threefold vow of poverty, celibacy, and obedience, dwelling together under a fixed rule of discipline. Benedictines, Cluniacs, Cistercians, Augustinians, Premonstratensians, Black Friars, Crossed Friars, White Friars and Grey, Knights Hospitallers, and Knights Templars, all at some time or other founded houses of varying degrees of importance within the limits of this large county. Indeed, Essex probably contained more religious houses than any other English county, save three or four. Individually, none of the foundations were possessed of great wealth, the revenues of Waltham and Barking —this latter the most famous nunnery in England—for example, being far less than those of a score of other foundations outside the county. Nevertheless, the combined revenue of the Essex foundations was considerable, probably amounting, early in the sixteenth century, to something like £100,000 yearly, as money value is reckoned to-day. But the demolition and destruction which was wrought on all these foundations was so thorough that even the ruins which remain are few and meagre. They are chiefly to be found at Waltham; St. Osyth's; Barking; St. John's and St. Botolph's, Colchester; Beeleigh; Bicknacre; and Maldon St. Giles'. Fortunately, however, the various official and other records enable us to form a fairly adequate conception of the numerous religious foundations of Essex, their importance and extent, prior to that fateful period when they were swept from the land at the bidding of a rapacious and tyrannical monarch.

Of the Essex foundations there were eight which belonged to the Order of St. Benedict, and whose members obeyed the celebrated Rule which this great ascetic framed in his dwelling at Monte Cassino in 529. In England, as elsewhere, monasteries had, of course, existed long before the introduction of the Benedictine Rule. Indeed, Mr. Willis Bund maintains that in their origin the earliest "monasteries" were mere settlements of Christians, clerical and lay, men, women, and children, who, for the sake of protection, lived together. And another recent writer, dealing more particularly with the early Church in Wales, says something very similar. In Wales, at all events, he believes the Church to have been essentially monastic, its whole organisation being built up round the monasteries:

"Its bishops were members, usually abbots, of monastic establishments, and they seem to have been non-diocesan. . . . Further, the constitution of this monastic church was essentially tribal. . . . Every great monastic establishment was a sort of spiritual clan, in which the abbot was chieftain, the officials represented the heads of the tribal families, and the monks were the tribesmen. . . . Thus, just as secular Wales consisted of groups of tribesmen clustering round powerful lay chieftains, so ecclesiastical Wales consisted of groups of tribesmen clustering round a few great monasteries founded by important Saints." [1]

Although by the close of the fifth century Monasticism had spread over the Christian world, it

---

[1] F. Homes Dudden, *Gregory the Great*, vol. ii., p. 135.

still retained many characteristics associated with the East, wherein it took its origin. There were solitary hermits, unattached to any foundation, and there were monasteries independent of each other. The Rule of St. Basil, though taken as a broad principle for the guidance of monastic life, was by no means binding or authoritative, but was modified to fit in with local circumstances or the personal wishes of individual abbots. Signs of weakness were not wanting in this monastic system, or rather lack of system; in fact, a reform was needed if the monastic life was to be perpetuated. The man who effected this reform was the great religious St. Benedict, who, as a recent writer has remarked, was to Monasticism very much the same power that St. Paul was to Apostolic Christianity. His little monastery at Monte Cassino attained a world-wide reputation, and was the nursery of the great Benedictine Order; while his famous Rule brought new life and vigour into the monastic system generally. Eventually this Rule, at once eminently aristocratic, and yet intensely democratic, proved irresistible, absorbing and supplanting for a time all other forms of Monasticism in Western Europe.

Of the eight Essex houses which owned obedience to it, Barking Abbey—first of the religious houses founded in the county, and undoubtedly the most famous of English nunneries—was quite certainly the richest. The only other nunneries in Essex, Wix and Hedingham Priories, were also Benedictine, and to these Benedictine houses must be added St. John's Abbey, Colchester (1096); Hatfield Peverel Priory (a dependency of St. Albans, Herts.); Colne Priory, (Saffron) Walden Abbey, and Hatfield Regis Priory.

From the Benedictines, at the close of the tenth century, sprang the Cluniacs, with their stricter rule and more centralized discipline. This eminently Continental Order, which never attained to great power in England,

had three priories in Essex—Prittlewell and Stanesgate,
cells to Lewes, in Sussex, where the Order established
itself in 1077 ; and Horkesley, a cell to Thetford, Norfolk.
The Cluniacs, while emphasising the severity of the
monastic code as to fasting and silence, laid stress upon
liturgical splendour.   The Cistercians, founded in 1098,
by Robert of Molesme, and to which the famous Bernard
of Clairvaux belonged, opposed to this principle the
utmost simplicity and severity in Divine service,
enjoining plain linen or fustian vestments, iron censers,
no pictures—nothing costly, in fact.   This Order, which
has been described as republican rather than monarchical,
had three abbeys in Essex—namely, Tilty, founded in
1153, and affiliated to Warden in Bedfordshire ; Stratford
Langthorne (West Ham), 1135; and Coggeshall, 1140.
The two latter, with their parent house of Savigny, in
France, joined the Cistercians in 1147.   This Order
spread rapidly during the first century of its existence,
the central house at Citeaux having at one time more
than fifteen hundred dependencies.   There were seventy-
five houses belonging to it in England and Wales at
the time of the general suppression.

Canons Regular—the second class of Orders existing
in England in pre-Reformation days—were very strongly
represented in Essex, the Augustinian Canons (so
called because they formed themselves on the rule
of St. Augustine) having twelve houses in the county,
including Waltham Abbey, wealthiest of all the religious
houses in Essex, and the most important Augustinian
foundation in England.   This abbey, originally founded
for secular canons by Harold, in 1060, passed to the
Augustinians on the expulsion of the Seculars by Henry II.
in 1177, at which period the Augustinians enjoyed great
popularity and exercised considerable influence in
England.   Nowhere were they stronger than in the
Eastern counties, and Essex comes fourth on the list as
regards the number of Augustinian houses it contained.

In addition to Waltham, with its mitred abbot, there was the priory of St. Botolph at Colchester, which claimed to be the first house of this Order in England. Dunmow Priory (1104), St. Osyth's Abbey (about 1118), Thoby Priory, founded under Stephen; Bicknacre Priory (*temp.* Henry II.), and the priories of Berden, Blackmore, Latton, Leighs, Thremhall and Tiptree, all founded about the close of the twelfth century, complete the number of Augustinian houses in Essex. At the time of the Dissolution there were nearly 170 foundations belonging to this Order in England, about a third of the whole being found in Norfolk, Yorkshire, Suffolk, Essex, and Lincolnshire. This Order was even more popular in Ireland, where some of its priors had seats in the Irish Parliament.

The habit of the Augustinian Canons was black, so they were often termed the Black Canons. The Premonstratensian Canons, on the other hand, by reason of their white habit, were known as the White Canons. Really an offshoot of the Augustinians, they took their name from Prémontré, near Laon, in France, where they were established by St. Norbert in 1119. Settling first in Essex, at Parndon, they responded later to the invitation of one Robert Mantell, and migrated to Maldon, there to found the Abbey of Beeleigh in 1180. In England, just before the Dissolution, there were thirty-four houses of this Order, which never possessed more than Beeleigh Abbey in this county.

Of the "Alien Houses" in Essex, five in number, the hospital or priory of Hornchurch was the only dependency in this land of the famous "hospice" of SS. Nicholas and Bernard, of Mont Joux, in Savoy. It was founded by Henry II. about 1159. Mr. Round suggests that it is very probable that the envoys sent by the King to the Emperor Frederick in the winter of 1158-59 crossed the Alps by the pass of the Great St. Bernard, and that the endowment, which consisted of land at Havering and Chislehurst, in Kent, may be traced to this connection.[1] The hospital at Writtle was a dependency of the hospital which Pope Innocent III. founded for the English at the Church of St. Mary, in Saxia, Rome—the Hospital of the Holy Ghost. It was sold, with all its belongings, including the church of Writtle and the chapel of Roxwell, to New College, Oxford, in 1391. The other Alien Houses were the priory of West Mersea, granted to the abbey of St. Ouen, at Rouen, by Edward the Confessor (1046?); Panfield Priory, founded under William I., a cell of St. Stephen's, Caen; and Takeley, a cell of St. Valery, in Picardy. This latter is generally considered to have been a thankoffering given by the Conqueror or his followers to the monks of St. Valery, to whose intercession was ascribed the change of wind which contributed to the success of the Norman invasion of England, September 27th, 1066. It was eventually sold to William of Wykeham, and, like Writtle, became the property of New College, Oxford, Pope Boniface IX. confirming the sale on February 2nd, 1392.

Passing to the Military Orders—the third class into which the religious foundations may be grouped—we find both the Knights Hospitallers and the Knights Templars were represented in Essex. The former Order, which began A.D. 1092 with the building of a hospital for pilgrims at Jerusalem, followed a modified rule of St. Augustine, and it is of interest to note that the chief house of the knights, at Clerkenwell, was founded by an Essex man, Jordan Briset, probably early in the reign of Stephen.[2] To this headquarters some fifty-three cells or "commanderies" were attached, one of these, dating from the reign of Henry II., being at Little Maplestead, in Essex. This hospital was dissolved in

---

1 *Victoria County History of Essex* (Constable), vol. ii., p. 195.
2 See Mr. J. H. Round in *Essex Archæological Society's Transactions*, vol. viii., p. 152.

1540. The Knights Templars came into England during King Stephen's reign, their first English foundation being very probably that of Cressing, in Essex. They obtained various manors and estates—indeed, as Abbot Gasquet, no unfriendly witness, puts it, " They became too rich and powerful "—and on these they frequently built churches and houses, in which some of the brethren lived. One such foundation, or " Preceptory," at Cressing, was granted them by Stephen and his Queen Maud, and when the Order was suppressed by Pope Clement V. (on account of its serious crimes) this, with some seventeen other estates, was handed over to the Knights of St. John of Jerusalem. John Lutterell, master of Cressing in 1381, was hated by the people; Cressing, therefore, suffered seriously from the peasants' uprising in that year, precious books, vestments, gold and silver being stolen and destroyed by the angry folk who attacked the " Preceptory."

The remaining branch of the Religious Orders, the Friars, was also represented in Essex: the Black Friars, or Dominicans, at Chelmsford (thirteenth century); the Grey Friars, or Franciscans, at Colchester (1279); the Crossed, or Crutched, Friars at Colchester (thirteenth century ?); and the White, or Carmelite, Friars at Maldon (1292). Differing from the monks, the friars were bound by their profession, "not to any locality or house, but to the province, which usually consisted of the entire number of houses in a country."[1] At first, too, they professed strict poverty, being by their profession mendicants, living on alms, and only holding the buildings in which they dwelt. The province of England was divided by the Grey Friars into seven wardenships, Colchester and eight other houses being included in that of Cambridge. In the old records we find the friars here and at Chelmsford being empowered to make conduits

---

1 Gasquet, *English Monastic Life*, p. 234.

from the wells to their houses, and to the hospital of the Crossed Friars at Colchester special privileges were attached. In 1401 or 1402 the Archbishops of Canterbury and York, and other prelates, granted indulgences to all who should visit and help this very needy foundation. Prior Deryks, in 1526, maintained the privilege of "sanctuary" for his foundation in connection with a charge of murder, the accused man being in the choir, near the high altar, where his would-be captor "durst not to enterprise." Maldon, "one of the very poorest of the religious houses of England," could boast of several scholars. Its Carmelite members—this was accounted the most learned of the religious orders— took their name from their place of origin, and observed a rule chiefly founded on that of St. Basil. The first European Chapter of their Order was held at Ailesford, in Kent, A.D. 1245, and in the sixteenth century there were about forty Carmelite houses in England and Wales.

In addition to the foundations already mentioned, Essex contained nine hospitals, some independent, and some belonging to other and larger houses. They were placed at Bocking, Braintree, Colchester, Hedingham, Ilford, Maldon, Newport, East Tilbury, and Brook Street, in South Weald. Several of these were leprosy hospitals, probably Colchester, Little Maldon, and Ilford. In each was a master, one or more chaplains, and a number of poor persons, who were either sick, infirm, or leprous. Of these hospitals two still survive—St. Mary's, Ilford, and St. Mary Magdalene's, Colchester. The former was founded by Adeliza (the sister of Payn Fitz John), who had been made the Abbess of Barking by King Stephen, preceding in this office Mary, the sister of Thomas Becket. By the statutes of Bishop Ralph, Stratford (1346), the proper number of thirteen leprous brethren (preferably from Barking) was to be kept up as far as the resources of the hospital would allow. There were continued disputes later over the respective rights of monarch and abbess, the latter generally coming off victorious. The house appears to have escaped at the Dissolution, but its tithes were "regulated" under the Commonwealth, owing to the loyal adherence of its master to his King. Passing through several hands to the Cecil family, the hospital (or almshouses) now exists for the accommodation of six aged couples, appointed by the Marquis of Salisbury, by whom the ancient chapel and hospital buildings are kept in repair. Standing in the midst of "London over the Border," this ancient building is one of the few remaining witnesses to those days when the Church was the nation's almoner and the guardian of the sick and needy. Memory of the terrible scourge of leprosy is preserved, too, in that other ancient hospital, remains of which still stand—St. Mary Magdalene's, at Colchester. Here, also, many vicissitudes and changes have been witnessed since the hospital was founded at the direction of Henry I.; many "abuses" have been corrected; its finances regulated; and its affairs generally brought up to date in a way that would doubtless surprise its pious founders. Of the other ancient hospitals few traces remain. Around some of them—e.g., East Tilbury, of which nothing is known since the middle of the fifteenth century—many disputes raged, the settlement of which was not always accomplished by legal and peaceable methods.

At Pleshey and Halstead there were colleges of secular canons; here and there hermitages were to be found; and throughout the county were many free chapels and chantries. In the list of English religious houses compiled by Abbot Gasquet for his book, *English Monastic Life*, there are some forty entries under Essex. As we have seen, no one of the greater houses was inordinately rich, though Mr. R. C. Fowler estimates the present equivalent of the total yearly value of all the Essex houses at about £100,000. The number of religious

in the Essex houses, again, was not very great, at any
rate at the time of the Dissolution.   At Barking there
were thirty-one; at St. Osyth's, sixteen; at Waltham,
eighteen; fifteen at Stratford; eleven each at Colne,
Dunmow, and Leighs; six at Tilty; ten at Hatfield
Regis; and eighteen in the six houses dissolved by
Wolsey. "Probably," says Mr. Fowler, "in the whole
twenty-seven monasteries in the sixteenth century there
were something less than 250, while in the four friaries
there may have been twenty-five more.   In earlier times
the numbers would have been considerably greater than
this."

In the space occupied by an article like the present,
it is impossible to deal in detail with so many religious
foundations as Essex contained.   Some there are,
however, which call for special mention, and notably
the abbeys of Waltham, St. Osyth, and Barking, and
the premier Augustinian house in England, St. Botolph's
Priory, Colchester.   The miraculous story associated
with the foundation of the Abbey of Waltham Holy
Cross has been well told by the old twelfth century
canon who wrote *De Inventione Sanctæ Crucis Nostræ*.
Briefly, a miraculous cross was discovered by a vision
at Montacute, in Somersetshire, and Tovi, or Tofig, a
wealthy landowner, built the Church of the Holy Cross
at Waltham for its reception, appointing two priests,
and providing endowment for them.   Subsequently the
estate was given to Harold, son of Godwin, by Edward
the Confessor, and by Harold the church was rebuilt
and the foundation developed.   The church was solemnly
dedicated in the presence of King Edward the Confessor,
most probably on Holy Cross Day, May 3rd, 1060.   It
was richly endowed by Harold, who was killed at the
Battle of Hastings in 1066, and whose body is said to
have been recovered and buried at Waltham.   This
question of Harold's burial is disputed, and cannot be
finally settled; Freeman, the historian, however, firmly

believed that it was at Waltham Harold was laid.
Speaking of the body of Edward I. resting in the
Abbey Church (*Norman Conquest*, vol. iii., p. 522), this
writer says:

" . . . The King with whom England fell might greet his first true
successor in the King with whom she rose again. Such were the men
who met in death within the now vanished choir of Waltham. And in
the whole course of English history we hardly come across a scene which
speaks more deeply to the heart than when the first founder of our
later greatness was laid by the side of the last kingly champion of our
earliest freedom—when the body of the great Edward was laid, if only
for a short space, by the side of Harold, the son of Godwin."

Despoiled to some extent by William the Conqueror,
Henry I. granted Waltham to his Queen, Maud, and
later this foundation belonged in turn to several
other queens of England. The year 1177 witnessed the
overthrow of the old foundation by Henry II., who had
vowed to build an abbey of Canons Regular in honour
of Thomas Becket, the murdered Primate, " for the
remission of his own sins." With permission of the
Pope, a new house was built, considerable sums being
given by the King towards the rebuilding of the church,
which was a costly work, and occupied half a century.
The new foundation was given to the Augustinian
Canons, the former dean and canons being compensated
for disturbance. Many privileges and favours were
bestowed upon the abbey, which eventually became the
richest in Essex, its net value being given in the *Valor
Ecclesiasticus* as £900 4s. 3d. Waltham managed to
survive every other abbey in England, formally
surrendering, at the hands of Robert Fuller, on March
23rd, 1540. The abbot and the other officers received
large surrender pensions, the abbey servants receiving
a year's wages. " Waltham," as Mr. Fowler remarks,
" on account of its size, royal patronage and proximity
to London, was one of the most important houses in
England; certainly the most important of those of the

WALTHAM ABBEY CHURCH: NAVE PILLARS.

Augustinian Order."[1] It is frequently mentioned in chronicles and records; the abbot was mitred, with a seat in Parliament; and in 1214, Abbot Nicholas, sent by the papal legate, deposed the Abbot of Westminster. On August 4th, 1307, the body of Edward I. was brought to Waltham, there to rest until its final removal to Westminster Abbey. From the *Letters and Papers of Henry VIII.*, it would seem that under the scheme for the establishment of new bishoprics at the Dissolution it was intended that Waltham should be made a Cathedral, but this was never carried out. The seal of Waltham Abbey, a remarkably fine one, more than three inches in diameter, shows on its obverse two angels guarding the Cross of Waltham upon a mount, and around it is the legend:

HOC [EST] SIGILL' ECCLESIE SANCTE CRUCIS DE WALTHAM.

The remains of this stately abbey, chiefly confined to the parish church of Waltham Holy Cross, are referred to in Mr. Grose Lloyd's sketch of ancient Essex churches (page 81). The splendid nave is to be seen, very much as it was left at the general destruction, with its immense Norman pillars, so like those of Durham Cathedral; and there are some carefully preserved fragments of Harold's tomb or shrine. The famous East window, given to the Abbey of Waltham by Henry VIII. to commemorate his union with Catherine of Arragon, now finds a place in the Church of St. Margaret, at Westminster.

The premier house of the Augustinian Order in this land was the Priory of St. Julian and St. Botolph, Colchester. It would appear that certain priests belonging to St. Botolph's, hearing of the Augustinian Rule—then unknown in England—and being desirous of joining some religious order, caused two of their number to study the Rule at Chartres and Beauvais. These

---

1 *Victoria County History of Essex*, vol. ii., p. 169

priests returning taught it to their brethren at Colchester.
"It thus appears that the Augustinian settlement at
St. Botolph's was not a new foundation, but a voluntary
transformation of a secular into a religious establishment,
somewhat resembling the forced change at Waltham in
1177."[1] In August, 1116, Pope Paschal II. granted to
the Canons a Bull, conferring upon their house authority
and jurisdiction over all other houses of this Order
which might be built in this country. The church of Holy
Trinity, London, was also to be obedient to them—an
obligation from which escape was compassed in the
thirteenth century. Charters were given or confirmed
by successive monarchs to this priory, the properties
belonging to which were spread over Essex, Suffolk, and
Cambridgeshire. The priory was not always on good
terms with the Benedictine Abbey of St. John in the
same town, and in the fourteenth century a serious riot
took place between these foundations. The abbot and
convent complained to the Pope that Prior John, with
two of his canons and several laymen, attacked one of
the monks with sword and dagger; blockaded them in
the abbey; and instigated others to enter the abbey and
injure the abbot. The Pope (Urban V.) ordered the
Archbishop of Canterbury, if the facts were as stated,
to excommunicate the militant prior and his followers,
but an amicable settlement seems to have taken place.
The priory fell, under the Act of 1536, and was given,
with all its possessions, to Sir Thomas Audeley.
Considerable ruins of the Priory Church remain,
presenting features of unusual interest to the student.
In its Norman walls there are ample traces of the use
of those Roman materials which this old walled city
supplied. Indeed, St. Botolph's is said to furnish the
earliest example of the use by Norman builders of
cement or stucco in their work. The great cylindrical

---

1 *Victoria County History*, vol. ii., p. 148.

ST. BOTOLPH'S PRIORY, COLCHESTER : WEST DOORWAY.

columns of the abbey were no doubt covered to some
extent with cement, and the rough projecting keys round
their summit indicate that their caps were finished with
the same material—an unusual method of treatment by
the Norman builders, due probably to the Roman
suggestion of the place and the abundant remains of
that period to be found there.

Colchester, too, contained the famous Benedictine
Abbey of St. John the Baptist, with its long and, at
times, exciting history, in which miracles, plots, political
and clerical dissensions play a large part. Founded
towards the end of the eleventh century by Eudo, the
son of Hubert de Ria, Lord of Colchester, it held manors,
tithes, fairs, and churches, and was by charter granted
the same liberties as Westminster. It held cells at
Writtle and Snape (Suffolk), the latter giving rise to a
serious dispute between monarch and Pope; and students
of the history of St. Thomas Becket may recollect how
some of the martyr's blood which was given to
Colchester Abbey was associated with certain alleged
miracles. Abbots of Colchester were frequently mixed
up in the political intrigues and dissensions of their
days, Abbot Geoffrey's rule being particularly noticeable
in this respect. Eventually this ancient house fell by
reason of the outspoken conduct of its last abbot,
Thomas Marshall, or Beche, who paid for his daring
with his life, being accused of high treason to the king,
and executed at Colchester on December 1st, 1539.
There is no room to doubt that Abbot Marshall was not
one of those divines who took the royal claims "lying
down." The evidence given by his servants and
"friends" at the several trials afforded proof that he was
a strong supporter of Rome, and a friend of the northern
insurrection. Indeed, he made bold to speak of the
king's "covetousness and tyranny," intimating "that the
nature of covettise is lyke to the dropsy, it is insaciable
and never content." After such sentiments as these the

Tower of London followed, and a trial by commission at Colchester, where the unfortunate abbot was found guilty and hanged on December 1st, the abbey and all its possessions, of course, passing into the hands of the king. The possessions of the abbey at the time of its fall were considerable, and included $2,244\frac{1}{4}$ ounces of plate, besides two mitres, jewels, etc.

The famous abbey of the Benedictine nuns at Barking was one of the two monasteries founded by St. Earkenwald, the successor of Cedd in the bishopric of the East Saxons (A.D. 675). Before he became Bishop of London, this holy man founded a monastery at Chertsey for himself, and one at Barking for Ethelburga, his sister. The abbey of Barking was probably founded in 666 or thereabouts, and was largely endowed by the East Saxon princes. In it Earkenwald died on April 30th, 693, and, later, his sister Ethelburga, the first abbess, who eventually shared with the Blessed Virgin in the dedication of the abbey. In 870 the abbey was burnt to the ground by the Danes, the whole congregation of virgins within its church being destroyed with it; and again it was granted to Wlfhildis, a nun, by Edgar, as an act of reparation, and by this king restored to its old magnificence. During the building of the Tower of London William I. resided in the abbey (1066), and there received the submission of Eadwine and Morkere. The roll of abbesses of Barking is a remarkable one, containing, as it does, many names of the very highest rank. Queen Maud, wife of Henry I., was temporarily its ruler; Stephen appointed Adeliza, sister of Payn Fitz John, to be its abbess; and upon her decease (probably in 1173) Mary, the sister of Thomas Becket, was made abbess by charter of Henry II., in reparation for her brother's death. Until 1214 the abbesses had been nominated by the king, but from that year free election was granted in England, and the nuns of Barking availed themselves of this privilege from 1215 onwards.

WALTHAM ABBEY CHURCH: NORTH ARCH.

FIRE BELL GATE, BARKING.

Kings, queens and nobles continually made gifts to the abbey, Stephen offering the hundred of Barstaple in person at its high altar. The manors of the abbey were found in Buckinghamshire, Middlesex, and Bedfordshire, as well as in Essex; the churches of Barking, Dagenham, Mucking, Horndon-on-the-Hill, Hockley, Tollesbury, Lidlington, and All Hallows-by-the-Tower belonged to it; also the advowsons of Abbess Roding, Bulphan, Ingatestone, Roding, Warley, Wigborough, and Slapton. The Abbess of Barking was a baroness in her own right, and to her was given license to hunt hares and foxes at Hainault, and free chase to hunt all beasts of the forest in season, including rabbits, badgers, cats, "and other vermin." Again, the abbess had precedence over other abbesses, being one of the four who were summoned with the bishops and abbots to do military service under Henry III. and Edward I. It was to this abbey that Eleanor, Duchess of Gloucester, retired after the murder of her husband in 1397, dying there in 1399. As one of the greater houses—its value was put at £862 12s. 3d. in the *Valor Ecclesiasticus* (1535)—Barking survived the Act of 1536, but was finally surrendered to the Royal Commissioner in the chapter-house at Barking, November 14th, 1539. The last abbess, Dorothy Barley, was granted 200 marks yearly, the thirty other nuns receiving smaller pensions, which, by the way, they most of them lived to enjoy until the reign of Philip and Mary. The site of the abbey, with the conventual house and lands, was granted by Edward VI. to Edward, Lord Clinton, in 1551. The wealth of this abbey was considerable; of the nunneries only those of Sion and Shaftesbury exceeded it. 3,586 ounces of silver and jewels; a jewel of 65 ounces (a "monstrance"); a beryl; and some vestments were amongst its treasures, the latest inventories of which are not discoverable.

The fragments of the abbey that exist to-day are few, chief of them being the fourteenth century Oratory

of the Holy Rood, over the entrance known as the " Fire
Bell Gate," of which an illustration is given ; but the
site of the stately abbey church may still be traced
outside the north wall of the churchyard, and we know
enough about the size and magnificence of the grand
old edifice to assure us that it was fully in accord with
St. Benedict's great principle that "nothing is to be
preferred to the *Opus Dei*," or Divine service, around
which the monastic life clustered.   According to careful
estimate, made during the eighteenth century, the length
of the cruciform church was 170 feet, its width 150 feet,
and the length of its choir 60 feet.   In addition to
the high altar, there were altars of Our Lady of the
Resurrection and of SS. Peter and Paul, and on either
side of the choir entrance stood the shrines of St.
Ethelburga and St. Hildelitha (the second abbess).

Of those monastic buildings some parts of which still
remain, Essex contains few finer fragments than the
great gateway of St. Osyth's Abbey.   A good deal
that is legendary surrounds the early history of this
foundation, but it is certain that an Augustinian priory
was founded here about 1118 by Richard de Belmies,
bishop of London 1108-27, and placed under the
patronage of the martyred St. Osyth.   The manor of
Chich and the churches of Clacton, Blythburgh, Althorne,
Mayland and Southminster were granted to the priory,
which became an abbey in the middle of the twelfth
century.   The records show several episcopal and
archiepiscopal visitations and consequent " injunctions,"
some of which point to serious breaches of discipline
occurring in the abbey.   In 1403 the Abbot of St. Osyth
joined the Abbots of Colchester and Beeleigh in aiding
the Countess of Oxford's plot to restore Richard II. to
the throne of England.   Upon the discovery of the
conspiracy warrants were issued for the arrest of those
concerned.   The Abbot of Colchester fled.   Eventually,
however, the three prelates concerned received pardon,

St. Osyth Priory: The Gatehouse.

indifference.   Finally, it is well to remember that the Dissolution was not altogether a sudden and unexpected blow.   It was led up to and suggested by various happenings.   The Dissolution of the Alien Houses, under Henry V., was succeeded by Wolsey's action in dissolving certain English priories a century later and diverting their funds to sundry colleges at Oxford.   In Essex six houses fell thus—Blackmore, Horkesley, Stanesgate, Thoby, Tiptree, and Wix.   These and other happenings served to familiarize the public mind with the idea of dissolution, and thus helped to prepare the way for that great confiscation eleven years later, under which Essex sustained a blow of such magnitude as we in our day and generation can but faintly appreciate.

THE MONUMENTAL BRASSES
OF ESSEX

By Miller Christy, W. W. Porteous, and
E. Bertram Smith

OF all our English counties, there is none, we believe, which is richer than Essex in the number, variety, and interest of its monumental brasses—with the possible exception of Kent. It is true that this preponderance is due, in part, to its large size; but, even allowing for this, Essex remains very near to, if not actually at, the top of the list.

The brasses laid down in the county before the year 1700, and still existing, number rather more than five hundred; and upon nearly three hundred of these one or more effigies are depicted. Moreover, there are few of the four hundred and odd Essex churches which do not contain at least one matrix from which a brass has been stripped. In some (as, for instance, those of Saffron Walden, Thaxted, and Hornchurch) there are many such matrices, showing that at one time these churches must have been almost paved with slabs bearing monumental brasses. Indeed, it seems probable that the brasses which have existed may be numbered by the thousand and that those still remaining are a little more than a tithe of them.[1]

---

[1] In various articles which have appeared during the last few years in *The Transactions of the Essex Archæological Society*, *The Essex Review*, *The Reliquary and Illustrated Archæologist*, and *The Transactions of the Monumental Brass Society*, we have figured some 320 of the more interesting brasses in the county (including nearly all those mentioned hereafter).

FIG. 1—BRASS OF SIR WILLIAM FITZRALPH
(ABOUT 1323) AT PEBMARSH.

In the following pages, we have endeavoured to give a general survey of the brasses of the county, figuring and describing in greater detail ten of the more interesting. We deal with them in twelve classes—(1) Men in Armour, (2) Civilians, (3) Ladies, (4) Priests, (5) Lawyers, (6) Shroud Brasses, (7) Palimpsest Brasses, (8) Flemish Brasses, (9) Cross Brasses, (10) Bracket Brasses, (11) Heart Brasses, and (12) Inscriptions.[1]

(1) BRASSES OF MEN IN ARMOUR.—Of the ten existing English brasses which date from the first half of the fourteenth century, no fewer than three are to be found in Essex. They are at

Pebmarsh (Sir William FitzRalph, c. 1323.: fig. 1).
Wimbish (Sir John de Wautone and w., c. 1345).
Bowers Gifford (Sir John Giffard, 1348).

Unfortunately, all these three compositions are now much mutilated. That at Pebmarsh is, nevertheless, one of the finest brasses in the kingdom; while the other two are two of the three brasses now remaining in Britain which illustrate the change in military costume from the "cyclas" to the typical jupon.

The brass to Sir William FitzRalph (about 1323) in the chancel at Pebmarsh (fig. 1) is the earliest now remaining in this county. The effigy of the knight (originally about five feet six inches in length) is slightly mutilated. The marginal fillet, which bore the inscription, the canopy, and two shields of arms have all disappeared, with the exception of three small fragments of the fillet (fig. 2), which are preserved at the vicarage. The knight wears a complete suit of mail, and over it a long surcoat, confined at the waist by a cord. The more exposed parts of the arms and legs are, however, further protected by plate-armour, and spiked roundels protect the arm-pits

---

1 Each of these sections is intended to deal with one class of effigy or device only. Therefore, even if no mention is made of a husband or wife (as the case may be) accompanying any particular effigy, it must not be assumed that none such exists.

and elbows. These portions render the figure of special interest; for it and the effigy of Sir — de Bacon (about 1320), at Gorleston, in Suffolk, are the two earliest existing brasses which depict the commencement of plate-armour. At his left side is his shield, which is rounded to his body. Though now mutilated, it bore originally his arms,[1] which appear also in one of the windows of the church.

When the Rev. William Holman, an Essex historian, visited the church in 1715, the greater part of the inscription remained.[2] It was in Norman-French. The portion missing was the beginning, but there can be little

FIG. 2—PORTIONS OF INSCRIPTION BELONGING TO THE BRASS OF
SIR WILLIAM FITZRALPH (ABOUT 1323), AT PEBMARSH.

doubt as to its general tenour; and, if our surmise is correct, the whole read:—

[+ ISSI : GIST : SIRE : WILLIEM : FITZRAUF : DE : PEBMERSH :] ET : VOUS : QE : PAR : ISSI : PASSEREZ : POUR : L'ALME : LE : DICT : WILLIEM : PRIEZ : POUR : UN : PATER : NOSTER : ET : UN : AVE : CENT : JOURS : DE : PARDON : ENT : AVEREZ.[3]

The Messrs. Waller (who engrave this brass) give a good deal of information[4] as to the family of FitzRalph, which held the manor of Pebmarsh.

Of brasses of the second half of the fourteenth century, Essex can boast the following five examples, the first three of which we figure:—

Chrishall (Sir John de la Pole and w., *c.* 1370 : fig. 3).
Little Horkesley (Sir Robert Swynborne, 1391 : fig. 4).
Aveley (Radulphus de Knevyntoun, *c.* 1370 : fig. 5).
Shopland (Sir Thomas Stapel, 1371).
South Ockendon (Sir Ingelram Bruyn, 1400).

---

1 [Or], three chevrons [gules], each charged with as many fleurs-de-lys [argent].

2 At that date, the effigy seems to have been still perfect, though the canopy and shields were already lost.

3 Here lies Sir William FitzRalph, of Pebmarsh; and you who shall pass by here, say for the soul of the said William a Paternoster and an Ave, and you shall have one hundred days of pardon.

4 *A Series of Monumental Brasses* (London, 1842-64).

FIG. 3—BRASS OF SIR JOHN DE LA POLE AND WIFE
(ABOUT 1370) AT CHRISHALL.

The latter two are very similar to the others, but are seriously mutilated.

The fine brass, at Chrishall, to Sir John de la Pole (about 1370) and his wife Joan (*née* Cobham), with a triple canopy and three shields (fig. 3), was hidden for many years beneath the flooring, but in 1849 it lay within the altar-rails. The canopy was then somewhat mutilated, but has since been carefully restored, and the brass, still affixed to its original slab, now lies at the western end of the south aisle. It is perfect, with the exception of the marginal fillet which bore the inscription, the whole of which is lost.[1]

The effigy of the knight (five feet two and a half inches in height) represents him wearing the mixed mail and plate-armour of his period. He wears an acutely-pointed bascinet, to which is fastened the camail of mail. This covers the neck and shoulders and overlaps the upper edge of his jupon, which has an escalloped lower edge and allows the hauberk of mail beneath to be seen at the arm-pits. The knight's legs and arms are encased in plate-armour. His feet, which rest upon a lion, are encased in pointed sollerets and armed with rowelled spurs. His right hand, which is bare, grasps that of his wife: his left, in a gauntlet, grasps the ornamented bawdric, from which is suspended a long sword.

The lady is described on page 141.

The fine triple canopy (eight feet high) consists of three cusped arches, the spandrils of which are filled with foliage and the finials handsomely crocketted.

Of the three shields, that on the dexter side bears de la Pole[2]; that on the sinister, Cobham[3]; and that in

---

[1] The three words shown (sa feme priez) have, we believe, been copied on to the new fillet from a fragment of the original one which in 1874 existed at the rectory.

[2] [Azure]; two bars nebuly [or].

[3] [Gules]; on a chevron [or], three lions rampant [sable].

the centre, de la Pole impaling Cobham. These bearings
enable us to identify the effigies, even though the
inscription is lost.

Sir John de la Pole was probably a son of Sir William
de la Pole, who held the manor of Chrishall-Bury from
1353 to 1358. Sir John married Joan, daughter of
Sir John de Cobham (died 1407), of Cobham, Kent.

The second brass of the series lies upon an altar-tomb
in the south chapel of the church at Little Horkesley
(fig. 4). Beyond any question, it is the most magnificent
brass in Essex, and it is equalled by few of contemporary
date elsewhere. It commemorates Sir Robert Swynborne
(died 1391) and his son Sir Thomas (died 1412), who are
represented beneath a very elaborate canopy, the whole
being surrounded by a narrow fillet bearing the inscription.
It is still almost perfect. As both father and son are
correctly represented as wearing armour of the date at
which each died, the brass depicts the changes in the
style of armour which took place in the twenty years
which elapsed between the deaths of the two knights.

Sir Robert Swynborne wears armour identical with
that of the Chrishall knight, with the addition of a dagger
or misericorde. The bawdric bears his monogram and
initials.

The figure of Sir Thomas Swynborne is described on
page 125.

The superb canopy is supported by a central shaft,
placed between the figures, and two lateral shafts. On
each of these latter are hung three escutcheons, but the
bearings on all except one are so defaced that it is difficult
to make them out.[1]

---

1 The Messrs. Waller give them as follows :—(1) [Gules] crusilly of
crosses botonées, three boars' heads couped [argent], for Swynborne;
(2) Paly-wavy of six [argent and gules], for Gernon; (3) Lost (It probably
bore [Or], a saltire engrailed [sable], for Botetourt); (4) Swynborne (as
above); (5) [Vert], an inescutcheon within an orle of eight martlets
[argent], for Erpingham; and (6) [Azure] a fess between two chevrons
[or], for Cornard.

FIG. 4—BRASS OF SIR ROBERT SWYNBORNE (1391) AND
SIR THOMAS SWYNBORNE (1412) AT LITTLE HORKESLEY.

The inscription, in Norman-French, reads[1]:

+ *Icy gist monsr. Robert Swynbo'ne, Seigneour de Horkesley Petite, Qe morust le jour de Seinte Steve l'an du Grace Mitt CCC Quat'vintz unszisme; De q'y alme [Dieu eyt mercye], AMEN. + Et Icy gist monsr. Thom's Swynbo'ne, fitz au dit monsr. Rob't, Sr. de Hammys, Mair de Burdeux, & Capitaigne de ffronsak, Qe morust en la veile de Seint Laurence l'an du G'ce Mitt CCCC xij: Del alme de q'y Dieu eyt pitee & mercye. Amen. Amen.*[2]

Between each word is a small floral device—a rose, a quatrefoil, an oak-leaf, or other; while each half of the inscription terminates with a boar's head—the badge of the Swynbornes.

The Messrs. Waller give a full account of the Swynborne family and of the two members of it commemorated by this brass.

The brass to Radulphus de Knevyntoun (1370), in the chancel at Aveley, is partly of foreign (Flemish) workmanship. It consists (fig. 5) of a rectangular plate (twenty-four inches by nine and a half inches) on which the knight is represented beneath a canopy, as is usual in the case of Flemish brasses; also of a smaller plate at the foot, on which is the inscription. Two shields, originally above the figure, have long been lost.[3]

The figure of the warrior is ill-drawn. The armour he wears is of a Continental, rather than an English, type, and agrees, in many of its details, with that worn by two wooden effigies in the choir of the cathedral at Bamberg.[4] In general, it approaches that of the two brasses just described, but the head and hands are bare, and across

---

1 The small portion placed within brackets is that now lost.

2 Here lieth Sir Robert Swynborne, Lord of [the Manor of] Little Horkesley, who died the day of Saint Steven [26th Dec.] in the year of Grace one thousand three hundred and ninety-one; upon whose soul may God have mercy, AMEN. And here lieth Sir Thomas Swynborne, son of the said Sir Robert, Lord of Hammys, Mayor of Bordeaux, and Captain of ffronsak, who died on the Eve of Saint Laurence [9th August] in the year of Grace one thousand four hundred [and] twelve; upon whose soul may God have pity and mercy. Amen. Amen.

3 They had gone when Holman wrote, about 1715.

4 *Archæological Journal*, ii., pp. 217-218 (1846).

his forehead he wears a narrow jewelled band or fillet. His jupon of leather is heavily studded with metal on the shoulders and round its lower part. The hauberk of mail below the jupon is seen at the neck and at the wrists, as well as at the waist, whence it hangs down to an unusual extent. To his bawdric are attached, as usual, a dagger and a sword, each of these being further secured by means of a long chain. Behind the sword is seen part of another weapon, probably a mace or club. This is very seldom represented on brasses. His thigh-pieces are heavily studded. His arms and the lower part of his legs are protected by plate. His sollerets are unusually long and pointed. His feet rest upon a hound. The canopy over his head, though richly cusped and crocketted, has a heavy and ungainly appearance owing to its square top.

There can be little doubt that the inscription, unlike the figure, was engraved in England, for the lettering is unlike that found on Flemish brasses, and resembles that met with on English brasses of the period.[1] It is in Latin, and reads:—

Hic jacet Radulphus de Knevyntōn ; obitus idem die Jovis ante festū Sci Nicholai Episcopi anno dni mittmo CCC lxx. Lr̄a d̄n̄icat F.[2]

Of the person commemorated by this brass nothing is known.

The commencement of the fifteenth century brought a radical change in the style of armour worn in England. The mixed mail and plate worn previously now gave place to suits of complete plate, the various pieces being

---

1 It is, perhaps, worth while to suggest that an inscription may once have run round the margin of the larger plate, as is usual on Flemish brasses, but that this has been cut off and a new inscription—that on the plate at foot—added. Possibly, even, the earlier inscription (supposing it to have existed) may have commemorated some other person ; in which case, the brass would be, in a way, palimpsest.

2 Here lies Ralph of Knevyntoun, who died on the Thursday before the Feast of St. Nicholas the Bishop [6th Dec.] in the year of our Lord one thousand CCC lxx; [when] the Dominical Letter [was] F. [The indication of the day of the week and the dominical letter of the year are both very unusual.]

Fig. 5—Brass of Sir Ralph de Knevyntoun (1370)
at Aveley.

comparatively few in number and simple in form. This style, known as the " Lancastrian," lasted for about half a century (until about 1450), but began to undergo changes during the latter part of that period.

It would be hard to find, anywhere in England, a finer or more characteristic example of armour of the Lancastrian Period than the effigy of Sir Thomas Swynborne (1412) at Little Horkesley, already figured (fig. 4). The knight is represented wearing a suit of complete plate-armour. The bascinet is now much less acutely pointed than formerly; the camail is replaced by a steel gorget, having a narrow fringe of mail below it; the cuirass takes the place of the jupon, and, at the bottom of it, covering the hips, are six rows of taces, below the lowermost of which the lower edge of the hauberk is visible; the arm-pits are protected by roundels or palettes, charged with the cross of St. George; but otherwise the knight's armour does not differ widely from that of his father. He wears, however, the Lancastrian badge, the Collar of SS.

An almost equally fine brass representing the same style of armour is that to Bartholomew Lord Bourchier (1409) at Halstead. Another fine example is that to William Loveney (about 1510) at Wendens Ambo. Other excellent, but smaller, examples are those at

Tolleshunt d'Arcy (John de Boys, 1419).
Bocking (John Doreward, 1420).
Felstead (a man in armour, *c.* 1420).
Springfield (Thomas de Coggeshall, 1422).
Harlow (a man in armour, *c.* 1430).
Arkesden (Richard Fox, 1439).
Ashen (a man in armour, *c.* 1440).
Willingale Doe (Thomas Torrell, 1442).
Little Waltham (John Maltoun, 1447).

The earlier examples are very similar to Sir Thomas Swynborne, but the last four, and especially the Arkesden figure, show transitional changes.

The Lancastrian style was followed by the " Yorkist," which lasted from about 1450 to about 1500. It was, of course, a development of that worn during the Lancastrian period. The difference lay chiefly in the addition of various new defensive plates, often extravagant in size and ugly in shape. The skirt of taces now becomes shorter (that is to say, it has fewer rows), and from the lowermost row a large tuille hangs down in front of each thigh.

Of the Yorkist style of armour, we have the following series of examples:—

Little Chesterford (George Langham, 1462: now lost).
Roydon (Thomas Colt, 1471).
Little Easton (Earl of Essex, 1483: fig. 6).
Latton (William Harper, *c.* 1485).
Little Bentley (Sir William Pyrton, 1490: mutilated).

Only one of these examples—that to Henry Bourchier, K.G., Earl of Essex (1483), and his Countess, at Little Easton—is of large size, and we have selected it for reproduction (fig. 6). This brass lies on the south side of the chancel, upon a large altar-tomb, which is surmounted by an elaborate canopy in Purbeck marble. The effigies of the earl and countess still remain and are in excellent condition, even retaining much of the coloured enamel by means of which the heraldic bearings were represented on their mantles. All else is, however, lost, including the marginal inscription on the chamfre of the slab and shields in quatrefoils on the sides of the tomb. Other missing parts consisted of two small scrolls; a design (probably a Bourchier knot) surrounded by the garter, above the earl's head; a representation of the fetterlock, the badge of the House of York, above the countess's head; twelve small Bourchier knots; and twelve small fetterlocks.

The earl (on a plate four feet four and a half inches long) wears over his armour the mantle of the Order of

Fig. 6—Brass of Henry Bourchier (1483), Earl of Essex,
and his Countess (1481), at Little Easton.

the Garter. The Garter itself surrounds his left knee, while the Collar of Suns and Roses (a Yorkist badge originated by Edward IV.) is seen round his neck. His head rests upon his helmet, which is surmounted by his coronet and crest.[1] The crest itself is broken away and lost, but the contoise, or lady's favour, which was attached to it remains. The mantling of the helmet is semée of water-bougets on the outer side and billetty on the inner ; these devices being taken from the coats of Bourchier[2] and Louvain,[3] which the earl bore quarterly on his shield. His feet rest against an eagle, as also do those of the countess. His armour is partly covered by his mantle, but one is able, nevertheless, to see the chief points in which the Yorkist style of armour differs from the Lancastrian—the flutings on the various plates ; the large defences for the shoulders, elbows, wrists, and knees; the shortness of the skirt of taces ; and the tuilles.

The dress of the countess will be noticed hereafter.

Sir William Bourchier, grandfather of Earl Henry, married Alianore de Loveyne. William, Lord Bourchier, father of this earl, was first cousin to Bartholomew, Lord Bourchier (died 1409), who is commemorated by a fine brass, already noticed,[4] at Halstead. Henry was created Earl of Essex in 1461 (at the Coronation of Edward IV.); died 4th April 1483; and was buried in the chapel of the Blessed Virgin Mary at Beeleigh Abbey, near Maldon, where his countess had been laid two years earlier. At the Dissolution, their bodies and monument were transferred to the church at Little Easton, where they held large estates.

Of brasses depicting armour of the first half of the

---

[1] An old man's (? a Saracen's) head in profile [proper], couped at the shoulders, habited [vert], collared [or]; on his head a ducal coronet [or], out of which rises a long cap [gules], tasselled [of the third].

[2] [Argent], a cross engrailed [gules], between four water-bougets [sable].

[3] [Gules], a fess [argent] between twelve billets [or].

[4] See *ante*, p. 125.

sixteenth century, several examples remain. Only one is of any great size, viz., that to William Viscount Beaumont (1507), which lies under a grand canopy (now, unfortunately, much mutilated) at Wyvenhoe. Smaller examples are very numerous in the county. The larger and more important are those at

Writtle (—— Bedell, c. 1500).
North Ockendon (William Pointz, 1502).
Writtle (Thomas Heveningham, 1513).
Tilty (Gerard Danet, 1520).
Roydon (John Colte, 1521).
Finchingfield (John Berners, 1523).
Ingrave (John FitzLewes, 1528).
Little Horkesley (Thomas Fyndorne, 1549).

The four last wear tabards.[1]

Of the men in armour of the second half of the sixteenth century, we have also many good examples, though all are quite small. The largest is that to Henry Fortescue (1576), at Faulkbourne. Others are at

Margaretting (a man in armour, c. 1550).
Great Canfield (John Wyseman, 1558).
Great Canfield (Thomas Fytche, 1558).
Tilty (George Medeley, 1562).
Stondon Massey (Rainold Hollingworth, 1573).
Stock (Richard Tweedye, 1574).
Rawreth (Edmund Tyrell, 1576).[2]
Runwell (Eustace Sulyard, 1587).[2]
Belchamp St. Paul (William Golding, c. 1595).

Practically all the Essex military brasses are fairly typical of the periods we have just been describing, but a few belonging to the sixteenth century deserve special mention.

The figure of Anthony D'Arcy (1540), at Tolleshunt D'Arcy, is engraved extremely rudely and is quite unlike

---

1 Others of less importance are at Hempstead (Thos. Huntingdon, 1492), High Laver (Edw. Sulyard, c. 1500), Stanford Rivers (Robt. Borrow, 1503), Little Braxted (Wm. Roberts, 1508), Theydon Gernon (c. 1520), Hutton (c. 1525).

2 These two are mural kneeling figures, see page 125.

others of that date. It seems to have been copied by a
very inefficient engraver—perhaps the local smith—from
the earlier figure of John de Boys (1419), already
mentioned, in the same church. The brass of George
Stonard and wife (1558), at Loughton, displays the
usual armour of the period, but it is curiously depicted,
and the arrangement of the figures and canopy all on one
large square plate, together with the costume of the lady,
suggest a foreign origin. The curious effigy of Gerhardt
d'Ewes (1591), at Upminster, is probably also of foreign
workmanship.

By the beginning of the seventeenth century the
custom of wearing armour, like that of laying down
monumental brasses, though not altogether obsolete, was
rapidly being discontinued. The brass to the memory of
Richard Bugges (1636) and his two wives, at Harlow, is
very fine and remarkably large for the period. The style
of armour represented upon it much resembles that worn
by most of the later figures mentioned above; but the
gentleman wears, over his armour, the large falling lace
collar of the Stuart period, and he stands with the aid of
a walking-stick (not in the usual attitude of prayer) and
with his helmet resting on the ground at his feet.

(2) BRASSES OF CIVILIANS.—Essex is very deficient
in early brasses representing civilians. There are now
in the county none of the fourteenth century, and very
few of the first half of the fifteenth. Of the latter
period, good matrices are to be found at Maldon (All
Saints'); but the only brasses that remain are poor
little effigies at Rayleigh, Blackmore, Widdington, and
Corringham. These are all either mutilated or worn;
are all both nameless and dateless, owing to the loss of
their inscription-plates; and are all very much alike, being
represented in the usual costume of this period—a
fur-lined gown, not reaching as low as the ankles, confined
at the waist by a belt, and having very full and loose

K

bag-sleeves, which are contracted and fit tightly at the
wrists. The hair is close cropped and the shoes are very
long and pointed.

During the latter half of the fifteenth century,
especially after the close of the Wars of the Roses, brasses
of civilians begin to be found more numerously in Essex,
and those examples which still remain are chiefly
interesting in that they illustrate the changes in civilian
costume which took place between the years 1460 and
1490. As a result of these changes, the gown became
longer (reaching below the ankles); the sleeves became
less full at the elbows and more so at the wrists; the toes
of the shoes became broader and more rounded (instead
of pointed); and the hair came to be worn long. They
are to be found at

> Leigh (Richard & John Haddok, 1453).
> Wenden Lofts (William Lucas, c. 1460).
> Hempstead (a civilian, c. 1470).
> Hempstead (a civilian, c. 1475).
> Littlebury (a civilian, c. 1475).
> Chrishall (a civilian, c. 1480: in profile: kneeling).
> Harlow (a civilian, c. 1480).
> Clavering (—— Songar, c. 1480).
> Barking (Thomas Broke, 1493).
> Brightlingsea (John Beriffe, 1496).

Two of the above—Hempstead (c. 1475) and Littlebury
—depict the cap and scarf, which is not commonly seen,
as the head is almost always shown bare.

Two fine matrices of brasses representing civilians of
about this date, both having been larger and more
magnificent than any of the brasses yet referred to,
remain in the county. In one (about 1480), at Saffron
Walden, the effigy stands upon a bracket and was
surmounted by a canopy. The second matrix is upon the
slab in St. Mary's Church, Maldon, commemorating
John Fenne, a merchant of the Staple of Calais. The
inscription is marginal and cut in the stone instead of
upon a brass fillet. This feature is unusual and suggests

foreign workmanship, which is probable in view of Fenne's close connection with the French port.

Just after the close of the fifteenth century, the low ebb to which the art of brass-engraving fell, at a period when England was already being stirred by the new learning, is extraordinary.   The mediæval arts were dying,

FIG. 7—BRASS OF THOMAS FRESHWATER AND WIFE (1517), AT TOLLESBURY.

to make room for others which were brought to England by the Renaissance, and brass-engraving was going the way of Gothic architecture and much else.   Yet brasses, while declining in quality, became more numerous than ever.

Further changes in costume also were taking place. The gown became open all down the front, and was worn as represented on the brass of Thomas Freshwater (1517) at Tollesbury (fig. 7). The toes are now much more broad-toed and ugly; hair is worn longer; and the face is always clean-shaven.

The brass (fig. 7) of Thomas Freshwater (1517), at Tollesbury, consisted, when perfect, of effigies of the man and his wife (each about eighteen inches high), two sons, and nine daughters, with a foot-legend, but the sons and the legend are lost. The children are represented (as usual on brasses of this period) in two groups—the sons below their father, the daughters below their mother. The group of sons remained when Holman wrote, about 1719; as also did the inscription, which read :—

Pray for the soules of Thomas Freshwater and Margaret his wife ; which Thomas deceased the 15th day of December in the yeare of our Lord 1517 ; on whose soules Jhū have mercy.

This style of costume—the Early Tudor, one may call it—appears with extraordinary uniformity upon all the Essex brasses to civilians of the first quarter of the sixteenth century. Examples, all very similar to that at Tollesbury, are at

Rainham (a civilian, c. 1500).
Stifford (John Ardalle, 1504).
Althorne (William Hyklott, 1508).
Littlebury (a civilian, c. 1510).
Saffron Walden (a civilian, c. 1510).
Writtle (a civilian, c. 1510).
Lindsell (Thomas Fitch, 1514).
Newport (Thomas Brond, 1515).
Hempstead (William Mordaunt, 1518).
Harlow (Thomas Aylmar, 1518).
Great Henny (William Fisher, c. 1520).
Great Coggeshall (a civilian, c. 1520).
Littlebury (a civilian, c. 1520).
Brightlingsea (John Beriff, 1521).
Netteswell (Thomas Lawrence, 1522).
Brightlingsea (William Beriffe, 1525).
Tollesbury (a civilian, c. 1525 : now lost).
Hempstead (a civilian, c. 1530).

About the year 1530, Essex brasses begin to show—
apparently almost suddenly—a further change in costume.
The gown now tended to become shorter; it was worn
slightly more open down the front, allowing the tunic
below it to be seen; and—most striking change of all—
it was provided with large false sleeves, hanging down
to the level of the knees, with holes or slits about on a
level with the elbows, through which the arms were thrust.
This style of costume—the Mid-Tudor we may call it—
was worn from about 1530 and onwards through the reigns
of Edward VI. and Mary. During these reigns, there is
a marked decrease in the number of brasses laid down.
The Essex examples of the period are mostly small.
The best are at

Elmdon (a civilian, c. 1530).*
Saffron Walden (a civilian, c. 1530).*
Upminster (a civilian, c. 1530).
Great Coggeshall (John Paycock, 1533).*
Toppesfield (John Cracherood, 1534).*
Orsett (a civilian, c. 1535 : kneeling).
Rettendon (a civilian, c. 1540).
Loughton (John Stonard, 1541).
Walthamstow (George Monox, 1543 : kneeling).
Upminster (Nicolas Wayte, 1545).
Lambourne (Robert Barfott, 1546).
Southminster (a civilian, c. 1560).
Colchester, St. Peter's (Aleyn Dister and Robert Leache, 1553).
Harlow (William Sumner, 1559).

All the above (except the Colchester figures) wear the
typical Mid-Tudor costume, but a certain number of them
(marked with an asterisk) have a peculiar character of
their own, which demands passing notice. These range in
date from about 1530 to 1540, and most of them occur in
a group of adjacent parishes in the north-west of the
county—that is, in the part nearest to Cambridge, where,
doubtless, some craftsmen, or school of craftsmen, had
a workshop from which they all emanated. Cole, the
antiquary, has left us sketches of others (about 1535)

which were, in his day, in the church at Chrishall, and the matrix of another still remains at Thaxted.[1] Curiously, however, the largest and finest of the series is the Paycock brass at Coggeshall, which is situated in the centre of the county, between twenty and thirty miles from the others. All these have a character which is easily recognizable, though the style of civilian costume represented on them does not differ, except in trifling details, from that on other brasses of the period. The style of female costume depicted on these brasses has, however, more distinctive peculiarities of its own, as will be noticed hereafter.

Commencing about the time of Elizabeth's accession (1558) and continuing through her own and the succeeding reign, a considerable revival in the art of brass-engraving becomes noticeable and the number laid down increases again. The plates of brass used are, for the first time, manufactured in England. They are somewhat thinner than formerly : consequently, the main engraved lines are all shallower. Further, shading and cross-hatching are much employed. The brass becomes more pictorial ; and there can be no doubt that, from this period onwards, effigies were intended to be actual *portraits* of the persons they commemorated, which they certainly had not been for nearly two centuries previously. Although, from the alteration in style of engraving, the general effect is very different, the actual costume of civilians changed very little, except for the appearance of small neck-ruffs and wrist-frills. The shoes were no longer abnormally broad-toed, the hair was worn short once more, and beard and moustache become almost invariable—a change of fashion which took place almost suddenly, if we may judge from Essex brasses.

The effigies of this period are represented not uncommonly as kneeling in the attitude of prayer before

---

1 Two brasses of the Early Tudor period—one at Littlebury (about 1520) and another at Hempstead (about 1530)—have also the same peculiarity.

a fald-stool, on which is an open book, with their children
kneeling behind them (the sons in a group behind the
father : the daughters behind the mother), the inscription
plate below them, and some shields above. Brasses of
this kind were generally mural, having never been intended
to be laid on the floor, as were brasses at all other periods.
Such brasses were let into a slab or panel, which was
built into wall or pillar.

FIG. 8—BRASS OF JOHN ALLEN AND WIVES (1572),
AT HATFIELD PEVEREL.

Examples of this kneeling type and of the new style
of costume just described are found upon brasses at

Terling (William Rochester, 1558).
Colchester, St. Peter's (John Sayers, 1563).
Colchester, St. Peter's (William Browne, 1572).
Hatfield Peverel (John Allen, 1572 : fig. 8).
Waltham Abbey (Thomas Colte, 1576).
Terling (John Rochester, 1584).

As an example, we figure the brass (fig. 8) to John Allen (1572), Esquire, at Hatfield Peverel. This is now on the floor of the chancel.[1] The brass, as we have it, represents John Allen and the first of his three wives, behind whom are her seven children (three sons and four daughters), all kneeling, with a long metrical inscription in English. Behind John Allen were kneeling effigies of his two later wives, both engraved on one plate, which is now lost, though Holman says it existed in 1715. Above were once also an achievement and two escutcheons, the latter of which remained when Holman wrote.

Other Essex brasses which represent civilians wearing the costume described above, but standing instead of kneeling, are those at

> Colchester, St. James' (John Maynarde, 1569).
> Roydon (John Swifte, 1570).
> Stondon Massey (John Carre, 1570).
> Writtle (Edward Bell, 1576).
> Brightlingsea (William Beriffe, 1578).
> Great Waltham (Thomas Wyseman, 1580: fig. 9).
> Great Coggeshall (Thomas Paycock, 1580).
> Great Waltham (a civilian, c. 1580).
> Harlow (a civilian, c. 1585).
> Great Parndon (Rowland Rampston, c. 1598).

The mutilated condition of the brass (fig. 9) to Thomas Wyseman (1580), at Great Waltham, is, unfortunately, characteristic of our Essex brasses. All that remains are the effigies of the man, his second wife, her children (a son and two daughters, mutilated), with an inscription below and an achievement above. The effigies of the first wife and her children, with the foot-legend, are lost. Thomas Wyseman is dressed in all respects like John Allen and the others just noticed; but, being represented standing, the front edges of his gown are parted slightly, allowing his tunic, tied with a sash at the waist, and his lower hose to be seen.

---

1 It was probably fixed upon the wall originally.

Fig. 9—Brass of Thomas Wyseman and Wife (1580)
at Great Waltham.

The inscription which was on the foot-plate, now lost, is recorded in an old manuscript book belonging to the Tufnell family, of Langleys, Great Waltham.[1]   It read:

Thomas Wyseman Obijt vicessimo die Novemb. Anno Regni Reginae Elizabeth. vicessimo secundo et Anno Domini 1580.

---

[1] Mr. F. Chancellor, *Sepulchr. Monum. of Essex*, p. 278 (1890).

The achievement displays the arms and crest of Wyseman.[1]

Essex civilian brasses of the next fifty or sixty years are very similar to the foregoing, except for changes in costume. The new style may be termed the Later Elizabethan. Its chief features (as seen in fig. 10) are the early disappearance of the wrist-frills, a remarkable increase in the size of the neck-ruff, the supersession of the short-skirted tunic by a tight-fitting doublet, reaching only to the waist and having practically no skirt, and the appearance of puffed-out trunk-hose or stuffed short breeches, worn over either long nether-hose or knee breeches. Over all these garments is worn an outer garment, either a long cloak (very similar to that worn in the preceding period) or a shorter sleeveless cape. Examples showing this costume under the long cloak are found on the brasses at

Sandon (Rev. Patrick Fearne, 1588).
Walthamstow (— Hale, 1588).
Hornchurch (Thomas Drywod, 1591).
West Ham (Thomas Stapels, 1592).
Loughton (William Nodes, 1594).
Barking (John Tedcastell, 1596).
Hornchurch (Thomas Hone, 1604).
Latton (Emanuel Woollaye, 1604).
Writtle (Edward Hunt, 1606).
Rettendon (Richard Cannon, 1605.)
Rettendon (Richard Humphrie, 1607).
Netteswell (John Bannister, 1608).
Writtle (Edward Bowland, 1609).
Newport (Geoffrey Nightingale, 1610).
Twinstead (Isaac Wyncoll, c. 1610).
Great Yeldham (Richard Symons, c. 1612).
Bocking (Oswald Fitch, 1613).
Great Waltham (Richard Everard, 1617).
Stifford (William Lathum, 1622).
Heybridge (John Whitacres, 1627).
Loughton (Abel Guilliams, 1637).
Matching (John Ballett, 1638).

---

1 [Per pale, or and azure]; on a chevron, two dragons combatant [all counterchanged]; on a chief [ermines], three cronels [argent]. Crest— A demi-dragon [sable] with wings endorsed [or] holding a broken staff [of the last].

An example wearing the sleeveless cape is the brass to John Alleyn at Fingringhoe (fig. 10). The effigy (thirteen inches high) is now mural, being affixed to the south wall of the chancel. The brass is peculiar in that it is undated, and, further, the inscription plate (both sides

HERE LYETH THE BODYE OF IOHN ALLEYN LATE OF WEVENHO AND AIL'SE HIS DAVGHTER

IEHOVA DEDIT IEHOVA ABSTVLIT SIT NOMEN BENEDICTV MORS ERVMARV META EST & I SALVTIS'. CVPIO ETIAM DISSOLVI & ESSE CV (

FIG. 10—BRASS OF JOHN ALLEYN AND DAUGHTER (ABOUT 1610), FINGRINGHOE.

of which we show) is palimpsest, having part of a Latin verse from Job i. 21 on the back.

Other figures represented wearing the short sleeveless cape are at

Harlow (Edward Bugge, *c.* 1582).
West Thurrock (Humphrey Heies, 1584).
Tillingham (Edward Wiot, 1584).
Clavering (Thomas Welbore, 1591).
Clavering (— Day, 1593).
Little Canfield (Ralph Pudsey, 1593).

> Eastwood (Thomas Burrough, 1600).
> Harlow (W. Newman, 1602).
> North Weald (Walter Larder, 1606).
> Berden (Thomas Thompson, 1607).
> Harlow (John Gladwin, 1615).
> Leyton (Tobias Wood, 1620).
> East Donyland (Nicholas Marshall, 1621).[1]

Many of these wear swords; most wear also large neck-ruffs; but (as at Fingringhoe) sometimes the broad collar of the cloak takes the place of the ruff. In some of the later examples (for instance, that of Nicholas Marshall, 1621), the ruff is replaced by the large falling lace collar which formed so prominent a feature of the Jacobean costume.

The reign of Charles I. marks the decay and final disappearance of monumental brasses, other than mere inscriptions. The few effigies of this period that remain are, for the most part, poorly designed and executed. Most of these have been referred to already. Others are at

> Leigh (Richard Chester, 1632).
> Southminster (John King, 1634).
> Leigh (a civilian, c. 1640).
> Harlow (Francis Reve, 1642).

The figures of John King (1634), at Southminster, the sons on the Chester brass (1632) at Leigh, and the civilian (c. 1640) at Leigh, are among the latest remaining in the county. All represent in some features the dress of the Cavalier.

(3) BRASSES OF LADIES are very numerous. We have, however, exceptionally few of very early date—in fact, only four belonging to the fourteenth century. The earliest, though smallest, of these—one of the earliest brasses to a lady in England—is that to Dame Ellen,

---

[1] Another example is the brass of Arthur Crafford (1606) formerly at South Weald, recently in the possession of the late Mr. John Sands, of the Priory, Noak Hill, Romford.

wife of Sir John de Wautone (1347), in the head of an elegant floriated cross at Wimbish. She wears, over a flowing cote, a plain but gracefully-draped mantle, fastening by a broad band across the breast. Her hair, which is uncovered, is arranged in large pleats on each side of the face and confined by a fillet across the forehead. Next in date comes the much-worn half-effigy of Isabel Clonville (1361), at West Hanningfield, in widow's garb.

A few years later in date is the largest and finest female effigy of this period in the county—that of Dame Joan, wife of Sir John de la Pole (1370), at Chrishall (see fig. 3). She wears a close-fitting kirtle, visible only at the sleeves, which are long, extending almost to the knuckles, and are buttoned throughout their entire length. Over this she wears a plain, low-necked, tight-fitting gown, buttoning down the front as far as the waist. The sleeves of this over-gown end at the elbows, from which hang long lappets or "liripipes," reaching almost to the level of the ankles. She wears the "nebulé" head-dress.

Another very large effigy is that of a widow (about 1390), at Stebbing, who wears over her cote a flowing mantle, with the barbe or gorget distinctive of her widowhood and a couvre-chef. Other widows in their distinctive dress are at

Halstead (Idonea, Lady Bourchier, 1409).
Little Chesterford (Isabel Langham, 1462).
East Horndon (Anne Tyrell, *c.* 1480).
Little Bentley (Katherine Pyrton, *c.* 1490).
Brightlingsea (Alice Beryff, 1536).

Brasses of ladies of the fifteenth century are to be found at

Halstead (Margaret, Lady Bourchier, 1409 : fine).
Tolleshunt D'Arcy (wife of John de Boys, 1419).
Felstead (Christina Bray, 1420 : half-effigy).
Bocking (wife of John Doreward, 1420).
Harlow (a lady, *c.* 1430).
Ashen (a lady, *c.* 1440).

Chrishall (a lady, *c.* 1450).
Rayleigh (a lady, *c.* 1450).
Wenden Lofts (Katherine Lucas, *c.* 1450).
Leigh (Christina and Margareta Haddok, 1453).
Hempstead (a lady, *c.* 1470).

All these (with the exception of the Halstead figure) wear a plain, long, loose gown, with very full sleeves, and confined by a girdle at the waist. With it, the earlier wear the " crespine " head-dress, and the later a more or less developed form of the " horned " head-dress. Ladies of high position usually wear instead a flowing sleeveless cloak over the plain or sideless cote-hardi, but this is not seen on any Essex brass between that of Lady Margaret Bourchier, at Halstead (1409), and those of Elizabeth Deyncourt at Upminster (1455), and Lady Arderne (1465) at Latton (see fig. 11, facing p. 152). These two show the horned head-dress in its most ornate form. Other fine figures of about this date are at

Ingrave (Margaret FitzLewes, 1466).
Roydon (Joan Colte, 1471).
Little Easton (Countess of Essex, 1483 : fig. 6).

The two former have " butterfly " head-dresses. The Countess of Essex (fig. 6) is a magnificent figure, wearing an ermine-lined mantle of purple velvet over a scarlet kirtle faced with ermine (the colours being represented by enamel). Her head rests upon a tasselled cushion, supported by an angel on either side, and her feet upon the back of an eagle. She wears her jewelled coronet ; also the Yorkist Collar of Suns and Roses (which her husband wears also), supporting as a pendant a lion couchant (the badge of the Earls of March), and she has jewelled rings upon her fingers.

After about the year 1480, the Essex brasses of ladies show an alteration in costume to a tight-fitting gown with a girdle and large fur cuffs to the closely-fitting sleeves. Of this series, there is one fine example, the brass at Dagenham to Dame Ann Urswyk (1479), who wears over this gown a cloak, as befits her station, a beautiful jewelled necklace, and an extreme example of the "butterfly" head-dress. The others are all small and poorly engraved. They are at

Harlow (a lady, *c.* 1480).
Saffron Walden (a lady, *c.* 1480).
Great Coggeshall (a lady, *c.* 1480).
Chrishall (a lady, *c.* 1480).
Clavering (— Songar, *c.* 1480).
Rainham (a lady, *c.* 1485).
Latton (William Harper, *c.* 1485).
Barking (Alice Broke, 1493).
Leyton (Ursula Gaspar, 1493).
Brightlingsea (Anna Beriff, 1496).

The first four wear "butterfly" head-dresses : the others either a simple kerchief or a modification of the "horned" head-dress, or an early form of the "pedimental" or "dog-kennel" head-dress noticed hereafter.

As with civilians, there is an extraordinary similarity amongst the brasses of ladies of the Early Tudor Period (1500-1530). A typical example is the Freshwater brass at Tollesbury (fig. 7, p. 131) showing the sleeved gown, the girdle and pendant, and the ugly pedimental or dog-kennel head-dress. Other examples are to be found at

Hempstead (Thomas Huntingdon, 1492).
High Laver (Edward Sulyard, *c.* 1500).
Writtle (— Bedell, *c.* 1500).
North Ockendon (Elizabeth Poyntz, 1502).
Stanford Rivers (Alys Borrow, 1503).
Brightlingsea (Mary Beriff, 1505).
Little Braxted (Jocose and Margaret Roberts, 1508).
Writtle (4 ladies, *c.* 1510).
Grays Thurrock (2 ladies, *c.* 1510).
Littlebury (a lady, *c.* 1510).
Great Coggeshall (a lady, *c.* 1510).
Saffron Walden (a lady, *c.* 1510).
Writtle (Heveningham, 1513).
Lindsell (Agnes Fytche, 1514).
Brightlingsea (Margaret Beriff, 1514).
Rochford (Maria Dilcok, 1514).

Newport (Margery Brond, 1515).
Harlow (Alys Aylmar, 1518).
Tilty (Mary Danet, 1520).
Cold Norton (a lady, c. 1520).
Dengie (a lady, c. 1520).[1]
Great Henny (Annes Fisher, c. 1520).[1]
Brightlingsea (— Beriff, 1521).
Netteswell (Alys Laurence, 1522).[1]
Brightlingsea (— Beriff, 1525).
Bradwell-juxta-Mare (Margaret Wyatt, 1526).
Tolleshunt D'Arcy (a lady, c. 1530).[1]

In some cases, ladies of position are represented wearing, over the costume described, long cloaks or mantles, handsomely blazoned with armorials. This is usually the case when their husbands are represented wearing tabards. Examples are seen at

Roydon (Elizabeth and Mary Colt, 1521).
Finchingfield (Elizabeth Berners, 1524).
Ingrave (Margaret FitzLewes, 1528).
Wyvenhoe (Countess of Oxford, 1537).
Little Horkesley (Brygete Marney, 1549).

The brass of the Countess of Oxford at Wyvenhoe is a magnificent life-size figure, which is still complete, although the elaborate canopy above it is now almost entirely gone.

Most of the brasses to ladies from 1530 to 1550 are very similar to those of the commencement of the century, except for a few slight details in costume. Examples are at

Messing (a lady, c. 1535).
Rettendon (a lady, c. 1535).
Loughton (Joan and Katheryn Stonard, 1541).
Walthamstow (Anne Monox, 1543).
Upminster (Ellen Wayte, 1545).
Lambourne (Katherine Barfott, 1546).

There is, however, one group of unusual type, and probably of local manufacture, which occurs in certain

---

[1] These ladies wear a plain kerchief, instead of the pedimental head-dress.

adjacent parishes in the north-western corner of the county, as noticed already.[1] The style of costume worn by the ladies represented on these brasses presents much more marked peculiarities than that worn by the men. In general, they wear the Early Tudor costume, but with variations.   Thus, the girdle is generally replaced by the sash, the long ends of which hang down ; a small short cape covers the shoulders; the dress is low-necked ; and a tam-o'-shanter-like cap is worn instead of the pedimental head-dress. Examples are seen on the brasses at

  Elmdon (two ladies, *c.* 1530).
  Saffron Walden (a lady, *c.* 1530).
  Hempstead (a lady, *c.* 1530 : no cape).
  Great Chesterford (Agnes Holden, 1532).
  Great Coggeshall (Joan Paycock, 1533).
  Toppesfield (Agnes Cracherood, 1534).

Another existed formerly at Chrishall and the matrix of yet another remains at Thaxted.

Another peculiarity of costume found on many of these locally-engraved brasses, and on some others of about the same date, lies in the form of the over-skirt. This is worn about twice too long, and has its lower edge turned up, either in front or at the sides, or both, and fastened at the waist, usually to the girdle, by means of hooks, pins, or buttons. In some cases, the skirt is lined with fur, which is seen, of course, when the lower edge is thus turned up.   This most remarkable fashion is shown on the following brasses :

  Great Coggeshall (Joan Paycock, 1533).
  Toppesfield (Agnes Cracherood, 1534).
  Rettendon (2 ladies, *c.* 1535).
  Walthamstow (Dame Anne Monox, 1543).

About the year 1550, the ladies on our Essex brasses changed markedly and abruptly in style of engraving and

---

1 See *ante*, p. 133.

L

in costume. The new costume may fitly be called the Elizabethan, because it came in shortly before the beginning of the reign of Elizabeth and continued to be worn, with only minor variations, until nearly the end of that reign. Its most marked feature was the entire disappearance of the pedimental head-dress, which was replaced by the French hood or Paris bonnet. This continued to be worn almost exclusively up to about 1585, and to a large extent up to about 1630 or even later. It is seen in figs. 8 and 9 (pp. 135 and 137).

Turning to the rest of the Elizabethan costume, we find that, in the earlier brasses, a small ruff surrounded the neck and small frills the wrists; but later the wrist-frills disappeared altogether and the neck-ruff grew very large. The over-gown had an opening all down the front, but was at first closed all down the breast, as far as the waist, by means of short ribbons tied in bows. Below the waist, however, the fore-edges of the over-gown, though furnished with rows of ribbon-ties which look as though intended to be tied, were always worn widely parted, displaying the front of the skirt of the under-gown. At first, the front of the under-gown was always quite plain, but after about 1560 the ribbons down each fore-edge of the over-gown disappeared, as in the Wyseman brass at Great Waltham (fig. 9, p. 137); and about 1580, the front of the under-gown came to be almost always embroidered, generally with a very elaborate floral, diapered, or arabesque design. The earlier examples of the Elizabethan costume are on the brasses at

Margaretting (a lady, c. 1550).[1]
Loughton (— Stonard, 1558).[2]
Tolleshunt D'Arcy (Philippa D'Arcy, 1559).
Upminster (a lady, c. 1560).

[1] The head being shown in profile, which is unusual, affords a side view of the French hood.
[2] This curious figure (probably of foreign workmanship) shows a late form of the pedimental head-dress.

Southminster (a lady, *c.* 1560).
Tilty (Mary Medeley, 1562.)
Fryerning (Mary Berners, 1563).
Writtle (Margaret Bell, 1567).
Stondon Massey (— Carre, 1570).
Great Waltham (— Wyseman, 1580; fig. 9).
Hornchurch (— Drywod, 1591).

The kneeling figure at Hatfield Peverel (fig. 8, p. 135) is another example of this costume, but does not show the front of the skirt.

After about 1580, figures with the front of the under-skirt elaborately embroidered and with the sleeves striped or slashed become the rule. Examples are to be found at

Littlebury (Joan Bradbury, 1578).
Willingale Doe (Ann Sackville, 1582).
Harlow (Jane Bugge, 1582).
Great Bardfield (Eleanor Bendlowes, 1584).
Chingford (Margaret Rampston, 1585).
Walthamstow (— Hale, 1588).
Tilty (Margaret Tuke, 1590 : kneeling).
West Thurrock (Katherine Redinge, 1591).
Writtle (Rose Pinchon, 1592).
Little Canfield (Ann Pudsey, 1593).
Barking (Elizabeth Tedcastell, 1596).
Faulkbourne (Mary Fortescue, 1598).
Bradfield (Joan Rysby, 1598).

The last few of these are, however, not altogether typical of the Elizabethan costume, for they show, in several respects, signs of coming changes. In some cases, the French hood is replaced by a broad-brimmed high-crowned " bowler " hat. Early examples of a lady wearing a hat are the wife of the Rev. Patrick Fearne (1588), at Sandon, and Katherine Redinge (1591), at West Thurrock. Other changes taking place about this time are the parting of the edges of the over-gown down the breast, leaving exposed the bodice of the under-gown, which is remarkable for its long, straight, peaked stomacher and is generally embroidered, like the front of the skirt of the under-gown.

These and other changes, commencing about 1590, gradually altered the Elizabethan costume, so that, by the end of the century, what may be regarded as a new style had been evolved. It may be called, for convenience, the Jacobean costume; for, although introduced during the latter years of Elizabeth, it attained its extreme development in, and was worn throughout, the reign of James I. In regard to details, there was greater diversity than is seen in connection with any earlier style of female costume. Consequently one seldom meets with two figures precisely alike.

Of the various forms of the Jacobean costume, we have many good examples. The best are

South Ockendon (Margaret Barker, 1603: with triple neck-ruff).
Hornchurch (Jane Hone, 1604).
Latton (Frances Franklin, 1604: skirt enormously distended).
Latton (Margaret Wollaye, 1604).
Writtle (— Hunt, 1606: kneeling).
North Weald (Marie Larder, 1606).
Berden (Ann Thompson, 1607).
Netteswell (Elizabeth Bannister, 1608).
Newport (Katherine Nightingale, 1608).
Writtle (Jone Bowland, 1609).
East Ham (Hester Neve, 1610).
Cressing (Dorcas Musgrave, 1610: wearing calash: skirt enormously distended).
Twinstead (Marie Wyncoll, 1611).
Great Waltham (Clemence Everard, 1611).
Great Baddow (Jane Paschall, 1614: wearing calash).
Writtle (Jone Bowland, 1616).

Before the end of the reign of James I. (say about 1615 or 1620), further changes began to appear. The French hood, though still worn, was now less common than the hat. The large starched neck-ruff was still fashionable, but the huge distention of the skirt had practically disappeared, as had the long-peaked stomachers and the embroidery on the front of the skirt.

The brasses of this period are neither very numerous nor very interesting. They are few, because, in the reign of Charles I., the custom of laying down memorial brasses was rapidly becoming obsolete; and they are of little interest, because the art of engraving them was undergoing final decadence. Among the best examples are those at

Leyton (Eliza Wood, *c.* 1620).
East Ham (Elizabeth Heigham, 1622 : with large calash).
Stifford (Susan Lathum, 1622).
Littlebury (Anne Byrd, 1624).
East Donyland (Mary Gray, 1627).
Stifford (Elizabeth Lathum, 1630).
Leigh (Elizabeth Chester, 1632).
Harlow (Elizabeth Bugges, 1636).
Loughton (— Gwilliams, 1637).
Matching (Rose Ballet, 1638).
Leigh (a lady, *c.* 1640).
Harlow (Joan Reve, 1642).

(4) BRASSES OF PRIESTS.—Of these, there are still in the county about twenty examples, as well as several fragments of effigies which have been found to exist on the reverse sides of palimpsest plates. There are also a remarkably large number of slabs bearing matrices which once contained brasses to priests.

All the earlier ecclesiastical figures are half-effigies represented in Mass vestments. The very earliest of these (three in number) were—for they are now lost, the matrices only remaining—each within, above, or beside the head of an elegant floriated cross, both effigy and cross being surrounded by a brief marginal inscription in uncial Longobardic characters. These commemorated Nicholas Ferrobaud (about 1315), at West Thurrock; a priest whose name is illegible (about 1315), at Felstead; and Sire Boneface de Hart, Canon of Aosta, together with another priest not mentioned in the inscription (about 1320), at Hornchurch. Four other half-effigies, which are scarcely later in date and fortunately still remain, are unaccompanied by a cross and have the inscription (still very brief) on a rectangular plate placed immediately below the half-effigy. Such are the brasses to Sire Richard de Beltoun (about 1340: very good), at Corringham; Sire Ralph Perchehay (about 1365: also very good), at Stifford; a priest (about 1370: head only remaining), at Great Leighs; and Ralph Strelley (1414: mutilated), also at Great Leighs. The example at Corringham has the apparel of the alb continuing all round the wrists: that at Stifford and the earlier of the two at Great Leighs have a very bold fylfot on the collar of the alb. Scattered about the county, too, there is a considerable number of matrices from which half-length effigies of priests of about the same period have been reaved.

From the beginning of the fifteenth century onwards, all our remaining brasses to priests are full-length, with the exception of one at Great Leighs, as noticed above.[1] The largest and finest example occurs at Great Bromley and represents William Byschopton (1432), beneath a handsome crocketted canopy. Another fine example at Saffron Walden commemorates (?) John Byrd (about 1425), over whose head was a pelican in piety, now lost. At Little Easton is a smaller figure, with a rhyming dateless inscription, to Robert Fyn (about 1425). A very poorly-engraved effigy to (?) John Kekilpenny (about 1480: holding chalice with wafer inscribed " I.H.C.") exists at Laindon. A very large matrix (about 1425) at Belchamp Walter and a smaller matrix (about 1490) at Pleshey, both once contained the brasses of a priest and a soldier, doubtless brothers. At Theydon Gernon, a large and fine effigy to William Kyrkeby (about 1485) represents him wearing a cope—our only remaining example of a pre-Reformation priest wearing this vestment, though the matrix of a very fine brass of a priest

---

1 Another exception was the brass to Sire John Smythe (1475), with very curious inscription, formerly in the Hospital Chapel at Great Ilford, but now lost.

in cope, beneath a handsome canopy, remains at Belchamp
Walter. At Stifford, a priest (about 1480), now nameless
through loss of the inscription, is represented in a shroud,
holding in his hands a heart inscribed " I.H.C."

Of brasses to priests in academic costume, we have
three examples—namely, at Thaxted (about 1450),
Strethall (about 1480), and Barking (about 1480 : holding
a chalice). All these are comparatively small and
all are nameless, through loss of their inscriptions.

Of priests represented on brasses to the memory
of their parents, there are two examples in Essex.
John Lucas, Lord Abbot of Waltham (resigned 1475),
wearing his robes and mitre and holding his crozier,
appears as the eldest son on the brass of his parents,
William Lucas (about 1460) and Katherine his wife, at
Wenden Lofts; and the eldest son of — Songar (about
1485) and wife, at Clavering, is represented as a monk.

The Essex brasses to sixteenth-century ecclesiastics
are few in number, small in size, and exceedingly
ill-engraved. The chief are those to a priest unknown
(about 1510), at Littlebury; to (?) Richard Bladwell
(about 1510), at Laindon; and to Thomas Westley (1535),
chaplain to Elizabeth Countess of Oxford (died 1537),
at Wyvenhoe. All these wear Mass vestments and hold
chalices with wafers. The Laindon effigy is so execrably
executed that one can only surmise it was engraved by
a local workman, perhaps the village smith, who tried to
copy the earlier figure of a priest, already noticed, in the
same church. At Sandon, there is the effigy of a
post-Reformation village priest—the Rev. Patrick Fearne
(1588)—who is described as " parson of this parishe,"
but appears to wear the ordinary civilian costume of the
time. He kneels with his wife at a table.

Of brasses of pre-Reformation abbots and bishops
wearing the Dalmatic, we have no examples remaining,
except certain small fragments engraved on the reverse
side of palimpsest plates; but, at Chigwell, there is the

huge late effigy of Samuel Harsnett (1630), Archbishop of York, who is represented in cope and mitre with pastoral staff.

(5) BRASSES OF LAWYERS are not numerous anywhere. In Essex we appear to have more than our fair share belonging to the fifteenth century, for we have three fine examples—those to Thomas Rolf (1440), Serjeant-at-Law, at Gosfield; Sir Peter Arderne (1465), Chief Baron of the Exchequer and Judge of Common Pleas, at Latton; and Sir Thomas Urswyk (1479), Chief Baron of the Exchequer and Recorder of London, at Dagenham.

The brass of Sir Peter Arderne (1465), at Latton (fig. 11), is upon an altar-tomb standing on the north side of the chancel, in a chantry which the judge built and endowed.[1] It is still in good condition and perfect, with the exception of the inscription, which is lost. There remain the fine effigies of the judge and his wife with four escutcheons. The figure of the judge (thirty-seven inches high) represents him in full judicial costume, consisting of the coif, a long tunic having tight sleeves narrowly edged with fur at the wrists, a hood, a tippet, and an outer robe, buttoned over the right shoulder, open down the right side, and reaching rather below the knees. The robe was lined with fur, represented by white metal or enamel let in, but now worn or broken away. The coif and hood have also been similarly inlaid.

The costume of the lady has been noticed already.[2]

The four shields bear respectively Arderne,[3] de Bohun,[4] ————(?),[5] and ————(?).[6]   All have at one time

---

[1] See Mr. C. E. Johnston, on "Arderne's Chantry at Latton," in *Home Counties Magazine*, iv., pp. 222-225 (1902).

[2] See *ante*, p. 142.

[3] Paly of six [or and gules]; on a chief [argent], three lozenges [of the second], the middle one charged with a chess-rook [of the first].

[4] [Argent], on a bend [sable], cotised, between six lioncels rampant, a mullet [of the first] for difference.

[5] On a bend, three mullets.

[6] A chevron engrailed between three chess-rooks.

FIG. 11—BRASS OF SIR PETER ARDERNE, JUDGE,
AND WIFE (1467), AT LATTON.

had enamel inlaid in them. They, together with the initials " P.K.A." (Peter and Katherine Arderne) carved on the stonework of the tomb, serve to identify the persons commemorated, in spite of the loss of the inscription. This was lost before Gough wrote in 1796, when what seems to have been a copy of it, written in Latin verse on vellum and framed, hung in the church.

Sir Peter Arderne probably came of an ancient Cheshire family of that name. He married Katherine, daughter of — de Bohun. He had a long and distinguished legal career, becoming Serjeant-at-Law in 1443, Chief Baron of the Exchequer and Judge of the Court of Common Pleas, both in 1448, and a Knight in 1460. He owned, and probably resided on, the manor of Mark's Hall, in Latton.

Sir Thomas Urswyk (1479), at Dagenham, wears the same tunic and gown, but lacks coif, tippet, and hood. His feet rest upon a lion, and a rosary hangs at his side. Our other legal effigy, that of Thomas Rolf (1440), Serjeant-at-Law, at Gosfield, is represented wearing a cassock-like gown, tabard, tippet, hood, bands, and coif. Of later legal effigies we have a few, though none of special interest, as all wear ordinary civilian costume.

(6) SHROUD BRASSES.—In this gruesome class of memorials, the corpse is represented as wrapped in the shroud, which is gathered and tied above the head and below the feet, but left partly open, so as to show the face and feet. This class is represented most numerously in the Eastern Counties, but, for some reason, very poorly in Essex; for there are two examples only—the brass (already noticed[1]) at Stifford (to an unknown priest, about 1480), and another at Little Horkesley to Katherine Leventhorpe (1500)[2] Formerly, however, there

---

[1] See *ante*, p. 151.
[2] This lady's family seems to have been fond of such memorials; for John Leventhorpe, Esquire (1484), and his wife, at Sawbridgeworth, Herts., are also represented in shrouds

was at Debden another shroud brass representing a lady (about 1490), a sketch of which[1] is preserved in Cole's Manuscripts in the British Museum.

(7) PALIMPSEST BRASSES.—The loosening of brasses from their matrices, which occurs from time to time, is always regrettable, because the detached plates are liable to become lost; but such detachment often discloses the interesting fact that there is, on the back of the plate, a portion of an earlier engraved design, the brass being thus what is called "palimpsest." We have in Essex a considerable number of brasses of this class, but they need not be noticed at length here, as they have been described exhaustively by Mr. Mill Stephenson, F.S.A.[2]

The most interesting are at Tolleshunt D'Arcy and Upminster, where there are several in each church. At Upminster, the figures of Nicholas Wayte and his wife are particularly interesting, as they have been cut out of the earlier effigy of a large abbot or bishop, whose chasuble was richly diapered, and two other portions cut out of the same figure are found to have been re-used in a brass (about 1545) at Bayford, Herts.

(8) "FLEMISH" BRASSES.—The brasses usually spoken of as "Flemish" (though they appear to have come, not from Flanders only, but also from other adjacent parts of the Continent) are so distinctive in character that they deserve separate notice.

In Essex, there are several brasses which appear to be of "Flemish" workmanship, but all are small. That of Ralph de Knevyntoun (1370) at Aveley has already been noticed.[3] Of later date are those to George Stonard and wife (1558), at Loughton, and Gerhardt D'Ewes

---

1 Figured by us in *Transactions Essex Archæological Society*, n.s., viii., p. 36 (1900).

2 *Transactions Monumental Brass Society*, iv., pp. 97-119 (1903); also published separately.

3 See *ante*, p. 123.

(1591), at Upminster. Fragments of others are found
on the reverses of various palimpsest plates already
noticed. A piece of scroll work (about 1375) at Tolleshunt
D'Arcy has charming designs in Flemish work on both
sides, and both apparently of the same date. The brass
of which it formed part must have been very large.

(9) CROSS BRASSES.—Not a single cross in brass now
remains in the county, with the exception of a tiny
fragment at Wimbish, though matrices which have once
contained such brasses are not very rare. Most of these
matrices are found in slabs belonging to the first quarter
of the fourteenth century and have brief marginal
inscriptions (usually in Norman-French and undated) in
uncial Longobardic characters. In all, the cross was of
very elegant design, having floriated arms and a tall slender
stem. Three such, having half-effigies of priests in or
above the head of a floriated cross, have been noticed
already.[1] Others exist at Tilty (to Maud de Mortemer),
Great Horkesley (to Richard Oliver, 1327, priest),
Tolleshunt D'Arcy, Great Dunmow, Blackmore, and
Heydon (the names of the last four all illegible).

Of the same type, but with a different kind of
inscription and slightly later in date, is (or rather was,
for only a small fragment remains) the elegant octofoil
cross at Wimbish, within the head of which are the effigies
of Sir John de Wautone (1347) and his wife. Its slender
stem rises from a "castle" on the back of an elephant.
The inscription, in French and probably in Longobardic
characters, was engraved on a brass fillet, but is now lost.

Later in date were the three cross brasses of which
the matrices remain at Danbury (about 1420), at Fyfield
(about 1420), and at Stapleford Tawney (William Scott,
1491).

(10) BRACKET BRASSES are scarce everywhere and
only a single one remains in Essex—that at Brightlingsea.

---

[1] See *ante*, p. 149.

It is elegant, but much mutilated. On it were originally
the figures of two priests (about 1400), but it has been
utilised for two later effigies, commemorating Dame Alice
Beriff (1536) and her daughter Margaret. We have,
however, two fine matrices of bracket brasses, both of
about the year 1400, at Saffron Walden and Birdbrook.

(11) HEART BRASSES, which form another small class,
are represented in Essex by one single example only.
It occurs at Elmstead, where a heart (about 1500) is
supported by the tips of the fingers of two hands, issuing
from clouds, conventionally represented. The heart
is inscribed "*Credo*," and the legend is continued on a
scroll above, which bears the words "*videre bona
donum*." The inscription is lost and the name of the
person commemorated is unknown.

(12) INSCRIPTIONS.—The inscriptions appearing on
our earliest brasses—those of the latter part of the
thirteenth century and beginning of the fourteenth—ran
round the margin of the slab. The characters were
Longobardic, each letter being cut separately out of a
sheet of brass and let into a matrix of its own. Colons
usually divide the words. Such inscriptions are always
very brief, usually dateless, and in Norman-French, though
Latin is used occasionally. Several such inscriptions,
associated with half-effigies of priests and floriated crosses,
have been noticed already.[1] On other such slabs there
was nothing but the inscription. The best of this kind
remaining in Essex are those to David de Tillebery (about
1330), at Stifford, and to Thomas-at-Nok (about 1310),
at Wennington; but there are others, very much
defaced, at Hempstead, Saffron Walden, and Blackmore.
Inscriptions of this kind were discontinued about 1330—
probably because it was found that the single letters were
easily detached from their matrices and lost. Of all the

---

[1] See *ante*, p. 149.

inscriptions of this kind we have in Essex, only *two* single letters on one slab—that at Hornchurch—now remain in position.

At an early date, therefore, inscriptions—still in Longobardic characters and still usually dateless and in French—began to be engraved on narrow fillets of brass. Our earliest example is that (fig. 2) to Sir William FitzRalph (about 1323), at Pebmarsh. Already, however, the use of Latin and of Black Letter characters had come in, as shown by the fragment of an inscription in Latin to John Bauchon (about 1325) formerly at North Ockendon. Yet a little later, inscriptions ceased to be engraved on marginal fillets and were placed on long rectangular plates, usually placed immediately below an effigy. Examples are those to Robert de Bokkyngg (1361), vicar, at Stanstead Montfitchet; Isabel Clonvill and her son John (1361), at West Hanningfield; and Sir Thomas Tyrell and wife (about 1380), at Downham.

Later inscriptions in Essex are too numerous and too varied to particularise. Of examples belonging to the fifteenth, sixteenth, and seventeenth centuries, we have about two hundred which seem never to have accompanied effigies and, of course, hundreds of others accompanying effigies and other devices. Up to about 1500, most are in Latin and in Black Letter. Later, English became common. Between 1550 and 1600, the use of Roman, instead of Black Letter, characters became almost invariable.

ESSEX AND THE CIVIL WAR

By Alfred Kingston

IT is unusual for the student of history to find a single county, or any definite local area, becoming a unit in the unfolding of a great historical drama; an exception to the general rule is, therefore, the more interesting. Such an experience was afforded by the great upheaval of the Civil War between King Charles I. and his Parliament—a war which, to a large extent, at any rate in the earlier stages of it, was waged by Parliament through its County Committees.

The Eastern Counties, as I have written elsewhere—

. . . " earned the distinction of presenting the one great historic unity which enabled these counties to hold their own, and, whether for good or ill, to practically determine the fate of the rest of the kingdom in the struggle. Here the essential elements of the Puritan revolution . . . came into sharpest conflict. In these counties arose the one man whose acts were destined to colour all our subsequent history; and here arose, too, the ever-victorious Ironsides, who, with the 'Soldier's Pocket Bible' in their knapsacks, went forth with sturdy purpose and resistless valour, to roll back the tide of war from their own borders, and to carry the Parliamentary cause to victory at Marston Moor and Naseby."[1]

Of the seven associated Eastern Counties,[2] Essex affords the most interesting example of a county marching into the war for Parliament with a practically free hand, so far as danger from without was concerned. So long as Parliament held London, the geographical situation

---

[1] *East Anglia and the Great Civil War*, by Alfred Kingston, p. 2.
[2] The seven associated counties were :—Essex, Hertford, Cambridge, Huntingdon, Suffolk, Norfolk, and Lincoln.

of Essex, with the other counties of East Anglia going solid for Parliament along its frontiers, left it practically unassailable. Nevertheless, its consistent following of Parliament was broken into from within by some of the most brilliant examples of loyal devotion to the King, and the most tragic experiences of some of its people.

It may be of interest to glance briefly at what was happening in Essex on the eve of the great struggle. What were the men of Essex—the county which gave Oliver Cromwell his wife[1]—doing while John Hampden was refusing to pay ship-money away in Buckinghamshire? From the sheriff to the petty constables there was no end of difficulty in getting the unpopular impost collected. In several Cambridgeshire parishes, on the north-west borders of Essex, riots occurred, and the collectors of the tax were maltreated. In 1640, a week after the dismissal of the Short Parliament, as the State Papers show, the Sheriff of Essex was sent for and examined for having collected very little ship-money, and for not having distrained upon those who refused to pay. At Dedham, Samuel Sherman and two other collectors were sent up to appear before the Council to answer for refusing to collect the tax in their parishes. Sherman was sent to the Fleet Prison, where he lay three weeks, and afterwards complained that in his absence "silver spoons were distrained upon for his own subsidy." [2]

Besides these conflicts over the collection of ship-money, there were loudly muttered complaints all over the Eastern Counties against the changes introduced into public worship in the churches, and when Charles I. would have imposed his ecclesiastical system upon Scotland, soldiers refused to march against the Scots. The Essex men, though living near it, did not like the

---

[1] Oliver Cromwell married a daughter of Sir Thomas Bourchier, an Essex magistrate.
[2] *Journals of the House of Lords.*

water, and "resolved to die rather than go by sea" to
Scotland. Lord Maynard, the Lord Lieutenant of
Essex,[1] gave this account of his troubles with the pressed
men of Essex:

"I am ashamed that I have to trouble you so often about the same
thing, but the insolences of the soldiers billetted in Essex are every day
increased by new attempts, insomuch as they have now, within these
few days taken upon them to reform churches; and even in the time of
divine service to pull down the rails about the Communion Tables, and
in Icklinton [*Ickleton, on the Cambs. border of the County*], in
Cambridgeshire, to force the minister to run over the river, and the
minister at Panfield near Braintree to forsake his charge and family
to save his life."

The county of Essex, in 1642, gave pretty clear
evidence of its readiness to take sides in the coming
struggle. In June this spirit is recorded in the "Petition
and Resolution of the Captains of Hundreds and other
inhabitants of the County of Essex":

"Thus, with our hands upon our swords, we stand ready at your
command to perform our vows to God and oaths of fidelity to His
Majesty, in taking up arms against these false flatterers and traitors
who abuse his Royal favour, intending under the glorious title of his
name and standard to fight against the peace and honour of their
Sovereign, against religion and the laws, and to make a prey and spoil
of three flourishing kingdoms at once; and so spend our dearest blood
in the defence of the lives and liberties of our countrymen; the laws
which are the life of our liberty and peace, religion more precious
than both; and the King and Parliament, in whose rights lieth bound
up the life of all the rest." [2]

But carefully guarded though the wording of this
petition was, there was a dilemma behind it which
puzzled Mr. Robert Smith, the High Sheriff for Essex.
He had received the King's proclamation forbidding the

---

1 Lord Maynard was at this time also Lord Lieutenant of Cambridgeshire and had to face a mutiny in that county, the injuries received in which,
having "kindled all the summer in his blood," were, as Lady Maynard
afterwards declared, the cause of "his violent fever, and consequently
of his soddaine death."—*Petition from Lady Maynard in "Carew
Transcripts," Public Record Office.*
2 *Journals of the House of Lords.*

trained bands to muster for exercise. In his dilemma he appealed to Parliament to know what he was to do, upon which Parliament declared the King's writ to be illegal, and assured Mr. Smith that he should be protected in whatever he did " in the service and by the authority of Parliament."

The clergy were in a similar dilemma, receiving rival and contradictory proclamations from King and Parliament. Some read both proclamations from the pulpit; others read that of the King and "threw away that of Parliament contemptuously," and became marked as "malignant priests" in consequence, especially where they took occasion to denounce the Parliament as well. The county families of Essex began to divide themselves into hostile camps so soon as an open rupture took place.

Meanwhile the King's standard was raised at Nottingham on August 22nd, 1642. Sir John Lucas had been secretly preparing to set out from his house at Colchester with horse and arms to go and join the King. But he had delayed his start until it was difficult to accomplish his purpose. At midnight on the Sunday everything was in readiness for the start northwards, when one of Sir John's servants betrayed the secret movements to the captain of the Parliamentary trained bands.

Between one and two o'clock in the morning Sir John Lucas and his followers set out by the back gate of his house, only to find the way barred by a strong guard, which sprang up from under the hedge. Then a gun was fired as a signal, drums commenced to beat, and immediately " the whole town was raised." Beacons were fired, horsemen galloped out of the town in all directions to "call in the country against the Cavaliers in Sir John Lucas's house." The house was entered with a rush, and the first person they encountered was Mr. Newcome, the Royalist parson of Trinity Church, Colchester, who was promptly lodged in the common gaol. In the ladies'

M

chamber they met Lady Lucas, and, putting a sword
to her breast, demanded of her to tell them where the
arms and the Cavaliers were. The arms were found,
carried off to the Town Hall, and Sir John and Lady
Lucas were taken to the Moot Hall. The house was
plundered, the servants made prisoners, and then, upon
a rumour being spread that Cavaliers were still concealed
therein, the house was " battered down, the deer killed
in the park," and it was alleged that St. Giles' Church
and the Lucas family vault were broken into, and " with
pistols, swords, and halberts they transfixed the coffins
of the dead." [1]

When Parliament heard of the affair, they sent down
Sir Thomas Barrington and Mr. Harbottle Grimston, the
Member and Recorder for Colchester, to " discountenance
such plunder." Sir John Lucas was taken prisoner to
London, and found guilty of treason, but afterwards
released on bail in £40,000.

Meanwhile, the people, in a frenzy of excited
partizanship, made their way to St. Osyth, the residence
of the Countess Rivers, a Catholic, who was naturally
suspect. Her house was plundered, but Lady Rivers
escaped to Long Melford, in Suffolk. The Earl of
Warwick was away at sea at the time, but his steward,
Arthur Wilson by name, " set off with some few men,
and a coach and six horses, to fetch the Lady Rivers
to Leighs Park for safety." Arriving at Sudbury, the
coach and six caused no end of commotion, the mob
failing to recognise it as that of the Earl of Warwick,
and declaring it to be that of Lady Rivers. Wilson
appealed to the mob, declaring that he was the steward of
the Earl of Warwick, " a lover of his countrie, and now
in the Parliament's employment." " The tops of the trees,"
he says, " were thronged with people, and there was an
ytching desire after the coach horses." [2] At length, after

---

[1] *Mercurius Rusticus.*
[2] Particulars of this incident may be found in Wilson's narrative in
Peck's *Desiderata Curiosa*, lib. lx., pp. 23-5.

producing letters, Wilson was allowed to go. At Long Melford he found that the Countess had escaped thence to Bury St. Edmunds, and had gone on to London.

After the battle of Edgehill, on Sunday, October 23rd, 1642, the fear that the King might march on London roused the home counties to the highest pitch of military ardour. A great meeting of gentlemen and freeholders of the county assembled at Chelmsford, and—

"With one consent resolved to unite themselves in defence of both King and Parliament, and at their own cost and charges set out 12,000 men to march towards the Lord Generall (the Earl of Essex, who was then falling back upon London, with the Royalist Army marching in the same direction) desiring that the Earle of Warwick might be made their Generall, which was condescended unto by both Houses of Parliament, and in pursuance of these, their valiant resolutions, agreed that such gentlemen hereafter named, in the severall places of their habitations in the County should raise what men they could, and have the leading and command of such as they should particularly raise in the places hereunder mentioned : —

"For the forces in and about Colchester, Kelvedon, Witham, the two Braxteeds and Cogshall and the County in those parts, Sir Thomas Barrington, Mr. Grimston, Sir John Sands, and Sir Thomas Wiseman, nominated.

"For the forces about Harwich, Felsteed, Maintree [Braintree?] and County adjacent, Sir Harbottle Grimston, Sir Samuel Luke,[1] Mr. Thomas Mildmay, of Teding, and Mr. William Wiseman, nominated.

"For the forces about Chelmsford, Baddow, Engerstone, and the hundred of Chelmsford, Mr. Wright, Sir William Stuckley, Sir Martin Lumley, and Mr. Talbot nominated.

"For the forces in the Hundred of Dengy, Bradwell-by-the-Sea, Burneham, Southminster, Tillingham, Ashledon, and Munden, Mr. Wiseman, Justice of the Peace, Mr. Alleston, Mr. Brown, Captain Mildmay, Captain Fleming, Captain Audley, and Mr. George Baker nominated.

---

[1] Sir Samuel Luke became Scoutmaster-General in the Parliamentary Army, Governor of Newport Pagnell, and among the men serving under him in that garrison was John Bunyan. Sir Samuel is said to have been the original of Butler's *Hudibras*. He had a keen eye for humour, even amidst the sordid and tragic side of war. The soldiers in Newport Pagnell were (about the time that John Bunyan was there) at one time in such sore straits that Sir Samuel wrote :—"There were 2 in my Company that had but one payre of Britches betweene them, soe that when one was up the other must upon necessity be in his bed."—Luke's Letter-book, in Stowe MSS., f. 236. See also Egerton MSS., British Museum Library.

" For the Hundred of Retchford, Mr. Thomas King, Mr. Whitaker, Mr. Peck, Mr. Sams, and Mr. White nominated.

" For the forces about Billerky (Billericay), Onger, the two Nortons, and that part of the County, Mr. Thomas White, Mr. Isaac Joyner, Mr. Haddow, Mr. Bradley and Mr. Hugh Kadley (or Radley) nominated.

" For the forces to be raised at Burntwood (Brentwood), Rumford, Horne-Church and the County between those towns and London, Sir Henry Fisher, Sir William Luckey, Mr. Thomas Harbottle of Baddow, and Mr. Ramsey nominated.

" These fore-named gentlemen, in pursuance of their noble resolutions, have raised about twelve thousand Horse and Foot, in the severall places before mentioned, and have now brought them up to London this 1st of November, and have listed themselves under the generall command of the Earle of Warwick in Finsbury and Moorefields, neer London, and there made a general mustering to fit and prepare them for their speedy march with the said Generall down to the Lord Generall, the Earl of Essex, and to join with his Excellency for the preservation of the peace of the Kingdome, and suppressing of the malignant party. God prosper their designes and good indeavours."[1]

At the end of 1642 and the beginning of 1643, the Eastern Counties of Essex, Suffolk, Norfolk, Hertford, Cambridge, Huntingdon, and Lincoln associated themselves together " for the maintenance and preservation of the peace of the said counties," and from this point the famous East Anglian compact was destined to become a determining factor in the long and painful struggle upon which the rival parties had entered.

Then into Essex there came, in the autumn of 1643, the sad tidings of the death of Hampden at Chalgrove Field, upon which Sir Thomas Barrington writes to the Essex Committee :

" Poor Hampden is dead, and I profess to you I have scarce strength to pronounce that word. Never Kingdom received a greater loss in one subject; never man a truer and faithfuller friend." Appealing for the support of the Essex people Sir Thomas added : " The power of Essex is great, a place of most life and religion in the land; and your power in the country is great too. The difficulties of this war need the utmost of both."

---

[1] A True Relation, King's Pamphlets, British Museum Library, E. 126 (16).

But Essex, like other counties, had its domestic needs pressing for attention. It had its harvest to get in, and for this reason some of its men had refused to march away to Cambridge, and some asked for more pay. Cromwell wrote to Essex:

"Hast, hast post hast. You see by this enclosed the necessitye of goinge out of our old pace. You sent indeed your part of the 2,000 foote, but when they came they as soon returned. Is this the way to save a Kingdom? . . . Hast what you can; not your part only of 2,000 foote, but I hope 3,000 foote att least. Lord Newcastle will advance into your bowells. . . . See your men come and some of your gentlemen and ministers come along with them, that so they may be delivered over to those shall command them, otherwise they will returne at pleasure. If wee have them att our armie wee can keepe them. From your faithful servant." [1]

The fact was that the raising of men for continuing the war was not so easy as in the full tide of zeal of the Puritan protest with which the war began, and some of the men Essex spared from the harvest field were in a sorry plight on their arrival. "Some companies of foot," wrote the Committee at Cambridge to Sir Thomas Barrington and his deputy lieutenants, "are sent hither from you, but in so naked a posture that to employ them were to murder them. Their demands are arms, coats, clothes, and shoes. If not sent at once there will be a mutiny." The Committee added in another letter: "We have provided red coats for such as we have sent away of yours; we shall trust to you to furnish the rest, and to send them with arms, drums, colours, and accoutrements."

Further glimpses of the state of things are afforded by the letters of Sir William Harlackenden and Sir W. Rowe, who were representing Essex on the Grand Committee, or Council of War, for the associated counties, sitting at Cambridge.

---

1 Letter from Cromwell in the *Barrington MSS.*

Meanwhile, desperate efforts were being made in Essex to meet the demands from headquarters at Cambridge. Edward Berkhead, a committee man, wrote from the "Dragon's Den" at Romford giving an account of his efforts, and declaring that "if fair play will not force the malignants, foul will." He declares that "it took a saddler ten days to mend the old saddles. The country brought in such trash that two-thirds were unfit for service. . . . I never saw such indisposition in men to the service in my life. . . . I think we must have another troop to force these out, but I hope this day to send them packing." Sir Thomas Nightingale, writing to Mr. Middleton (also an Essex committee man) about Stanstead having to find three nags, with three muskets and able riders, adds: "Besides, we are to find men well-affected to Parliament, but where we shall find them, God in heaven knows, for we do not." In the same class of documents[1] there are further glimpses of recruiting obstacles from three poor Essex constables, who complained that "altho' they have impressed men, the men will not obey the warrants; the constables being poor men, they ask for authority to charge persons better than themselves to assist them." The poor constables got little sympathy from Parliament, but were fined £10 each.

The Earl of Manchester, "getting within musket shot of the town of Lynn," then being besieged by the Parliamentary forces, wrote to Essex: "I have here divers men sent out of Essex, and as many of them I believe are run away as are come; and those whom you have sent have no arms, clothes, nor colours, nor drums. Hasten hither all the force you can with money and arms, for otherwise they are far more dreadful to me than any enemy." Sir William Harlackenden sends another eloquent appeal to his neighbours in Essex from

---

1 *The Barrington MSS.* at Barrington Hall, in the possession of the Lowndes family.

headquarters at Cambridge: "Your labours I doubt not shall be rewarded from heaven, your names clothed with honour on earth, and your posterity receive eternal mercy. . . . There are 200 coats ready for the soldiers. The poor soldiers long for them, and the time of year calls for them."

At this time, the autumn months of 1643, Essex was threatened with a Royalist incursion into its borders by a force under its own neighbours, Sir John and Sir Charles Lucas, to whom it was alleged the King had given a commission "to go into Essex with 8,000 foot, ten troops of horse, and 1,200 dragoons." In the story told by a captured scout, it was added that he had "also heard that 10,000 hands in Essex were ready to stand with them when they marched, and that they had men come in every week from Essex informing them how every man stood affected, one of whom came in the guise of a pedlar, and brought horse-hair and tobacco on his back." [1]

During the month of October there had been an alarming advance of the Cavaliers across Bedfordshire towards Cambridge. As they drew near, Sir William Rowe, the Essex representative in Cambridge, wrote thus pathetically to Sir Thomas Barrington: "If you would do a seasonable service to the State (not to speak of your friend, who is a lone and naked man here), let what help you can be instantly sent hither. Alarums come thick and very near us." In Lincolnshire, as the winter drew on early, the Essex soldiers were thus described by Captain Rich: "The winter has already come, and our lying in the field hath lost us more men than have been taken away either by sword or bullet, notwithstanding which we are ready to persist, and unwilling to wait any opportunity of doing God honour and our

---

[1] *Barrington MSS.* Fairfax (*Short Memorials*) says that Newcastle's instructions were "to go into Essex and block up London that side."

country service." [1] Captain Rich adds that at the time
of writing he had only 2s., and his troop without money,
even for shoeing their horses and repairing saddles, etc.
He begs that the common soldiers may be constantly
paid, though the officers go without money at all.

But the Essex men, and those of the other Eastern
Counties, passed through the crisis of a most trying time
for the association. Some of the forced levies raised
to repel the expected invasions of their borders were sent
back to their homes, and the rest did their part valiantly
at Marston Moor. Loyal to the new model army, which
came under the more personal command of Cromwell,
and put an end to the war by county committees, Essex
came out not only in the men from her shire who fought
at Naseby, but more especially in the powerful reserve
force of three regiments which she sent to the borders
of the association, in case the issue of the great battle
had been unfavourable to the Parliamentary arms.

On Sunday, August 24th, 1645, after the battle of
Naseby, the King marched southwards with 2,200 horse,
and was met at Stilton by 400 horse raised in Essex
and Suffolk, which, after a skirmish, retired before
superior numbers into Huntingdon, where the King
arrived in the evening. All the country round was
plundered by the Cavaliers, and the Eastern Counties
were in a state of panic. "During that Sunday evening,
and all day on Monday, drums were beating and
trumpets blowing all over East Anglia, and before
Monday evening men were leaving the harvest field and
marching to the rendezvous at Cambridge once more.
In Essex the rumour went that Cambridge itself had
fallen into the King's hands."[2] It is interesting to notice
that amidst all this hurly-burly at Huntingdon, the
diarist Richard Symonds, an Essex man, whose
antiquarian pursuits amidst the clash of arms form one

---

[1] *Barrington MSS.*
[2] *East Anglia and the Great Civil War*, p. 220.

SAFFRON WALDEN CHURCH, FROM WINDMILL HILL.

of the curiosities of the Civil War, had got his sword in its scabbard, and, with pencil and note-book in hand, was strolling round the churches. His notes and miniature sketches may still be seen in the British Museum Library (*Harl. MSS.*, 944).

The Earl of Warwick wrote thus of his doings in Essex: " Upon this alarm of the enemy's coming to Huntingdon, I drew up all the forces of Essex, being 6,000 foot and 900 horse, as also 4,000 foot and 500 horse came out of Suffolk, for the guard of Cambridge and the Isle of Ely."

In the spring of 1647, Essex was the scene of stormy debates over the disbanding of the great army of Fairfax and Cromwell, which it had done so much to help to raise. Fairfax's own regiment was lying near Chelmsford, and the other regiments were along the borders of the county next Cambridgeshire. The Essex people felt the inconvenience of, and petitioned against, having a vast army lying along its borders, and " so near Parliament, which makes us feel that there is some design for an aweing influence upon the proceedings of Parliament." [1] Parliament sent down Commissioners to induce the soldiers to disband or volunteer for service in Ireland.

" Our general commanded that all our officers should meete in the greate church at Saffron Walden to hear what the Commissioners had to say unto us." [2] Fairfax and Cromwell delivered speeches to the officers, who nearly filled the church. Captain Reynolds, one of the agitators, made a violent scene with Cromwell, and the conference came to nothing. Fresh Commissioners were sent down from Parliament, and met two hundred officers in the church. " Fairfax and Cromwell, and we all go," was the shout that rang round the church when the question of the choice of officers and going to Ireland was being discussed:

---

[1] *Journals of the House of Lords.*
[2] Colonel Wogan's Narrative in the Clarke Papers.

"On Saturday, May 15, the spacious aisles of the parish church at Saffron Walden once more resounded with the clanking of swords, when upwards of 200 officers, and a certain number of representatives of the private soldiers, assembled for the Convention at which the officers were to report the views of their regiments scattered over the Eastern Counties. The scene must have been a brilliant and impressive one. Skippon, the veteran soldier, bearing the scars of Naseby fight, presided, and opened the proceedings in conciliatory tone :—'Gentlemen, fellow soldiers, and Christian friends.' . . . The debate was, however, a stormy one, and did not end that day. The great Convention re-assembled in the church on Sunday. The speeches were sometimes loudly applauded and sometimes provoked angry signs of dissent. . . . After sitting until a late hour Skippon wound up the stormy debate with a conciliatory speech, and 'soe good night.' As a result of it all, the next day the 'Declaration of the Army' was drawn up and signed by 223 officers and sent up to Parliament. Its main purpose was to ask for more definite proposals for paying arrears."[1]

When, shortly afterwards, the Commissioners went down to Chelmsford with £7,000 to persuade Fairfax's regiment to disband, it was said that "they may as well send them among soe many beares to take away their whelps." They found the soldiers had revolted and marched away towards Newmarket, and when one thousand of them were overtaken at Braintree, they exclaimed: "What doe you, bringing your twopenny pamphlets to us?"

In the following year, 1648, the King having been taken a prisoner, there occurred a reaction, with fresh Royalist outbursts all over the Eastern Counties, in which the family of Lucas was once more to assert their allegiance to the Royal cause with such tragic results to their neighbours in and about Colchester. It was "an interesting coincidence that Parliamentary East Anglia had its toughest struggle with the two extremes of its area—with the Lucases of Colchester, and the Earl of Newcastle in the Fens. Margaret Lucas, of Colchester, was the wife of Newcastle, the commander of the "White Coats." Her brother, Sir Charles Lucas, had been

---

[1] *East Anglia and the Great Civil War*, pp. 237-8.

SAFFRON WALDEN CHURCH.

Newcastle's lieutenant-general, and was now, in 1648, a force to be reckoned with among his own neighbours about Colchester.

The Grand Jury at the Spring Assizes at Chelmsford in 1648 presented a petition in favour of a personal treaty with the King, a disbanding of the army, and satisfaction of their arrears, and suggested holding a great meeting at Stratford-Langthorne on May 4th; but Parliament declared it would be " prejudicial to the peace of the kingdom in these distracted times." Instead of the meeting at Stratford-Langthorne, the Grand Jury and freeholders marched up to Westminster—two thousand persons on horse and on foot, representing " thirty thousand inhabitants of the county "—and presented a petition praying that the King might be satisfied and the army disbanded. Parliament replied in diplomatic phrases, but found it necessary to caution the Earl of Warwick to be careful in assembling the trained bands so as not to prejudice the peace of the county " at this juncture of time and of ill-affected humours." [1] In pursuance of their petition, the Grand Jury, freeholders, and other inhabitants of the county of Essex entered into an engagement and declaration refusing to pay " any more excize or other taxes till all the desires expressed in our said petition have been fully obtained by us." They further resolved to stand together and defend one another and King Charles, and even suggested a method of putting their views into practice—all of which was " offered to the consideration of the gentlemen and the trained bands at their severall rendesvouz." [2]

The fears that the trained bands might not be trusted were not altogether groundless, and with the Kentish rising it was confidently predicted that the twenty thousand Kentishmen would be joined by an equal

[1] *Journals of the House of Commons.*
[2] *King's Pamphlets*, E. 443 (13), British Museum Library.

number of men from the other side of the Thames in
Essex.   The Essex Parliamentary Committee were sitting
at the time at Chelmsford for the purpose of appeasing
these " ill-affected humours," when " a rabble of mutineers,
commanded by Lieutenant Farre" (apparently the
Captain Farre who stood out for the old captains at
the beginning of the war), entered the Committee Chamber
and carried off the committee men prisoners.   Parliament,
on hearing of the turn affairs were taking, became
alarmed, and next day passed an Ordinance offering
an indemnity for the inhabitants of the county for what
they had done, providing that all persons should disband
and go peaceably to their homes within twelve hours
of its publication, and that the imprisoned committee
be liberated.   The inhabitants of Chelmsford were
disposed to accept the offer, but the aged Earl of
Norwich and Sir Charles Lucas appeared, and prevailed
upon the trained bands to remain under arms.
Meanwhile, Lord Capel had come across out of
Hertfordshire with a number of followers, and, with
the remnant of the Kentishmen, came to Chelmsford,
where the Essex trained bands were in doubtful
allegiance; and with the Parliamentary committee men
still imprisoned in the town, and supplies coming in
for the scratch Royalist force " from all parts of the
kingdom," things began to look ominous.   At Bury St.
Edmunds, where the people shouted " for God and King
Charles," they were joined by " divers from Colchester
and those parts."   On Saturday, June 10th, Colonel
Whalley and the Parliamentary forces drew near, and
the Royalists marched away from Chelmsford, and, by
the way, paid a visit to Leighs Park, the Earl of
Warwick's house, and carried off a quantity of arms
and ammunition, and " one great brass saker," and
marched on to Braintree.   At Braintree the increasing
Royalist force rested for the night, and spent Sunday
in " digesting the volunteers into several troops," under

the command of Lord Norwich, Lord Capel, Lord Loughborough, and Sir Charles Lucas. It is said their intention was to march into the Isle of Ely, and then to march "up to the very walls of London, and be joined by their friends in plundering that rebellious city." [1]

It so happened that when the Essex committee men were taken prisoners, some of their number were absent from the meeting. The absent ones were Sir Thomas Honeywood, Colonel Harlackenden, Colonel Cooke, and Colonel Sparrow, who got together one regiment of horse and two of foot, marched over to Braintree and secured the powder magazine there, and took up a position at Coggeshall, which the Royalists would have to pass on their way to Colchester. Fairfax, tormented with gout, and nicknamed by his enemies "King Gowty-leggs," rode on to Coggeshall and joined the Essex men there. The Royalists had to make a detour, and when they arrived before Colchester they met with a divided allegiance, for while "neere a thousand of the townsmen broke through their guards to give them welcome, there was opposition from horsemen of the town and of Bardfold and Dedham. At this point Sir Charles Lucas rode up, and counselled his neighbours to let them into the town."

"The gates were opened and wee marched through the towne in greate order, and drew our men into the lower courte of my Lord Lucas his house, which having been formerly an abbey was capable of receiving them all. . . . But the inhabitants of the towne . . . were so distracted with the noveltie of their business—having never seene an army before—that they suffered our souldiers to want, which created soe great a mutinie that it was above the skill of the authoritie of the officers to appease. . . . Soe we were forst to let them march into the towne before their quarters were made, where wee reposed that night." [2]

Sir T. Honeywood, with the Essex trained bands, had followed closely upon the Royalists, and arrived

---

[1] Rushworth's *Historical Collections*, viii., 1160.
[2] Narrative of the Siege in the *Beaufort MSS.*

before Colchester, when Fairfax also came up, and brought up the total force to "5,000 disciplined troops against about 4,000 new levies, only partly armed, within and about the town of Colchester." Fairfax sent a summons to surrender, and thus save "much blood that is like to be spilt," and to save the town from ruin; but the Earl of Norwich slightingly asked the trumpeter "how his general did, telling him that he heard he was ill with the gout, but he could cure him of all diseases." There was, therefore, now no alternative but for the inhabitants, as well as the soldiers, to face one of the greatest tragedies of the Civil War.

There was still, however, fighting to be done on the outskirts of the town before its investment was complete. Across the approach to the town by the London Road Sir Charles Lucas drew up his defending forces, and three times in succession the Royalist centre drove back the Parliamentary foot; but the cavalry, here as in other great theatres of the war, turned the scale, drove in the right wing of the Royalist horse, and the whole of the defending forces were soon making their way into the town as best they could. At the narrow entrance by the Head Gate a stubborn resistance was made, of which the contemporary chronicler writes:

"The enemie advancing boldly upon us, forced our men to retreate and pursued them to Head Gate, where stood the Right Honourable Lord Capell with a partie of horse to receive the enemie, but justly apprehending that the disorder of our men retreating and the narrowness of the place would render his horse unserviceable—like himselfe, that is a man of incomparable honour and presence of judgment in the greatest danger—hee alighted and tooke a pike, who was presently seconded by Sir Charles Lucas, Sir George Lisle, and two or three others, and these worthies—like Horatius Cocles—opposed themselves to the furie of the enemie, whilst under cover of their courage the remains of our men saved themselves within the porte.

"Then those bucklers of their partie retreated with their faces to the enemie, selling every foote of the ground they parted with at the

---

1 Morant's *History of Colchester*, vol. i., p. 59.

price of the invaders' lives : an action without flatterie to the living or the memories of the dead, that would be thought worthy of a place in a chronicle as any that is legible in ancient storie."[1]

The account of the same fight given in the Diary of the Round MSS., states that in the rush for the Head Gate a portion of the Parliamentary foot were carried inside " quite into the street of the suburb, and most of them that had so rashly entered were cut in pieces," when Lucas ordered the gate to be closed, and fastened the bar with the cane he held in his hand. On the other hand, by the hurried closing of the gate a number of Royalists were shut out and were made prisoners. An attempt by Fairfax to fire the gate having failed, the attack on the walls near the Head Gate and St. Mary's Church continued until midnight, the loss on both sides being very heavy. Fairfax, " weary of the last night's work," next morning contented himself with settling down before Colchester, with the support of Sir Thomas Honeywood and the trained bands, and the reluctant Suffolkers hemmed in the town on their side, and it was declared " that the enemy had no means of escape but by betaking themselves by sea." Within the walls of the town, says the Royalist narrative :

" Like the Jews in Jerusalem, with our swords in one hand and our trowels in the other, we began to repaire the ruines of our walls, which are many : this town being one of the antientist foundations in the kingdome. There were above five hundred places without any fortifications at all. . . . Wee looked into the magazine of the towne, where wee found 70 barrells of powder with some match, and in private houses are a thousand armes ; then we searched the stores for provision, and at the Hythe, a parte of the east suburbs, where a small river runns into a creeke of the sea, wee found two thousand quarters of rye with a greate proportion of salte and wine, which wee brought into the towne. . . . The inhabitants were as much amaz'd at this plenty as ourselves, for the market day before wee enterd the towne the poore were complayning in the streets that they could not gette corne for their money ; those bowell-lesse merchants having ingross'd it to enhanse the price."

---

[1] Narrative of the Siege in the *Beaufort MSS.*

Outside the walls the Suffolk men were hesitating, and the Royalists, not yet quite cut off on the east side, had seized Sir Harbottle Grimston's house at Bradfield. Sir Charles Lucas sent out an appeal asking his Suffolk neighbours to declare on which side they were going to be—whether as enemies or friends. The answer to this appeal was that the Suffolk men, on June 15th, completed the bridge over the Stour, and marched over and took their place outside the walls by the side of the Essex men, who "had stood so many cannon shots that they deserve to be called Essex lions." Outside the walls of the town, Fairfax's men were lying on the sodden ground in one of the wettest summers on record. "The weather being very rainy, it rotted divers of Fairfax's men, and had cost him more had not the provisions and shelter the county brought in to him made him so well struggle with that difficulty." [1]

As for the unfortunate committee men within the walls, Sir Thomas Honeywood wrote a pathetic letter to Parliament that "the sad condition of our worthy friends in Colchester doth everyday heighten our compassion." It was alleged that the committee men were placed "under the mouth of our only advantageous battery," so that "with all our care a bullet passed through the roof where they are all in durance." Sir William Masham, one of the committee, was exchanged for a Royalist prisoner, and Parliament left it to the general to make exchanges for the rest, but several of them endured all the horrors of the siege.

Notwithstanding some "grand sallies" on the east side, by July 7th the line of investment was drawn closer, "my Lord Lucas's house was taken in, and after that the Hithe church, and then we were wholly invested," says the narrative in the *Beaufort MSS*. Of the

---

[1] Warwick's *Memoirs*, p. 314.

horrors of the siege space will not permit a detailed
record. Of the concluding stages of it I have written
elsewhere an account, from which I take the following
passages :

At last the situation became too desperate to live on
hope; the townspeople and the women, with their
children, appealed to the humanity of Norwich, but
the commanders still held on to the hope of Langdale
and the Scots reaching them. The Mayor of Colchester
appealed to Fairfax to allow civilians to pass the lines
of communication; but, like Norwich inside, Fairfax
without had to set aside private feelings, and, while
pitying their condition, found that " it did not stand
with his trust to permit it." Again a famished crowd
of women and children appealed to Norwich, and, rather
than give way, he threw open the gates and told them
" to go to the enemy with their complaints." In their
dire extremity it is said that a woman and five children,
one sucking at her breast, came outside the fortifications.
" She fell down at our guards, beseeching them to let
her pass beyond the lines ; the people in the town were
watching to see if the woman and children were allowed
to pass, and resolving to follow them. But the guards
were necessitated to turn them back, or otherwise hundreds
would come out, which would prejudice the service. The
woman said that could they but get dogs and cats to
eat it were happy for them, but all the dogs and cats
and most of the horses are near eaten already." No
wonder the writer adds : " Some sad things of necessity
must befall the town suddenly (presently)."[1]

Towards other women who came out, the sentries
could only fire shots over their heads to frighten them
back; and at last were obliged to threaten to strip them
of their clothing and send them back naked. In the

---

1 Rushworth's *Historical Collections.*

N

face of this threat they retired, but huddled themselves together, and took shelter in a mill just outside the walls for the night.

At last, on August 22nd, says the Royalist writer inside the walls, " all hope was cut off by the news of Cromwell's victory over the Scots (at Preston), of which the enemy sent in a printed account by trumpet. At first we refused to believe it, but, after two days, further news convinced us, and a Council of War was called, which decided that overtures should be made to the enemy." Other risings had been crushed at Linton (Cambs.), Cambridge, and St. Neots, Hunts. Two of the imprisoned Essex committee men were induced to address a letter to the commanding officer to allow them, " out of their tender bowells to the starving inhabitants of the towne," to wait upon Fairfax and mediate an accommodation. Fairfax, knowing that it was the defeat of the Scots that had prompted the device, sent back answer that they had held out and defied his summons so long, that the best conditions they could expect would be to submit to mercy.

On August 27th, terms of capitulation were signed; a Council of War decided that Sir Charles Lucas and Sir George Lisle should suffer death, and they were led out to be shot. Lucas was the first to fall, justifying his action in his last words by " all the laws of the kingdom " and his commission from his sovereign. Lisle caught his body in his arms, and kissed the dead man's face. Then, taking his fallen comrade's place, Lisle called to the firing party to come nearer, to which one of the soldiers replied: " I'll warrant you, sir, we'll hit you." " I have been nearer you when you have missed me," Lisle smilingly replied, and then fell, as the bullets pierced his body. The peers were dealt with by Parliament, and the scene at the execution of Lord Capel at Whitehall is part of the history of England.

From the starved, empty shell of a town now in ruin and in ashes,[1] with only a barrel and a half of powder left in it, but "plenty of the enemy's great shot" in place of food, sixty-five gentlemen, seventy-two lieutenants, sixty-nine ensigns and cornets, 183 sergeants, and 3,067 private soldiers, with gaunt, hungry looks, filed out in charge of their captors, and on August 28th Fairfax was in possession of the town.

Many of the prisoners were marched across the county into Hertfordshire, and there for a time were accommodated in the churches, revelling in the new found luxury of the bread and cheese doled out to them, but with the harder fate in store for many of them of being shipped off to the West Indies. For the inhabitants of Colchester an equally rigorous punishment was meted out by the victors in the £12,000 exacted from them for the soldiers in lieu of plunder, of which £2,000 was returned by Fairfax to be given to the poor. The Essex and Suffolk trained bands received £2,000 as their share, the other £8,000 going to Fairfax's soldiers.

The prisoners taken at the entrance to the suburbs of Colchester at the beginning of the siege were drawn out. "Everye thirteenth man of the Essex Batchellours to die; every tenth man of the married men, and every fifth of Londoners and Kentish men that were engaged in this new designe; the others that are left of Batchellours to be sent beyond the seas, and the remainder of the married men to their families."[2]

Behind the heroic acts of individuals and the tragic events which belong to the fighting side of the struggle between King and Parliament, there was the interesting

---

[1] Rushworth (*Historical Collections*) says that when riding roundabout the wall of the town "it was a sad spectacle to see so many fine houses burnt to ashes, and so many inhabitants sickly and weak with living upon horses and dogs." It was stated that 800 horses were eaten during the siege, and that three hundred houses were burnt.

[2] *King's Pamphlets*, E. 448 (18), British Museum Library.

problem of the effect of the struggle upon the social and industrial life of the people. When voluntary contributions failed, Parliament was able to enforce a war tax, and thus to exact substantial contributions, not only from its own supporters, but "from the very men who hated the name of Parliament." At the critical period of the strife, in the spring of 1644, the following were the weekly assessments made upon the associated counties :

				£	s.	d.
Essex	...	...	the weekly sum of	1,687	10	0
Suffolk	...	...	„	„	1,875	0	0
Norfolk	...		„	„	1,875	0	0
Lincolnshire	...		„	„	1,218	15	0
Hertfordshire	...		„	„	675	0	0
Cambridgeshire	...		„	„	562	0	0
Huntingdonshire			„	„	330	0	0
The Isle of Ely	...		„	„	221	5	0

In the Duke of Manchester's Papers, in the Public Record Office, there is a complete account of the assessments for five of the associated counties for the complete year 1644. For that year the amount actually received from the county of Essex was no less than £60,664 6s. 10d. The estates of noted Royalists in Essex, in their absence fighting for the king, were taken care of by Parliament, "sequestered," and farmed by its agents, and made to contribute to the defeat of the King. By the time the Royalist had "compounded" and purged his "delinquency" with a heavy fine, there might be very little of the estate left for him to come into. For example, a son of the Lord Lieutenant of the county, the Earl of Warwick, had, at the beginning of the war, marched away to the King at Oxford, and for this "delinquency" was later to be called to account. His case, as disclosed by the Royalist Composition Papers, presented "a remarkable complication of

Royalism, money-lending, imprisonments for debt, and curious turns in the wheel of fortune." Before the war began young Rich had outrun the constable, and mortgaged his annuity, allowed by the Earl, to a city money-lender named Gosse. For a £600 loan Lord Rich and two sureties gave £1,000 in bonds. Being unable to recover either principal or interest, Gosse, in the time of the war, arrested one of the sureties, who was, however, rescued by Lord Rich and other officers, who beat and wounded Gosse "to his great damage." Sticking on like the proverbial leech, Gosse, "thinking that Lord Rich had not the privilege of a peer," caused him to be arrested for the debt. But Rich was released by order of the House of Lords, and the unfortunate Shylock, Gosse, was himself cast into the Fleet Prison, and four of the sheriff's officers into Newgate, for causing the arrest. They were detained fourteen days, and poor Mr. Gosse, "by reason of his ill-accommodation, contracted such a weakness that he was constrained to keep his bed," and died shortly afterwards, but not without casting up the costs and damages, which by now had swelled the original £600 into £6,300! Rebecca Gosse, his widow, next comes upon the scene, pressing her suit for the debt, and lamenting that "there hath not any progresse beene made, unlesse to ye unhappiness of yr petr." Unfortunately, the young Lord Rich had been fined £2,000 for going to the King at Oxford, and, notwithstanding that the Earl of Warwick, his father, "believed in the reality of his repentance for his errors," and pleaded for him, the committee thought it reasonable that he should pay something out of his annuity to widow Gosse before his fine could be remitted.

In a rare book of proclamations, broadsides, and other contemporary documents, preserved in the British Museum Library, there is given a "Declaration and Address of the Gentry of the County of Essex who have adhered to the King and suffered imprisonment or sequestration during the late troubles."[1] The declaration is addressed to General Monk, and is dated Chelmsford, April 17th, 1660, and is signed by the following: Edward Russell, Esq.; Sir Henry Appleton, Bart.; Sir Benjamin Ayloffe, Bart; Sir Denner Strutt, Bart.; Sir Humfrey Mildmay, Knight; Sir John Tirell, Knight; Sir C. Harris, Knight; Sir Edmund Pierce, Knight; Sir Henry Wroth, Knight; William Ayloffe, Esq.; James Altham, Esq.; Gamaliel Capel, Esq.; Anthony Brown, Esq.; Charles Fytch, Esq.; Thomas Argall, Esq.; Stephen Smyth, Esq.; Salter Herres, Esq.; Henry Pert, Esq.; John Fanshaw, Esq.; Thomas Roberts, Esq.; Richard Humphrey, Esq.; John Lynn, Esq.; Dr. John Michaelson; Richard Symonds, Esq.; Anthony Kempson, Esq.; William Herris, Esq.; William Brampston, Esq.; John Brown, Gent.; Nicholas Sarle, John Vavasour, Gent.; James Cookson, Gent.; Edmund Coole, Gent.

No account of the Civil War as it affected the county of Essex would be complete without reference to the Puritan stronghold which Parliament found in Essex and in the other Eastern Counties, for in these counties, at least, the struggle was largely one of a revolt against the ecclesiastical tendencies of the times. The Puritans in Essex had a poor opinion of the preaching of the Royalist clergyman, and would either absent themselves from his church and go to hear sermons elsewhere, or, if they attended, would make a note of his extreme doings and sayings to be used against him afterwards. On the other hand, the Royalist clergyman had a contempt for the habit of going out of the parish to hear sermons. Thus, Henry Osbaldeston, D.D., of Much Pardon, is said to have declared that " It was never a merry England since there had been so much preaching," and of the Puritans who went out of his parish to hear

---

1 British Museum Library, 669, f. 25.

sermons that "they stanke of two sermons a day." Mr.
Cherry, parson of Much Holland, was accused of
"bowing twelve times to the East when he goeth into
the chancell"; and Mr. Cuthbert Dale, of Kettleborough,
on the other hand, declared of one who sat in church
with his hat on, that he was "a sawcy unmannerly
clown, a scabbed sheepe, and none of his flock."

From such incidents as these, and from the acts of
pulling down of images, etc., both during and after the
war, it may be seen how keen was the part of the
conflict which surrounded the parish churches and the
ceremonial of public worship.

HISTORIC HOUSES

By Miss C. Fell Smith

ALTHOUGH Essex cannot now boast of having within her borders any great palace of world-wide reputation and renown, nor, so far as that goes, a single principal seat of duke, marquis, or even earl, the county is incontestably able to bear away the palm from almost every other in England, in so far as Tudor, Elizabethan, or Jacobean mansions of more or less pretension may be reckoned.

Her Abbeys and Priories are dealt with elsewhere in this volume. Of her Castles, Norman, or even (as Colchester) earlier, there is something to be said; but the chronicle of the old-world moated halls and many-gabled manor-houses that lie scattered up and down, hidden in sheltering thickets of trees, approached by small by-roads, and affording protection only to some hamlet or small cluster of cottages, would take many pages to tell. Some, alas! are fallen into ruin and sad disrepair; others, having been continuously inhabited, are now modernised with every latest device of civilization and luxury, yet manage still to preserve something of the stately grandeur and peculiar aroma of the past.

In the space of a short article such as this, it cannot be hoped to deal exhaustively with any one of them, or indeed to mention every picturesque old mansion that is known to me. The best that can be attempted is to take a few of the most important seats now remaining and endeavour to present the reader with an outline of their history and chief features, in the hope of securing something of their indestructible charm and their once vivid human history. This is the more grateful task, because in the few attempts that have already been made in this direction (apart, of course, from the general notices included in the county histories) no real sense of proportion or chronology has been aimed at.

It is a striking fact that although for several centuries past no king, queen, or prince has chosen Essex for his or her residence, in spite of the obvious advantages of proximity, bracing air, etc., that we can offer, it was quite otherwise in the past. We must entirely decline to accept this fact as bearing any relation to the long period of decline, depression, and utterly unmerited defamation on the score of natural beauties, from which the county so long suffered, but is now triumphantly emerging. Rather we would attribute it to lack of opportunity in the prosperous years before that decline, when Essex estates came seldom into the market—perhaps, too, to the absence of country tastes and pursuits shared by the Hanoverian Georges, which possibly a closer acquaintance with the well-watered, wooded charms of the Essex corn-lands would have directly fostered.

In former days Essex, as we know, was particularly selected for royal residence. It was at his favourite retreat at Havering Bower that the saintly Edward the Confessor (more suited to a cloister than to rule over hardy Englishmen) received back the ring he had given to a beggar, with the injunction to set his house in order, for within six months he should leave it for heaven. Then only did he divine the "fair old man," disguised in rags and asking alms in the name of God and St. John, to have been the Blessed Evangelist himself. In the fulness of time Edward died here; the nightingales, whose unceasing music was wont to disturb him at his prayers, and for whose absence he had uttered many a petition, are said to have avoided for a century this once familiar haunt, and

contented themselves with warbling outside the park pales.
From evil John to amorous Henry all the kings
hawked, hunted, or played the lover here; Mary
and Elizabeth as girls, and as queens, spent some
of their happiest hours in Havering Bower, and from
her Palace here Elizabeth started four times for her
progresses through Essex, and again for the martial
exploit of reviewing her troops at Tilbury before
they set sail to the Spanish Main. An ominous and
fitting close to the regal occupation of Havering was
the last visit of " the White King," in 1637, when he came
to meet his mother-in-law, Maria de Medici, who had
landed at Harwich a day before. Exiled from France, she
was soon again to be dismissed from England by a
powerful Parliament and a douceur of £10,000. She
was entertained at Gidea Hall near by, whilst Charles
slept for the last time at Havering. No royal head ever
lodged there again. The glories of the place sadly
departed, and when a survey was taken in 1650 the Palace
was described as a confused heap of old, ruinous, decayed
buildings, the materials of which were valued at £480.
A couple of years later, this ancient estate of the Crown
was divided and sold for about £9,000, the eastern park of
five hundred acres and the Palace becoming the property
of Richard Deane, one of the judges who signed the King's
death warrant. He cut down the splendid trees and
destroyed the Palace. A stone from its ruins, bearing the
arms of Edward III., was long preserved in the
neighbouring Bower House, built in 1729. A modern
mansion, Havering Park, occupies the site of the Palace,
which was acquired by the Mackintosh family in 1828,
when the royal manor, with all its rights and privileges,
was finally disposed of.

Near by the King's Bower stands Pyrgo, another royal
Palace, which descended from queen to queen, usually as
a part of her jointure, and formed the asylum to which
in comparative retirement the royal ladies came upon their

widowhood and release from courtly cares. Here the
child-queen, Isabella of Valois, received the tidings of the
murder of her husband, Richard II., in Pontefract Castle;
here, at her favourite home, in July, 1437, died Joanna
of Navarre, the queen of Henry IV.; and here the
gentle Elizabeth of York, born heiress of the crown
of England, whose marriage to Henry Tudor, Earl of
Richmond, afterwards King Henry VII., healed the
long strife of the Red and White Roses, came often to
visit her motherless nieces, housed for safety in her
Palace at Havering. The nine days' queen, Lady Jane
Grey, was sometimes at Pyrgo with her uncle, Sir John
Grey, to whom it was given by Elizabeth, and perhaps
it was during these visits that she played with her young
cousin, Edward VI., or studied Greek and Hebrew with
the learned young ladies at Gidea Hall close by. Like
the Bower, no trace of the original Palace of Pyrgo
remains. Its site is covered by a modern mansion now
belonging to Lord O'Hagan, from whence the views
over South Essex, the Thames, and Kent—in fact, over
five counties—are almost unrivalled.

The history of Havering has carried us down the
centuries, but we must return to an earlier queen, whose
troublous fortunes ended in Hedingham Castle in May,
1151. Only the massive keep or dungeon tower of this
splendid fortress has survived the storms of battle and the
elements. Standing upon a high mount overlooking the
village, its four square walls, crowned at two corners by
square turrets, make it an object of mark from all the level
country round. It was built probably between 1088 and
1107, by Aubrey de Vere, a general who fought for the
Conqueror at Hastings, and who was rewarded by him
with fourteen lordships in Essex alone. He founded
Colne Priory, a few miles away, and was the first of that
proud race of de Veres, hereditary Great Chamberlains of
England, who lived here in splendour for six hundred and
thirty years, and whose name is immortalised by Tennyson
as identical with the bluest of blue blood.

His grandson, the "grim" Earl Aubrey, fought for Queen Maud against her haughty cousin, the Empress Matilda, sheltered her last days, and was created Earl of Oxford by her son, Henry II. Faithful to John, his castle was besieged and taken by the sturdy barons, and once again by the invading Frenchmen in 1217. These mighty earls were renowned fighters at home and abroad; tradition says that the well-known mullet of their armorial bearings was added to commemorate a star that fell from heaven upon the shield of Aubrey, the third earl, while fighting a Crusade in the Holy Land.

Five tall stories high the Norman tower stands. A flight of steps conducts to the principal entrance, once portcullis-guarded, as the well-worn grooves in the stone will show. In its bowels lie the dungeons. To the ground floor, built for safety, light and air are only admitted through narrow slits. Above are double windows, round-headed and richly ornamented, lighting an arcaded gallery that surrounds the splendid hall or armoury, whose roof is supported by pillars and round arches, the base and capitals each embellished with a different design. In this hall it was, no doubt, that John, the thirteenth earl, entertained Henry VII. so magnificently, conducting him through a lane of such splendidly apparelled gentlemen and yeomen that he had afterwards to pay his avaricious monarch a sum of £10,000 for an offence against the Statute of Retainers. His passion for display evidently followed him to the end, for, by his desire, there were given at his burying "black gowns to the number of nine hundred or more." In this hall, too, Queen Elizabeth was entertained in August, 1561. In 1703 the last Earl of Oxford died without male issue, and the castle was sold to the Ashurst family, from whom it descended to the Majendies, who now own it.

A daughter of the first Aubrey de Vere became the wife of Geoffrey de Mandeville, first Earl of Essex (and indeed the earliest patented earl in England), who is

credited with having built the castles of Walden and
Pleshey. Of the former only a few ivy-covered ruins now
remain, enclosed within the pleasure grounds of the town.
At Pleshey little is to be seen except the deep fosse
(evidently of Roman formation), and the fine brick bridge
of one arch which crosses it to the high mount upon which
stood the seat of the High Constables of England for four
hundred years.

> "Yet still remains and marks the ancient bound
> The bold abutment of the outer mound;
> Still with a slow and pausing step we tread
> High o'er the lofty arch, and thence are led
> To mount the keep whose hard access of yore
> A moat defended, but defends no more;
> For where of old did guardian waters flow
> Now spreading ash and humbler elders grow."

Stephen graciously presented Pleshey (his wife
Maud's property) to Mandeville, whose son William
obtained a licence from Henry II. to fortify the castle.
He celebrated here with much pomp his marriage to
Hawise, Countess of Albemarle. The beauty of this spot
and its accessibility from Chelmsford make it a favourite
resort for picnics. How many of these gay visitors, I
wonder, cast a thought to the dramatic story of a king's
treachery that was unfolded here one hot summer's
afternoon so long ago?

Froissart, in his own quaint style, has told us the tale,
but we must re-tell it in our own words. Pleshey passed
through the female line from Mandeville to the Bohuns,
Earls of Hereford, and was carried by Eleanor de Bohun,
a vast heiress, in marriage to a royal prince, Thomas of
Woodstock, Duke of Gloucester, sixth son of Edward III.

The hapless Richard II., son of the Black Prince and
"the Fair Maid of Kent," weak but winning, finding
himself on becoming king somewhat overweighted with
uncles, was fain to rid himself of this one, for
Gloucester, an honest man, was opposed to Richard's

favourites and evil advisers. The King set out one
morning in September, 1397, from Havering, with a
handful of followers only, as if to go a-hunting, but
his quarry was a human life. Covering the twenty miles
across country in a few hours, he arrived at Pleshey just
as the duke, "who was a small eater," arose from supper.
The Duke and Duchess, their children, the priests from
his newly-founded college hard by, the boys from the
song-school kept by the warden and chaplains, all received
the unexpected guest, and a banquet was spread for him
in the base-court of the castle. When he had eaten, he
bade Gloucester have five or six horses saddled and ride
with him at once to London, for the advice of the three
uncles on important matters was greatly needed. With
only seven attendants, and avoiding the high road through
Brentwood, the party rode rapidly southwards until they
were nearing Stratford-le-Bow. Here the King and his
men outpaced Gloucester, who was suddenly seized by a
troop of men in ambush, under Mowbray, the Earl Marshal.
They carried off their prisoner to Tilbury, and embarked
him for Calais, where on his arrival he was "piteously
murdered"—smothered, it is told, with a feather bed.
Gough, the poet of Pleshey, has fallen into a curious
mistake about Gloucester's age, and calls him "old
Gloucester," "the good old man," and even "the hoary
sage." He was, in fact, only forty-two, some twelve years
the senior of the King, his nephew. His body was
brought back to Pleshey to be buried by his canons,
but was removed thence to Westminster Abbey, where
it lies beside the dust of his mother, Queen Philippa,
on the south side of the Confessor's shrine. His faithful
wife, Alianore, retired to spend her widowhood at Barking
with the nuns. She made her will at Pleshey, and,
though she lived only two years after her lord, she saw
Richard deposed and a prisoner.

The castle and parks and manor of Pleshey
were granted by Edward VI. to Sir John Gates, his

Vice-Chamberlain, who had already received from Henry VIII. the spoils of Pleshey College, Beeleigh Abbey, and other religious houses. Gates ruthlessly destroyed the castle, college, and chancel, nave and aisles of the church, which it adjoined on the south side. Not a trace is now left of the pious foundations of these noble and princely donors, whose stately tombs and bones even have perished. Only the name " College Field " remains hanging to a parcel of ground adjoining the rebuilt church.

Three other ruined castles in Essex can only be mentioned, viz., Stanstead Mount Fitchet, built by William de Montfichet, the founder of the Abbey of Stratford ; Hadleigh, built by Hubert de Burgh in 1231 ; and Ongar, whose history is lost in antiquity. The unique and perfectly spared castle of Colchester, which is the pride of the county, and where a wonderful museum is housed, hardly falls within our scope to describe. It has never been a domestic residence since it was built by Eudo, one of Norman William's nobles, and for long was the county gaol.

Palaces and castles, whether fortresses, dwellings, or prisons, having now been glanced at, we must turn to the mansions, and especially to two : Audley End and New Hall, Boreham, which outstrip all others in the county both in splendour and extent, although only a portion of either now remains. Both at one time were royal residences.

Audley End, as everyone knows, derives its name from Thomas Audley (see page 235), Chancellor to Henry VIII., who bestowed upon him, among other spoils of the Church, the Abbey of Walden. Audley's sole surviving child, Margaret Audley, married that Duke of Norfolk who aspired, after her death, to become the husband of Mary Queen of Scots, and paid for his ambition by death at the hands of Mary's jealous cousin, Queen Elizabeth. Margaret's son Thomas was created Baron Howard de

Walden and Earl of Suffolk. He was the builder of a magnificent palace here, upon which he is said to have expended over £190,000, and thus to have impoverished his heirs. His widow, ingenious though she was in obtaining money by various means, lawful and unlawful, ended her days eluding the serjeants-at-arms who daily sought to arrest her. Her son Theophilus, famous at the tilt, patron of merchant-adventurers, and something of a poet, was in much favour at Court, and a companion of the young Prince Henry of Wales.

The building of the great house was begun in 1603, and is said to have occupied thirteen years ; at any rate, the date 1616 remains, or did remain, upon one of the gateways. Whilst it was progressing, King James I. twice visited the builder, who was keeper of his Privy Purse. The " canny " Scot surveyed the works narrowly, and astutely remarked that though the house was certainly too large for a king, it might not be for a Lord Treasurer. Incomes of the monasteries had gone, as we have seen, to enrich the builder through his mother ; now his property in the Midlands, and the Charterhouse, which he sold to Mr. Sutton, went as contributions to the building fund. So magnificent a palace was reared that no after possessor was able to maintain an establishment fitted to its splendour. A series of plans and drawings made by Henry Winstanley (see page 237), clerk of the works to Charles II. there, give us an idea of its extent ; for the merry monarch " took a liking " to this fine place, and acquired but never paid for it. Havering and many other of the royal residences were demolished, and his fancy turned, it seems, to Essex.

The style of architecture was, Evelyn tells us, " 'twixt antiq and modern." He calls it one of the stateliest palaces in the kingdom. The two entrances to the house were reached through a large outer courtyard, the sides of which were open cloisters, having apartments above. " The kitchen and cellars," says Evelyn, " are very large " ;, the

AUDLEY END: THE GREAT HALL.

hall, though fair, he thinks too small for so august a pile.
Pepys, who went later, was chiefly impressed with the
cellarage. Escorted by the landlord of the White Hart
and the housekeeper of the mansion, that gay and
irresponsible creature penetrated to these underground
labyrinths, drank the King's health in "a most admirable
drink," and afterwards played on his flageolet, less,
presumably, to test the echo than to impress his
companions. After this little display, everything—ceilings,
chimney-pieces, pictures—are found "exceedingly worth
seeing." Seven years later he came again, bringing his
wife. He was now a blasé man of the world. The ceilings
he finds "not so good as he took them to be"; the
staircase is "exceeding poor"; there is but one good
picture in the house—a Holbein portrait of Henry VIII.;
the hangings are ancient things such as he would not
give the hanging up to in his house; the beds and
furniture are all according. Only the gallery is good,
and, above all things, the cellars. Yes, the cellars.
"We went down to the cellars and drank of much
good liquors, and here my wife and I did sing to my
great content." Amiable egotist, how he loved to pose
and excel, whether in song, fine clothes, a fine wife,
or even in impropriety!

Queen Catherine of Braganza and her ladies sometimes
stayed at Audley End after this, and once they went,
disguised as country lasses, a-frolicking to Walden Fair.
They bought yellow stockings and long gloves stitched
with blue, at a booth, but the country folk soon discovered
them by their foreign "gibberish," and the royal
masquerader was almost mobbed by crowds of people who
had come to the fair, and thought a queen buying a fairing
was a merry sight. Whilst Audley End was in the King's
hands, Suffolk retired to Chesterford Park, but the Palace
was conveyed back to the fifth earl on condition of his
relinquishing all claim to the £20,000 which had remained
on mortgage and on which no interest was ever offered.

o

The royal tenants, moreover, had annexed some of the treasures of the house, notably some tapestries valued even then at £4,500, which Horace Walpole says were hung at Windsor. About 1721 the great kitchens, chapel, and the whole outer court were demolished by the advice of Sir John Vanbrugh. The work of destruction went on under Lady Portsmouth, who bought the house and park in 1747. The building was decaying and unsafe; and later the splendid gallery was sacrificed, a portion only of the costly palace being spared. Her nephew, Lord Howard de Walden, who succeeded in 1762, found it in a very dilapidated state; at enormous cost he restored and repaired the mansion, improved the grounds, and added to the park. Much also was done by his successors, the Lords Braybrooke. Like them, the present tenant—once more a Lord Howard de Walden—is descended in the female line from the third Earl of Suffolk.

The glory of New Hall, once a splendid palace rebuilt and decorated by a king, has even more thoroughly departed; although it still remains the most stately house in the county save Audley End. This estate formed part of the possessions of the Abbey of Waltham until the time of Edward III., when the abbot and convent exchanged it for land in Epping, lying nearer to their seat. After being held by the de Coggeshall family and the Botelers or Butlers, Earls of Ormond, for some generations, it lapsed during the Wars of the Roses to the Crown. James, Earl of Ormond, a zealous Lancastrian, fought for Henry VI. at St. Albans, Wakefield, Mortimer's Cross and Towton, where his followers, the Essex archers, died in their hundreds. Ormond was taken prisoner there, beheaded and attainted. To a younger brother Henry VII. restored his father's seat, granting him licence to build walls and towers about the mansion, for it had fallen into ruin and decay. His grandson was Sir Thomas Boleyn, father of the two handsome daughters who, and especially Ann, fixed for a time the fleeting fancy of that

much-married monarch, Henry VIII. Having seen the
young lady at Court, Henry seems to have proposed himself
as a purchaser of her father's Essex seat, which he coveted
not much less than the owner's daughter. Kings are not
to be gainsaid, so he acquired it, rebuilt and adorned it,
renamed it Beaulieu (a name that, as we well understand,
"never prevailed among the common people"), and
celebrated there in lavish and royal fashion the Feast of
St. George of Merrie England (April 23rd) in 1524. The
handsome gateway leading to the inner courtyard was
of his building, and bears his arms and an inscription in
stone over the gate. It was not till eight years after that
he actually married Ann Boleyn; meanwhile his daughter,
Princess Mary, separated from her mother, the divorced
Queen Catherine, passed most of her time at the early
home of her greatest enemy, the new rival in her father's
affections. At New Hall she studied Latin with her
governess, Lady Salisbury, and enjoyed the quiet of the
country, far apart from plots and counter-plots of which
she, as presumptive heiress to the throne, was the
unconscious object. In December, 1533, her household at
New Hall was suddenly broken up by the arrival
of the Duke of Norfolk bearing a peremptory order
for her to go to Hatfield and live with Ann Boleyn's
daughter, the baby Elizabeth, then three months old.
When Ann's very brief power ended Mary was free
to return to New Hall. Here she mostly lived during
the short reign of her brother Edward, and here she
entertained, in July, 1552, her unfortunate cousin,
Lady Jane Grey, whose life was the forfeit of a
father-in-law's ambition and a cardinal's bigotry. When
Edward died, Mary was on her way from New Hall to
her Norfolk home of Kenninghall. She heard that Jane
was proclaimed Queen, escaped disguised as a beggar
woman from a lodging near Cambridge, and was first
proclaimed Queen of England at Norwich. She seems
never to have revisited New Hall after this, although

doubtless the place was always associated in her mind with some of her most happy hours.

Queen Elizabeth kept house here for five days in July, 1561. In commemoration of the visit, either she or the Earl of Sussex, to whom she gave the estate in 1573, added her arms over the porch. The notorious Buckingham bought it of the Radcliffes for £30,000, and the next purchaser (for very much less) was the redoubtable Oliver Cromwell. Misliking it, however, he exchanged it for Hampton Court. The next purchaser was that engine of the Restoration, Monk, Duke of Albemarle, who with his blunt but honest Duchess, a farrier's daughter, kept great state in the palace. After his time the house stood empty and neglected, and, finally, was robbed of many of its splendid ornaments and materials by a later purchaser, Benjamin Hoare, banker, who used them to build his elaborate mansion of Boreham Place, on the other side of the high road. He sold New Hall, bereft of all its land, save the splendid approach through an avenue of lime trees a mile long, to John Olmius, Lord Waltham, who reduced the rambling palace to a compact and moderate-sized mansion. It has now for fifty years been the secluded home of a colony of nuns of the Order of the Holy Sepulchre, who carry on educational and philanthropic works of mercy.

No other house in the county approaches these two in antiquity and splendour. In the early and middle eighteenth century a wave of financial prosperity and philistine decoration swept over Essex, demolishing or transfiguring most of the Tudor and Elizabethan mansions into pseudo-classic temples or massive, square Georgian blocks.

Probably the largest house after New Hall is Terling Place, the seat of Lord Rayleigh, built by his ancestors, the Strutts, on the site of a more ancient house, where Henry VIII. used occasionally to reside. But there is nothing of the old mansion left, and we may turn to more ancient associations, beginning with the southern part of the county.

Gidea Hall, standing a little way back from the high road between London and Romford, was built—or, at any rate, begun—by Sir Thomas Cooke in 1467. Born in humble life at Lavenham, in Suffolk, Cooke, like Dick Whittington, went to London to make his fortune, became a wealthy draper, sheriff, and Lord Mayor, and, although a Yorkist, married the daughter of a prominent Lancastrian. The building of his "castle of stone and chalk," which by royal licence was permitted to be "turreted, moated, embanked, and machiolated," was sadly interrupted by his being indicted for high treason (he had refused to lend money to Queen Margaret) and thrown into prison. The rear portion of the house was added by his great grandson a hundred years later. This was the learned Sir Anthony, whose careful training of his own children, and other young noblemen committed to his charge, called forth Protector Somerset's famous epigram: "Some men govern their families with more skill than others their kingdoms." He was a believer apparently in co-education, for his five daughters, as well as his sons, became masters of the classics, and it has been said that Lady Jane Grey and the Princess Elizabeth, when living at Pyrgo near by, at some time or other participated in his teaching. His other royal pupil, the young King Edward VI., made no great pretence to learning. Cooke's eldest daughter, Mildred, married the great Lord Burleigh; Ann, the second, became the wife of Sir Nicholas Bacon and mother of the great philosopher, Francis Lord Bacon. Queen Elizabeth visited Gidea in 1568, but one cannot be sure if she ever saw with her own eyes the flattering inscriptions recording this visit which Cooke learnedly placed upon the mansion's front—an index, says one writer, to the library within. Certain Hebrew words and characters were engraved upon it, but the lines referring

to the Queen were in Latin, and have been roughly
translated as follows:—

> " This mansion's ancient front my grandsire Thomas gave,
> Anthony's tardy hands the other portions made.
> Each builds his own, but few God's house repair,
> Yet meaner things should claim the lesser care.
>
> " At thy bidding, gracious Queen,
>   All adverse fortune flies.
> My house, my groves and meadows green
>   Shall sing thy eulogies."

The old house was demolished early in the eighteenth
century, when the present one was built by Sir John Eyles
It has since received additions and alteration. Maria de
Medicis slept here on her journey from Harwich to
London, as has been already mentioned.

Quite near to Gidea is Marks, once an ancient
embattled mansion built around a quadrangle and
surrounded by a moat. It was long the property of the
Mildmays, and is now much reduced. Gobions, Stewards,
Dagenhams, Valentines, are all in the near neighbourhood,
and many other country seats, old and new, which we
cannot pause to enumerate. At Goosehays, in Havering
parish, lived Alured Cornburgh, the founder of a rich
chantry at Romford. The house was rebuilt by Lord
Dudley and Ward, who afterwards sold it to the Mead
family. Here, with his friend and stepson, William
Mead, the champion of the right of juries to give a
verdict in accordance with their conscience, George Fox,
the founder of Quakerism, used to stay.

Few of the splendid houses which adorned this district
now remain. The wealthy city merchant and the ministers
of State who built them now go much farther afield, and
the erections of the suburban builder encroach like a
great growing fungus farther and farther over the fields.
Of Wanstead and the Earl of Leicester's wild
extravagance when he entertained his doting queen
for four days, produced a woodland masque of

Sir Philip Sidney's, and spent a fortune; or of Sir Richard Child's grand mansion, built upon the site of Leicester's, nothing but an avenue of lime trees now remains. The park and beautiful lake, with its large heronry, have fortunately been acquired for public enjoyment. Eastbury, a massive pile of ruinated brick, in Barking parish, stands overlooking the Thames, vacantly watching the barges and vessels sail down the river between the green marshy fields of Essex and the hills of Kent. Parsloes low old house in Dagenham parish, with its trees peering into the ghost-haunted corners of the empty panelled rooms, will soon disappear.

A little farther from London, and on the old Roman road to Ipswich, is the fine mansion, partly old but largely rebuilt, of Weald Hall, where lived Sir Anthony Browne, Chief Justice of the Common Pleas and founder of the Grammar School at Brentwood in the days of Elizabeth. It has now been in the Tower family for one hundred and fifty years or more. To the noble Tudor building of gables, mullioned windows, and vast chimney stacks, a former owner, of unaccountable taste, ill-advisedly added, about 1730, a classical front with Ionic columns. Ten miles or so away southwards is the fine house and park of Belhus, named from the Norman family of Belhouse, who flourished in the time of King John. The ancestors of Sir Thomas Barrett-Lennard, its present owner, were of even earlier record, and appear on the roll of Battle Abbey, where the Conqueror's followers are enumerated. They enjoyed this estate through marriage with a Belhouse co-heiress, and derived also from the house of Dacre. The ancient mansion was moated and stood near a corner of the churchyard of Aveley, in which parish Belhus lies. The present mansion was built after the time of Henry VIII., but was much added to by Lord Dacre. Perhaps it was still building in 1578 when Queen Elizabeth lodged a night " in a farmhouse belonging to Mr. Barrett " here. It contains a magnificent collection of family portraits, and its park is one of the finest in the county, measuring three miles in circumference.

Hill Hall, between Epping and Ongar, is one of the least known yet most interesting places in the county. Its splendid park and high situation provide magnificent views, and its fine approach through an avenue of elms adds extremely to its charm. For over three hundred years it has been the seat of the Smyth or Smijth family. The house was built about 1548 in the then prevailing Renaissance fashion by Sir Thomas Smyth, who is said to have derived the design, during his travels in Italy, from John of Padua, a famous architect. About 1713 Hill Hall, like so many old Tudor houses in Essex, underwent severe treatment in order that it might more closely resemble the prevailing fashion of classical architecture. Many features of the old house were preserved; a grand entrance hall fifty-six feet by twenty feet is a later feature. Sir Thomas Smyth must be sought for among the Essex Worthies (see page 236), for he is one of our shining lights. Some Holbein portraits of his time are still among the treasures of the house.

Contemporary with the modern portion of Hill Hall a number of houses may be named. Copt, or Copped, Hall, Epping, overlooking the famous Forest, was originally built soon after 1564 by Sir Thomas Heneage, and was said at that time to be the "noblest house in Essex." It had a fine chapel and a gallery fifty-six yards long, which was blown down in a hurricane in November, 1639. It was built by John Conyers, whose family held it for more than a hundred years; it is now the property of E. J. Wythes, Esq., a former High Sheriff of the county. Barrington Hall, Hatfield Broad Oak, was erected about the same time by John Barrington Shales, near the site of the Benedictine Priory founded by the "grim Aubrey," first Earl of Oxford, where the Barrington family had resided since the dissolution of the monasteries. It is a fine mansion, although never actually completed. In springtime the grass grows yellow with daffodils among the ruins of the priory.

Thorndon Hall, the seat of Lord Petre at Ingatestone, was erected about 1766, but destroyed by fire in 1883. The wreck remained standing for many years, but a wing has now been restored for use. The park is one of the largest in the county, and is well stocked with deer. It is also a perfect paradise of roses and honeysuckle in the leafy month of June. Sir William Petre, founder of the family, born in Devonshire, buried under a fine monument in Ingatestone church, was one of the principal Secretaries of State to Henry VIII., Edward VI., Queen Mary and Queen Elizabeth.

Felix Hall, Kelvedon, the ancient home of the Abdys, and of the famous Whig, Lord Western, was built about 1760, but was almost entirely rebuilt by Lord Western in the then prevailing classical style. It was filled with treasures brought from Italy by this liberal patron of the arts, but although it still belongs to the grandson of his heir, Sir Thomas Burch Western, no Western has lived there for many years. The real seat of the Westerns is Rivenhall Place, a couple of miles away, one of the famous old houses of Essex which have lately been restored and inhabited after a long period of decay. A beautiful lake intersects the park, which can boast some splendid timber. The Westerns lived here from 1693 until Lord Western moved to Felix Hall, Kelvedon, leaving Rivenhall to the Rev. Sir John Page Wood, vicar of Cressing, and once chaplain to the unfortunate Queen Caroline. Perhaps he is better known to the present generation as the father of that popular hero, Field-Marshal Sir Evelyn Wood, V.C. A granddaughter of Sir John now resides at Rivenhall, but it is pleasant to learn that a Western has once more come to take up his abode in the county, in the person of Colonel C. M. Western, R.A., now of Goldsmiths, Laindon Hills.

In its remote and rural northern portion, Essex
possesses in Gosfield Hall one of the most beautiful and
interesting specimens of domestic architecture in the
kingdom. The beauties of the magnificently planted park
and its fine large lake attracted the approbation of no less
an authority than Arthur Young. The village itself, with
the church situated in the park and only divided from it
by a sunken wall, is one of the prettiest in Essex. Others,
no doubt, preserve more ancient features, such as the
village green, but Gosfield can boast, as well as the
highly decorative and sanitary cottages built by
Mr. Samuel Courtauld when rural housing in Essex
was at its lowest ebb, some gabled, thatched, and
whitewashed buildings that vie with any in Finchingfield
or Stebbing, for instance. The Hall presents an
example of a residence designed for strength and
protection, yet not either castle or fortress, the building of
these, after the Wars of the Roses, being prohibited by
law. Its western front, with a fine Tudor gateway leading
to the inner quadrangle, remains almost unchanged, and
shows how impregnable the mansion must once have been.
Its thick massive walls are unpierced by windows in the
lower story ; the upper floor mainly consists of a long
oak-panelled gallery, with heavily barricaded windows.
This apartment, one hundred and six feet in length, goes
by the name of Queen Elizabeth's gallery, for the great
queen in her " Progresses " twice visited Lady Maltravers
here—in 1561 and 1579—on her way to and from Leighs
Priory. Her hostess was the widow of Sir Hugh Rich,
re-married to Henry Fitz-Alan, Lord Maltravers. Both
husbands died very young, leaving her to enjoy a long and
peaceful widowhood at Gosfield, which she inherited from
her father, Sir John Wentworth, the builder of the Hall,
who died in 1567. After her, the estates passed to a
cousin, John Wentworth, of Horkesley, and eventually
to the Earls Grey. About 1715, they were sold to
John Knight, who rebuilt the north-east and south fronts

and lessened the apartments on the ground floor by cutting off a passage on either side of the courtyard, because the rooms all opened into each other. Mrs. Knight, when a rich and rather eccentric widow (of whom there is a curious wax effigy in the church), re-married with Lord Nugent, from whom, in 1788, the estate passed to the Marquis of Buckingham. It became the shelter for a year or two of the exiled King Louis XVIII., and about the same time a number of other French emigrés resided in the village, including a small colony of Poor Clares exiled from Gravelines. After many vicissitudes, this beautiful house was purchased, in 1854, by Samuel Courtauld, descended from a French refugee and goldsmith, and then the head of the large firm of silk and crape manufacturers of Bocking, Earls Colne, and Halstead. It passed to his adopted daughter, who now resides there.

Of far greater pretension than Gosfield Hall, but now still more reduced in size, are the three mansions of St. Osyth Priory, Leighs Priory, and Layer Marney Tower. The beautiful gateway of St. Osyth leads to a quadrangle around which the monastery stood ; one side is now occupied by the modern house. At Leighs there is also a fine outer gateway, through which the two courtyards of Lord Rich's handsome mansion were reached. But only a portion of the outer range of buildings remains, and the splendid isolated tower which formed the entrance to the inner courtyard, where was a beautiful little fountain, with a leaded roof of conical shape, which remains on the grass-grown site. One wanders dreamily through the heavy gateway, with Elizabeth's rose and the Rich motto, " Garde ta Foy," overhead, and thinks of the stir and bustle of that day in 1641 when the Royalist Sir Charles Lucas and his mounted troops clattered into the courtyard, searched the armoury for weapons which the faithful steward, Arthur Wilson, had concealed, frightened a pack of undefended women, and rode off again to their long siege and death in

Colchester. Lord Warwick, the steward's master, away
in the army of the Parliament, would have been none
too pleased to have provided arms for the King. Across
the winding stream lies the Wilderness, once a retired
garden, where his daughter-in-law, the pious Countess
Mary, daily performed her morning devotions, like
St. Francis, in the open air.

The tower of Layer Marney Hall, which is illustrated
herewith, is even more beautiful and far more perfect
than Leighs. The tragedy of this fine old building
is that it was never finished, and that its days of
splendour began and ended within a span of twenty-
five years. Then, for hundreds of years, it was
neglected and decayed, until within this present century
alien hands have reverently repaired and restored it to
something less than its former greatness. The Lords of
Marney came to this country with Norman William, fought
at Hastings, and held land in Essex at least from 1166.
Sir Henry de Marney, the builder of the tower, was made
a baron by Henry VIII., having been in great favour at
Court both with his father and himself. He was a Privy
Councillor, Captain of the Guard, and Keeper of the Privy
Seal. A man of cultured tastes, well-known abroad at the
Courts of France and Italy, it is not surprising that when
he began to build his mansion, soon after 1500, his selection
of style was influenced by foreign ideas. Terra-cotta was
extensively used in elaborate modelling upon the windows
and parapets of the tower; the fine red brick which is
such a beautiful feature of old Essex was unfortunately
partially covered with plaster, but it has crumbled away
sufficiently to show the diaper patterns of black brick
which one meets again at Leighs Priory, Nether Hall,
Belhus, and a number of old houses in Essex. The fluted
and scrolled chimneys remain magnificent examples of the
workmanship of an age that saw Wolsey's Hampton Court
and Henry VII.'s Chapel at Westminster built. St. John's
College, Cambridge, built by the Lady Margaret, Countess

LAYER MARNEY HALL : THE TOWER.

of Richmond, the King's mother, was then in course of
erection, and to this generous lady Henry Marney was
executor. He died a year after he received his title, and
before his mansion was finished. Sad to say, his son died
in the following year, leaving no heir to the title, and the
very workmen who were engaged in fashioning the parapets
and window ornaments upon the lofty tower were now
employed upon the two tombs in the little church a
stone's-throw away. One wing only of the new mansion
was finished ; adjoining it is a long range of outbuildings,
massively built, with an upper apartment under a highly
decorative roof, windows, and a huge fireplace, evidently a
sleeping-place for the retainers, and still called the
dormitory.

Layer Marney, from its high situation, can be seen a
long way off. Not so another mansion with a tower,
Faulkbourne Hall, near Witham, for it is, like most of
the old houses, situated in a hollow and enclosed by
skirting trees and the uplands of a wooded park.
Faulkbourne has been added to by many owners. Although
reputed to have been begun in the time of Stephen, so
much antiquity cannot be claimed for it. It is, however,
a highly interesting Tudor house, connected with Sir John
Montgomery, Keeper of the Exchange to Henry VI., and
after 1637 with the Bullocks. Its present appreciative
owner is Mr. Christopher Parker, who was High Sheriff
of Essex a few years ago.

In the north-western part of the county, and twenty
miles or more from Layer Marney, is the interesting old
mansion of Horham Hall. Few persons visit this place,
for it lies (until the proposed light railway appears)
in one of the most inaccessible parts of Essex.
Only a small remnant is left of the " very sumptuous "
house built by Sir John Cutts, Treasurer of King
Henry VIII.'s household, and enlarged and completed
by his grandson of the same name. Here, this last
Sir John entertained, in 1571, his capricious queen,

making upon her so good an impression of his liberal housekeeping that she afterwards despatched her sick ambassador from Spain to be nursed into convalescence amid the high and healthy surroundings of Thaxted. From the battlemented tower the whole open country between Cambridgeshire on the north, and Hertfordshire on the west, may be surveyed, with the wooded acres of Easton Park and Lady Warwick's rebuilt mansion in the nearer view. If we enter the grand hall through its Tudor-arched doorway, we shall discover in the wide window recess some beautiful old stained-glass, and we may admire the flat-arched roof, divided by oak beams into squares of three feet or so apiece. A similar ceiling, with badges and shields and finely-carved and gilded leaves and flowers, is to be seen in "Queen Elizabeth's bedroom" upstairs. Some splendid brass fire-dogs which stood in the great open fireplace, where a cartload of wood might be burned at once, have lately been sold at a fancy price, together with other relics from this fine old house. Everyone interested in Tudor architecture should visit Horham, for seldom is there to be seen such a display of varied forms of building. In its palmy days, with moat and drawbridge in full play, Horham was truly a palace fit for a queen.

None of the melancholy of these once stately and now abased mansions belongs to Spains Hall, Finchingfield, a place almost unrivalled in the county as an example of Tudor domestic architecture. Having been continuously occupied since it was built in the time of Elizabeth, its fabric at least has not been suffered to decay, nor does it bear those unmistakable marks of having been adapted to a lesser purpose which characterise many of those houses we have considered. Its fine hall, large and lofty, is lighted by a magnificent bay window extending along the greater part of the front. When William's Domesday Survey was made, this manor belonged to the Spain or Hispania family, from whom, of course, it has taken its name. Through marriage it passed to the Kemps in the

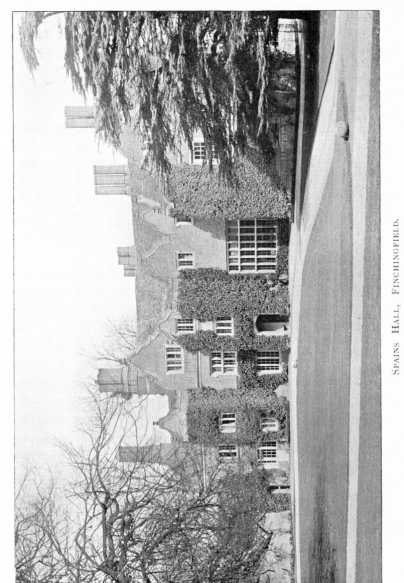

SPAINS HALL, FINCHINGFIELD.

time of Edward I., and in that family remained until 1736. There is a delightful story about one of the Kemps —William the Silent he has been called—which is known to everyone in the district, yet will bear to be told again. William's wife, Philippa, it is perhaps no disloyalty to woman to say, occasionally called for some display of forbearance on the part of her husband. One day his self-control absolutely broke down, and he indulged in an unseemly passion of speech. So sincere was his penitence that he imposed on himself a rigid vow of seven years' silence, which he faithfully kept. They must have been dull years for the poor lady, his wife, and one trembles to think how terribly it lay in her power to torture the speechless penitent with reproach.

Not many houses in the county can show such a stable record of ownership as Moyns Park, Steeple Bumpstead, some three miles to the north of Spains Hall. From Domesday until a few years ago this estate remained in a single line, although conveyed by Joan le Moyne, heiress of the first Norman owner, on her marriage to William Gent, into a family which had lived at Wimbish near by since 1328. Sir Thomas Gent, serjeant-at-law, one of Queen Elizabeth's Barons of the Exchequer, built the handsome turreted front about 1580, but the domestic offices, surrounding a flagged courtyard at the back, are of at least a century earlier. With their gabled roofs, black oak timbers, and thin red bricks, in which the leaded casements are set high and narrowly, they show their date to be that of Shakespeare's Stratford, and make the lilied moat, the bowling green, and the crumbling mulberry tree appear, by comparison, almost modern.

A word must be added, in conclusion, about the fine manor houses which are thickly spread throughout the county. Some, like Feering Bury, Spaynes Hall, Yeldham ; Beaumont Hall, near Harwich ; White Notley Hall, or Rayne Hall, the ancient seat of the Capells, have been constantly occupied; others have fallen from bad to worse, and are now only tenanted by bats and owls, who perhaps permit a small corner to shelter a farm bailiff and his family. Of such are the remarkable farmhouses in the Rodings which have been illustrated and described in the *Essex Review* by Mr. Miller Christy. Colville Hall, with its quarry of armorial glass and window paintings of the husbandries of ten of the months; Rookwood Hall, which entertained Queen Elizabeth in 1578, and gave a title to Sir Henry Selwin Ibbetson when he was called to the peerage; moated New Hall, with its enormous barn of herring-bone red brick; and Camoys, or Cammas, Hall, modernised almost beyond hope, may be mentioned.

Sir Martin Lumley's Great Lodge in Bardfield parish has lost the greater part of its park, but its fine embattled clock-tower remains. Rickling Hall shows some features of brickwork not elsewhere to be found. Porter's Hall, Stebbing, is completely encircled with its moat, and only approached by three bridges. These and many more such fascinating old manors and farmhouses lie hidden away amid Essex lanes and commons, uninvaded as yet by the railway and its attendant modern craze for a " week-end country cottage."

ROUNDELS FROM COLVILLE HALL.

DENEHOLES

By Francis W. Reader

ESSEX is fortunate in possessing many of the ancient excavations known as Deneholes, and notably the remarkable group at Hangman's Wood, near Grays, where perhaps the finest examples yet discovered are to be seen.

The name "Denehole" is one that has been applied locally, and is thought to have been derived from the Anglo-Saxon *Den, dene, denn*=a cave, though by some it is said to mean Dane. The term in this part of the country refers to workings in the chalk, which, although subject to considerable variation as to size and arrangement, all fall into a class having a vertical shaft leading from the surface, the base of which is opened out into a chamber or a cluster of chambers. Excavations in the chalk have been numerous from very remote times, and have been undertaken for many purposes, so that in considering deneholes it is essential to keep them distinct from the galleried mines, such as have been found at Cissbury and Brandon, which were clearly dug in order to obtain flint; the chalk mines with communicating tunnels, like those of Chislehurst; and from the pits which abound in some chalky districts, which bear evidence of having been formed for storage, or as a receptacle for rubbish.

Deneholes occur most plentifully along the riverside of Essex and Kent, though they are found in many other parts of Kent, notably at Rochester and Sittingbourne. They are also said to occur in Hertfordshire, Bedfordshire, Norfolk, Suffolk, etc. Some artificial caves in the limestone rocks of Durham are known as Danes' Holes, but would seem not to belong to the same group as the deneholes of the chalk district, as they have no vertical entrance. At the present time considerable numbers of deneholes still remain, some showing on the surface as a shallow depression, owing to the collapse of the roof of the chambers; but others, which have remained intact, still preserve an open shaft. Most of them have become filled in and obliterated, but they are frequently met with in quarrying operations. Local conditions have in some instances influenced the size and arrangement of the shafts and chambers, but in others the variation of type seems to indicate their construction at widely different periods. In the simplest form the shaft is merely enlarged into a single, roughly circular chamber. This type is not only simpler and ruder, but is usually much shallower than those of the later and more elaborate pattern; while they occur in places where the chalk comes to the surface or is covered only with a slight thickness of sand or other deposit. The shaft is carried at once into the chalk, leaving enough to form a roof of sufficient strength, below which it becomes gradually enlarged into the chambers. There is reason to suppose that some of these were formed as early as the Neolithic period, and they are known as the bell, or beehive, type (fig. I A). Such pits discovered near Crayford, Kent, are described by Mr. F. C. J. Spurrell.[1] One of them was thirty-six feet six inches in total depth from the surface, the depth of the shaft and that of the chamber being about equal, and its greatest diameter was eighteen feet:

"The floor reached to the layer of flint which all the other caves reached, and part of the flint had been taken up and piled in a heap at one side of the cave. From the floor rose an obtuse cone of sandy clay, very hard, six feet high, washed in very slowly and evenly by the rain. In the cone was found several flakes, worked scrapers, and a 'core,' but no pottery; above this lay coarser soil, several sorts of

1 *Archæological Journal*, vol. xxxvii., p. 332.

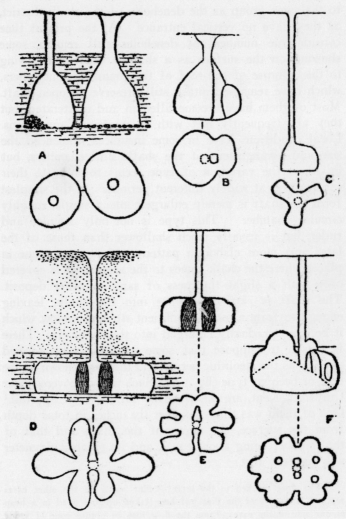

FIG. 1—DIAGRAM SHOWING VARIOUS TYPES OF DENEHOLES.

A Crayford.　　B Stankey.　　C Jordens.　　D Grays.
E and F Stankey.

pottery, some made with shells, some with chalk, and ornamented by the finger nail; higher still Roman pottery, a fine Samian plate and bones, and rubbish to the surface. The time which has elapsed since the deposit of Roman remains we can calculate. It is well within bounds to date the commencement of the deposit of mud at half that period earlier, and that would not reach the time of its excavation."

In some cases bays are worked out of the side of this chamber, sometimes with pillars left to support the roof. An instance of a single subsidiary chamber (fig. 1 B) which has been formed in this manner occurred at Stankey, Kent, and it is referred to by Mr. Spurrell in his well-known and excellent paper, "Deneholes and Artificial Caves with Vertical Entrances."[1] It appears that these secondary chambers are sometimes the results of later re-working of the pits, as it has been noticed that the sides bear marks of a different method of removing the chalk. In this earlier work the chalk seems to have been forced away with wedges, while the later caves show distinctly the marks of metal picks.

More developed deneholes often have the shaft carried through gravel, Thanet sand, etc., of a great depth, commonly fifty to eighty feet. The shafts vary, from being just wide enough to admit the body of a man to pass down them, to about four feet. Where the soil through which the shaft passes is of a tenacious character, such as Thanet sand, the natural sides have been left; but in softer soils the sides are steined with flints or brick. In some are found foot-holes, or holes in which timbers have been placed to aid the descent, but most of them appear to have been descended by a rope, the marks of which often remain. The shaft is carried down into the chalk, and from it chambers are driven, forming in plan a trefoil, or a double trefoil. These chambers vary in length generally from fifteen to thirty feet, and from twelve to thirty feet in height, leaving a thin roof of chalk, often only two

---

[1] *Archæological Journal*, vol. xxxviii., pp. 391-409 ; vol. xxxix., pp. 1-22.

or three feet thick. An exceptional pit discovered at Plumstead[1] had its shaft carried through twenty-four feet of Thanet sand, after which it passed twenty feet into the chalk before opening out into two long chambers in opposite directions (fig. 2). Of the single trefoil type the chambers usually radiate equi-distantly (fig. 1 C).

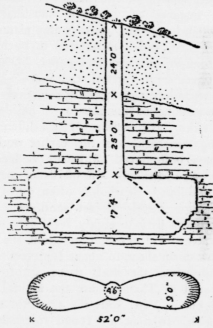

FIG. 2—DENEHOLE DISCOVERED AT WICKHAM LANE, PLUMSTEAD.

Another example on this plan in Jorden's Wood had the chambers of the unusual length of fifty feet, others being only fifteen or sixteen feet long, and of almost equal breadth and height.

The double trefoil is the form most commonly met with, and these have two primary or terminal chambers in the same longitudinal direction, and from the base

[1] *Woolwich Antiq. Soc. Proc.*, 1897-8, pp. 20-41.

of these are two lateral branches, generally inclining slightly towards the outer end of the terminal chamber to which they are attached (fig. 1 D). A further development sometimes occurs where the partition walls are broken through, leaving the roof supported by columns. A double trefoil pit having two columns was found at Cavey Spring, Bexley (fig. 3), while one found at Stankey (fig. 1 E) has one column, and another (fig. 1 F), which may be regarded as the full development, has had each of the walls removed, leaving, in its original state, six columns, and having an additional bay worked in the spaces between the terminal and lateral lobes of the trefoils. In addition to the types above mentioned, there are many variants, some of no regular plan, as, for example, a pit at Frindsbury[1] (fig. 4).

The deneholes of Essex are mostly situated in the district between Purfleet and East Tilbury, and at a distance of from one to three miles from the Thames. They are mentioned by Camden, who says:[2] "Near Tilbury are several spacious caverns in a chalky cliff, built very artificially of stone, to the height of ten fathoms, and somewhat strait at the top. A person who had been down to view them gave me a description of them." He adds some curious representations of them, which are interesting, although not strictly accurate (fig. 5). Large numbers of them have occurred near Purfleet, Stifford, and West Thurrock, many of which are said to have been filled up during recent years, while others have been dug away in the chalk quarries. Although no precise details of them are given, Mr. Spurrell mentions that among them were some of the "rudest and earliest caves," and that near Purfleet flint flakes are abundant on the adjacent surface. Quite recently further details of some deneholes at Purfleet have been recorded by Mr. T. V. Holmes,[3] who gives a plan of one having a longitudinal passage sixty-six feet in length, with

1 *Rochester Naturalist*, April, 1887.   2 *Britannia* (1610).
3 *Essex Naturalist*, vol. xv., p. 8.

several lateral passages of an irregular plan, which suggests a rough specimen of the double trefoil type. Shallow pits also occur at East Tilbury, and Mr. Spurrell believes the pits at both Purfleet and East Tilbury to belong to an early period, and he strongly urged the examination of the pits in these districts. During the present year (1908) a denehole was discovered in a field

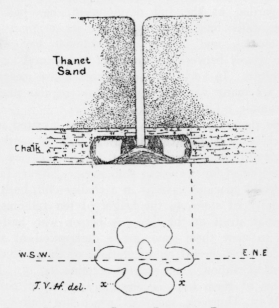

Thanet
Sand

Chalk

W.S.W.

E.N.E

J.V.H. del.   x   x

FIG. 3—SECTION AND GROUND PLAN OF A DENEHOLE IN
CAVEY SPRING, KENT.

at West Thurrock; this the writer visited at the invitation of the Rev. J. W. Hayes, who has given much attention to the subject. The total depth of this pit was only about twelve feet, the chambers being ten feet long, six feet wide, and seven feet high. It was a simple matter to crawl into this pit, with the aid of a waggon-shaft and a rope. Although partly filled up, the chamber seemed to be arranged on an irregular double-trefoil plan. Mr. Hayes says that about forty similar pits have been found on this field, and nine or ten were revealed a few years ago after a heavy rain, these being stopped up with faggots and rubbish. The local tradition is that they continued to be dug until comparatively recent times, to obtain chalk for manuring the heavy clay land of the district.

The only deneholes in Essex that have been systematically examined are those already referred to at Hangman's Wood. The work was undertaken by the Essex Field Club in 1884 and 1887, a full and elaborate report of which was drawn up by Mr. T. V. Holmes and Mr. W. Cole.[1] Mr. Miller Christy, who also took part in the exploration, has contributed an able article on this subject.[2] The number of pits that are still to be traced in Hangman's Wood is said to be between fifty and sixty. Mr. Spurrell gives the number as seventy-two, and it is said that formerly they were even more numerous, many having been filled up from time to time. Several shafts are still open, and the descent has been made accessible by private enterprise, so that they are now widely known and visited. The chalk is in this part overlaid by a thick deposit of Thanet sand, extending to a distance of fifty or sixty feet below the surface, and capped with a thin layer of gravel. The pits are of the double trefoil type, and are placed very close together, but care seems to have been used to keep the chambers of the different pits distinct, although the thin partition walls are in a few places broken through. It seems probable that this was accidental, or done by some later agency. The height of the chambers was found to be usually from sixteen to eighteen feet, but in one case it was as much as twenty-one to twenty-two feet. The roof varied from

---

1 *Essex Naturalist*, vol. i., pp. 225-276.
2 *Reliquary*, 1895, N.S., vol. i., p. 65.

two to six feet in thickness. The total depth of the floor of the pits from the surface varied from seventy-eight to eighty-one feet, and the width of the chambers at the widest part was from ten to fifteen feet. A large quantity of the debris forming the cone which had fallen in through the shafts was removed and carefully examined, but the labours of the Exploration Committee

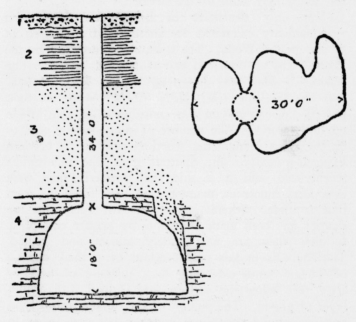

FIG. 4—PLAN AND SECTION OF THE FRINDSBURY DENEHOLE.

1 Soil and Flints.   2 Brickearth.   3 Thanet Sand.   4 Chalk.

were not rewarded with the discovery of relics throwing light on the origin of these pits. A fragment of pottery of the late Celtic period was found on or close to the floor of one of the pits, while another yielded a piece of Niedermendig lava, probably a portion of a millstone. Some fragments of mediæval pottery also occurred. A number of bones were found, mostly of small animals, the most numerous of which were rabbits and dogs. There were also some of the ox, donkey, sheep, etc., and the remains of a human skeleton. None of these bones, however, appear to have had any connection with the makers of the deneholes, but seem to have been the remains of victims of the pitfall formed by the open mouths of the shafts, into which they had fallen during later times. Mr. E. T. Newton, F.R.S., who reports on these remains, observes: "It is somewhat strange that up to the present time the deneholes have yielded no remains which indicate any great antiquity; indeed all those characteristic forms which are usually met with in prehistoric deposits are conspicuous by their absence."

Describing the excavations, Mr. Holmes says:

"We found the upper part of the mound was composed almost wholly of Thanet sand with occasional pebbles, the lower consisting of gravel with a slight admixture of sand. The gravel formed a low cone extending to the very ends of the chambers, the sand a much steeper cone of much smaller horizontal extent. Occasionally lumps of chalk, the result of its weathering towards the base of the shaft, appeared here and there. . . . We found as we got nearer the floor the lumps of chalk became much more numerous, and that close to the shaft were great numbers of large flints, frequently more or less squared. There can be little doubt that these large flints had once been used for 'steining' or lining the uppermost six or eight feet of the shaft sunk through the surface gravel, which would be a most treacherous and dangerous material around the mouth of a shaft if unprotected by steining. And it is not unlikely that much of the chalk, so specially abundant close to the floor, had been used for the same purpose, courses of chalk having been found alternating with others of brick in the shaft at Eltham Park,[1] already mentioned."

The foregoing refers to the cone beneath the shaft of the first pit examined, but the same general description applies to those subsequently explored. The floors of the chambers were noticed to be smooth, while the sides are rough, and bear plainly the marks of metal picks. There were no ashes, or signs that fires had been lighted in the caves. Little, in fact, was found as the

---

[1] *Archæological Journal*, vol. xxxv. p. 179.

result of the exploration of the Hangman's Wood pits, in which respect they agree with the accounts given of those destroyed in the quarries.

In a pit near Grays, however, a remarkable find is recorded by Mr. Meeson, who says: " I have opened one full of Roman burial vases, crushed by the fall of the roof, but from which I extracted one nearly perfect, containing the bones of a female and child with bronze armlets and a spindle whorl of lead."[1] This find is quite exceptional, and it seems to admit of little doubt that the objects were placed in position during the Roman period. The few relics found in the Hangman's Wood pits afford no such evidence, and might have lain in the soil above before the pits were formed, and have fallen or been washed in subsequently.

As regards the age of deneholes, it is generally agreed that they date from an early period, and have continued to be made down to comparatively recent times. Very different views have been expressed, however, respecting their purpose. They have been variously held to be: pit dwellings, storage-pits, places of hiding or refuge, flint mines, pitfalls, burial-places, and holes for obtaining chalk. Of all these solutions, the last, which is the simplest and most practical, is the one that is now most generally held, and it is supported by the analogy of very similar workings which are practised at the present time. It should be pointed out, however, that neither Mr. Spurrell nor Mr. Holmes believes in the chalk-works theory, and as both these authorities have devoted so much time and study to the subject their views are deservedly worthy of great consideration. In the paper referred to earlier, Mr. Spurrell has collected a great deal of information regarding subterranean excavations in other parts of the

---

1 *Stifford and its Neighbourhood*, p. 41 ; *Archæological Journal*, vol. xxvi., p. 190.

world, and he instances many that have been used as granaries, dwellings, and hiding-places. The difficulty comes in ascertaining the details and conditions to establish a parallel with the deneholes, and also in determining whether the pits were originally excavated for the purposes to which they had subsequently been put. The distinctions also between excavations definitely made for dwellings and storage, and those which are the result of mining, are often difficult to determine.

Fig. 5—Illustrations of Deneholes from Camden's
Britannia (1610).

In speaking of pit dwellings, Mr. Spurrell says: "In Kent almost every gradation may be traced between such and the deepest caves with narrow shafts." It is by no means clear that the various pits recorded as deneholes are all of a similar character, although they may be included under the definition of a chamber or chambers having a vertical entrance. There must of necessity be some features which, in a general way, would be common to such pits, whether dug for the material or for the space. Experience would, in the course of time, determine the best method of excavation consistent with safety of life and economy of working. In Wiltshire and elsewhere[1] many pits have been found in the chalk which bear evidence of having been used for storage and occupation. It is indeed seldom that these pits fail to yield indications of such use, and their method of construction often leaves little doubt that they were intentionally dug for these purposes. It is quite otherwise with the more numerous and typical deneholes. They reveal no signs of occupation and contain but few ancient relics, and in very rare cases only do these relics provide reliable evidence in favour of extreme antiquity for their formation. In some of these exceptional instances, such, for example, as the discovery by Mr. Meeson at Grays, no details of the character of the pit are given.

Mr. Holmes has always strongly controverted the idea of deneholes being chalk workings, principally on the ground of each group of chambers being kept distinct and requiring a separate shaft, and the great depth at which the chalk lies beneath the overlying soils in the case of many deneholes, particularly at Hangman's Wood, when at only a short distance away, chalk could have been obtained on the surface. No trace of chalk was found on the surface above the deneholes in Hangman's Wood, although the Thanet sand excavated from the shafts is said to have been spread evenly over the ground, and from this Mr. Holmes concludes that secrecy was one of the objects of those who constructed deneholes, in order to provide a safe storage for grain. He compares them to the pits found in the Isle of Portland.[2]

If the fact of chalk occurring near by on the surface possessed the advantage, which, at first sight, may appear evident, these arguments might be unanswerable, and

---

[1] *Flint Chips*, E. T. Stevens, p. 57; *Early Man in Britain*, Boyd Dawkins, p. 268; *Excavations in Cranborne Chase*, Lieut.-Gen. Pitt-Rivers, vols. i., ii.

[2] *Proc. Geol. Assoc.*, vol. viii., p. 404.

under this impression, the writer of this article was led to express the same view in a former short notice on deneholes.[1] Having since submitted this question to the opinion of several quarry managers, the writer is assured that there is nothing whatever in this argument, and that even at the present time it would be easier and cheaper to

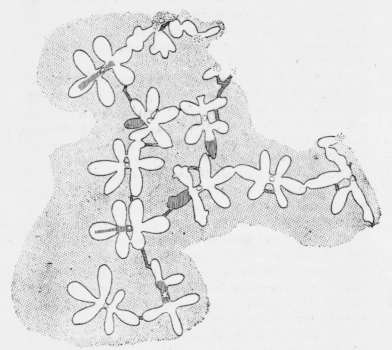

FIG. 6—GROUND-PLAN OF GROUP OF DENEHOLES AT HANGMAN'S WOOD.
(Scale, 40 ft. to 1 in.)

haul it up on the spot than to transport it from an even less distance than would be necessary at Hangman's Wood. This, of course, implies that the material was used on the spot. A practical instance exemplifying this point can be seen in operation at the present time in a

1 *Essex Field Club Museum Handbook*, No. 5, p. 26.

brickworks near Plumstead, where chalk is procured in this way, and the proprietor declares that it is a more practical plan than carting it from the surface—a distance of a quarter of a mile. This has been pointed out by Mr. Charles Bird,[1] among others, who also quotes the opinion of Mr. James Pye, that deneholes were mostly dug to get chalk to manure the land, a custom which he has known to take place as late as 1886 at Strood. Pennant[2] also, in alluding to deneholes, says they were dug for chalk, and that the same method was still followed at the time he wrote.

A system of sinking chalk wells for the purpose of top dressing the land is described by Mr. F. J. Bennett as an appendix to the Report of the Hangman's Wood explorations. Mr. F. W. Elliott has also called attention to chalk shafts at a tileworks in Buckinghamshire.[3] which, he states, more nearly resemble the deneholes of Essex than the chalk wells referred to by Mr. Bennett. There is, further, the celebrated passage from Pliny,[4] who speaks of chalk being obtained "by means of pits sunk like wells, with narrow mouths, to the depth, sometimes, of one hundred feet, where they branch out like the veins of mines, and this kind is chiefly used in Britain." On the strength of this, C. Roach Smith appears to have based his opinion of deneholes, which led him so strangely to oppose their further investigation when undertaken by the Essex Field Club.

The number of deep shafts so close together, and the apparent care taken to keep the chambers from communicating, seem difficult to understand when judged by our modern ideas of mining; but the pits at Brightling, Sussex, described by Mr. C. W. Dawson, F.S.A.,[5] provide a striking and convincing parallel in

[1] *Rochester Naturalist*, 1887.
[2] *Journey from Chester to London*, 1811.
[3] *Essex Naturalist*, vol. i., p. 254.
[4] Pliny, *Natural History Lib.*, xvii., cap. 8.
[5] *Geol. Mag.* N.S., Decade iv., vol. v., pp. 293-302, July, 1898; see also *Report at the South-Eastern Union of Scientific Societies*, 1898.

this system of operation (fig. 7). Here hundreds of
shafts have been dug, and continue to be made, on
precisely the same principle as the deneholes of Essex,
only they pass through forty to fifty feet of Purbeck
shales in order to reach a seam of limestone, a few feet
thick, which is used for road-metal. Above the stone the
base of the shaft is expanded into a bell-shaped cavity,
in the sides of which arched bays are worked out in a

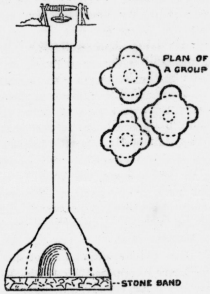

FIG. 7—BELL PITS AT BRIGHTLING, SUSSEX.

somewhat irregular manner. The size of the excavation
depends on the stability of the material, in some cases
having a diameter of only fifteen feet, but sometimes
considerably larger. When a fresh pit is started,
measurements are carefully taken so as to utilize
as much surface as possible without allowing the
pits to encroach on each other. The material removed
before reaching the stone is thrown down the shaft of

a pit that has already been worked out. It is said by the workers that this is the most economical and practical method for their requirements. Such being the case to-day, and with the object of obtaining only a thin stratum of stone, how much more likely is it to have been the purpose of deneholes in earlier times, and where all the material excavated was of use.

If the primary reason of the formation of deneholes was to obtain chalk, there is no doubt that the flint met with was also utilized, although it was not specially sought, as only in a few instances do the flint bands appear to have been followed. Some of the other explanations that have been put forward probably have their origin in the subsequent use to which deneholes have been put. It is difficult to suppose, however, that any race of men ever excavated the deneholes as dwelling-places, or even to any extent occupied them. The length of time during which deneholes appear to have been formed would require that men of different races and culture, in certain restricted districts, all adopted this laborious method of dwelling, the entrance and egress to which was attended with such difficulty and danger, and yet without leaving any trace of their occupation. As store-houses or for refuge they may occasionally have been resorted to, in the way that smugglers are said to have used them; but that so many hundreds of vast holes could have been deliberately formed for such purposes seems to be inconceivable. Evidence of burial in one example, and a general resemblance in form to a Roman Columbarium, is no warrant for supposing that they were excavated for burial purposes.

The simpler explanation of deneholes being mines for chalk may seem prosaic, but it is more reasonable and consistent with all the ascertained facts.

Q

ESSEX WORTHIES

By Miss C. Fell Smith

THE roll-call of notable persons born in Essex is a long and honourable one, and contains the names of not a few whose memory is imperishable, and cherished all the world over. Of these are John Ray, pioneer of natural science; Thomas Audley, Lord Chancellor; Samuel Harsnett, Archbishop of York, and founder of Chigwell Grammar School; Francis Quarles, the quaint poet of the *Emblems;* Sir Thomas Smith, statesman; Jane and Ann Taylor, with their father Isaac; and Joseph Strutt, of the *Rural Sports and Pastimes.* To these names may be added, surely, that of one of the foremost living scientists, a descendant of the last-named, John William Strutt— Lord Rayleigh.

In the few pages available, we cannot do more than glance at the many, while dwelling more at length upon about a dozen; and, passing chronologically over several names for the moment, we must place at the head of our list the great naturalist of the seventeenth century.

Ray, the illustrious, foremost naturalist of his age, and founder of all modern scientific botany, was born in the village of Black Notley. The entry of his baptism, on June 29th, 1628, may still be deciphered in the crabbed handwriting of the parish register. His parents, Roger and Elizabeth Wray, were in quite poor circumstances—the father is generally said to have been

226

a blacksmith. The boy, however, received a good education under Mr. Dove, master of the small grammar school then recently founded at Braintree, two or three miles away, by James Cocker, a Black Notley man. From Braintree, Ray passed to Cambridge, at the cost of a far-sighted patron, Squire Wyvill, whose philanthropy was amply repaid by the distinguished university career of the unknown Notley boy. At the age of twenty-four he won the appointment of Greek Lecturer; at twenty-six he was Mathematical Lecturer; and a couple of years later Humanity Reader for the University. Later in life, when etymology had become the pastime of his leisure, the naturalist dropped the initial letter of his name, and became Ray. The Church was then the opening for all men of letters, and Ray, a good Hebrew scholar, became noted as a preacher of "sound and solid divinity" even before his ordination in 1660. His clerical career was soon abandoned, for although his views were generally in harmony with the Church of the Restoration, Ray declined to subscribe to the Bartholomew Act of 1662, and, with thirteen other fellows of colleges and four thousand ministers and clergy, he resigned all church preferment on August 24th of that year, and became a private and unbeneficed individual, in lay communion with the Established Church until his death.

Ray's claim to pre-eminence lay in his studies of animal and plant life, and the Synopsis or Catalogue of plants that he made. He began in 1658 a series of botanical tours throughout England and Wales, observing and noting in diaries the plants he met with by the way. His companion for many years was a Cambridge friend and sometime pupil, Francis Willoughby, of Middleton Hall, Warwickshire, with whom a close friendship began at Cambridge, and ended only with Willoughby's death. For three years the pair travelled through Europe to study plants and insect

precious manuscripts and drawings for the books then
printing for the naturalist in London and Leyden;
scientific additions and commentaries added by learned
correspondents; unique collections of specimens, whether
dried plants, fish, or impaled beetles and butterflies; and
rare books of reference, for the loan of which Ray,
in his country retreat, was indebted to fellow-workers
in town. In spite of constant physical suffering, the
gentle old naturalist worked away at his labour of
classifying the natural kingdom with untiring energy,
that may be exemplified by one out of a number of
similar passages in his letters. Towards the close of his
life he turned to the study of insects, and it was
proposed that he should undertake an examination of the
most famous collections of the kind belonging to private
individuals, with a view to publishing a *History of
Insects*. The precious cases were to be submitted to
him at Dewlands, for the state of his health did not
permit of his leaving this place. They could only reach
Notley by way of the carrier's cart, and one shudders
to think of the state of these insectivoræ when they
arrived after hours of jolting in that springless
vehicle upon those unkept roads. This, however, is
preamble, and we return to a letter of the doctor's on
the subject of the generation of gnats. Ray writes,
about 1702 : —

"For my own part I am now almost threescore and fifteen years of
age, so that it is time for me to give over these studies and inquiries;
and besides I am so lame, and almost continuously afflicted with pain,
that I cannot attend any study. It is true of late years I have diverted
myself by searching out the various species of insects to be found
hereabout, but I have confined myself chiefly to two or three sorts, viz.,
Papilios, diurnal and nocturnal, beetles, bees and spiders. Of the first
of these I have found about 300 kinds, and there are still remaining
many more undiscovered by me, and all within the compass of a few
miles. How many, then, may we reasonably conjecture are to be found in
the whole world? The beetles are a tribe near as numerous as these,
and the flies of all sorts not fewer. I have now given over my
inquisition by reason of my disability and my approaching end."

One is reminded by such passages as these of the long patience and rewarded experiments of Ray's great spiritual successor, Charles Darwin, in his studies of the habits of earth worms.

The pathetic side of his life is strangely evident in the letters of this gentle, pious, and philosophic old naturalist. His sufferings arose from the constant state of ulceration of both his legs, for which all his science could only provide remedies which to medical knowledge now appear the most pitiful and childish. Nothing can better make us realise what the study of medicine has achieved for us in two hundred years than to read his theories of the cause of this skin affection, and the cures—suggested at random by accidental callers or stray correspondents—with which he vainly tried to win relief. Six years or more after he had first suffered from constantly recurring sore legs, he came to the conclusion that the eruption proceeded from " invisible insects making their burrows under and nestling in the' cutis, spreading in spots around which may be their nests, like anthills, they seeming to be gregarious." To kill the creatures thus lodged, he imbibed strong doses of flower of sulphur, half a drachm at once. At the same time he used outwardly a decoction of elecampane, dock-root, and chalk, steeped in whey. The diascordium from the Braintree apothecary is pronounced "pitiful slop, with neither the colour, consistency, taste, nor virtues of diascordium," so conserve of roses is preferred, and sounds a delicious exchange.

When Ray's little daughter Mary, one of the twins, is lying desperately ill with jaundice, he fears to give her the appetising drink which had cured him of the same complaint years before, so he earnestly prays Sloane's advice as soon as possible, "physic not being my calling." The precious concoction was an infusion of horse-dung, steeped all night in ale, strained and sweetened and flavoured with saffron. Alas! before within the last ten or fifteen years that one of the foremost electricians of the day, Professor Silvanus P. Thompson, F.R.S., has rescued his name and great work on the magnet from partial oblivion, and has collected the few details that are known about his life. He was never married, and died in his own house on St. Peter's Hill, London, in 1603, after several years of travel to universities abroad, and an honourable, if perfunctory, fulfilment of the post of physician to that robust dame, Queen Elizabeth.

In the lists of Essex worthies the Bourchier family must always occupy an important place. Henry Bourchier, created Earl of Essex in 1461, was great-grandson of Robert Bourchier, Member of Parliament, or knight of the shire, for Essex from 1330 to 1339, who fought at Crécy, and was the first lay Chancellor of England. He founded a college for priests at Halstead, near his own house, and lies buried in the church there. Henry, by his marriage with Anne of Woodstock, was uncle of Edward IV. His brother Thomas became Bishop of Ely and Archbishop of Canterbury, and enjoyed an episcopal and archiepiscopal career of unparalleled length, for he wore the mitre during fifty-one years. He it was who solemnised the marriage between Henry VII. and the daughter of Edward IV., an alliance which brought peace to England after the long civil wars, and laid the foundation of a fruitful future. As old Fuller quaintly observes : " His hands first held that sweet posie where red and white roses are tied together." To another member of this family, the archbishop's great nephew, John Bourchier, Lord Berners, we are indebted for a famous, if not the first, translation of the ever fascinating *Chronicles of Froissart* (1525).

We may next glance at a group of persons who deserve grateful remembrance in Essex as pioneers of education and founders of schools. Sir Walter

Mildmay, of Chelmsford, treasurer of Queen Elizabeth's household and chancellor of the exchequer, founded Emmanuel College, Cambridge; Samuel Harsnett, the baker's son, of Colchester, who died Archbishop of York, established, as has been already said, a grammar school at Chigwell (where he had been eight years vicar), as a "mite of gratitude and thanksgiving" for his success in life; Sir Anthony Browne, of Weald Hall, queen's serjeant and judge, gave us the grammar school at Brentwood; to Dorothy Petre, daughter of Sir William of Ingatestone, and survivor of her husband, Nicholas Wadham, of Merefield, Somerset, Oxford is indebted for Wadham College; and, finally, Thomas Sutton, founder of Charterhouse, came, in 1582, from Littlebury, near Saffron Walden, endowed his foundation with Essex lands, and appointed the vicar of Littlebury first master of the school, which, according to the original patent, was first intended to be set up at Hallingbury in this county.

In the north-western corner of Essex lies the town of Saffron Walden; its high red-roofed houses climb up one hill and down another to encircle the tapering spire of a church that is one of the chief beauties of the county. Walden has the honour to be connected with more of her distinguished sons than any other place in Essex. Thomas Lord Audley and Sir Thomas Smith had close ties with it, one by residence, the other by birth. The Harveys, that trio of remarkable brothers, emanated thence; and another pair of Waldenian names are little less memorable, those of Henry Winstanley, builder of the Eddystone Lighthouse, and his brother William, the "Poor Robin" of almanac fame.

Audley, though born at Earls Colne, and a burgess and town clerk of Colchester, is inseparably connected with Walden, where his name is perpetuated in the hamlet and mansion of Audley End. A student of the Inner Temple, the young Essex lad rose rapidly to the

highest offices of the State. He was Speaker of the
Parliament by whose aid Henry VIII. separated his
kingdom from allegiance to the Pope, and, upon
Wolsey's fall and Sir Thomas More's resignation,
became Lord Chancellor, and keeper of that very
negligible quantity, the conscience of King Henry VIII.
Henceforth Audley seems to have been little more than
a submissive instrument in the hands of Henry and
Cromwell, ready to acquiesce in condemning or elevating
man or woman, as it suited the royal whim or pleasure.
The history of Audley's connection with Walden, and
the passing of his gorgeous palace to the heirs of his
only child, is touched upon elsewhere in this volume
(see page 194); here it may only be added that Audley
lies buried under a handsome tomb erected by himself
in Walden Church, with, as epitaph, some doggerel
verses said to be his own composition.

Sir Thomas Smith, a statesman of very different
calibre, a true scholar of high attainments, and author
of a classic volume upon the constitution of England,
was born at Walden on December 23rd, 1547, of a
family then in high position, claiming descent from
Sir Roger de Clarendon, son of the Black Prince. At
eleven Smith went from Walden Grammar School to
Cambridge, and soon held several appointments in his
university, where he was known as a staunch Protestant.
He entered the service of Protector Somerset, was
employed on diplomatic missions abroad, became
Ambassador to France, Provost of Eton, and Dean of
Carlisle. He represented Essex in Parliament, and
reached his highest honour as Secretary of State to
Queen Elizabeth, over which capricious lady he gained,
indeed, considerable influence. Smith acquired Hill
Hall with his second wife, Philippa, widow of Sir John
Hampden, of Theydon Mount, and in 1557 and 1568
rebuilt portions of this fine old manor house, which is
still in the possession of the descendants of his brother

George, for he had no children of his own. He is buried in the chancel of Theydon Church.

Gabriel Harvey—the satirist of venomous pen, whose quarrel with Nash and Greene, two contemporary poets, has rendered the little Essex town immortal in his vituperative *Have with you to Saffron Walden* (1596)—John and Richard Harvey, the three sons of a Walden rope-maker, were all related to Sir Thomas Smith. Gabriel Harvey celebrated Smith's death with an elegy in Latin, elegantly entitled *Smithus*, etc.

The vivid career of Henry Winstanley belongs to a century nearer our own time than Smith's. It appeals more to popular taste than that of his brother William, the "Poor Robin" to whom reference has been made. From a small scholar at the historic grammar school, founded at Walden in 1421 by vicar John Leech and his sister, Dame Johane Bradbury, Winstanley emerges in 1665 as a young porter or carrier employed in the reconstruction of Audley End. On the sale of the palace to the King, Winstanley obtained the appointment of clerk of the works there and at the royal sporting box at Newmarket. He spent his leisure in drawing and engraving a set of twenty-four plans of Audley End. He designed a novel place of entertainment, "The Water Theatre," in Piccadilly, which continued a profitable source of income to his widow even after his death. At his house at Littlebury, near Walden, he had also many ingenious and strange contrivances. On the strength of all this, and the somewhat slender architectural experience it afforded, he was entrusted with the construction of a lighthouse for the Eddystone Rock, off Plymouth, and commenced building it, after twice modifying his original design. From the beginning he was unlucky, and once was carried away prisoner by a French privateer, who destroyed his work so far as accomplished. He began again, and proceeded slowly for seven years, when, on a winter's night, November 26th,

1703, the whole flimsy and fantastic structure was swept away, with its builder and all the workmen, in a fearful storm at sea.

William Winstanley began life as a barber, but, as an old writer remarks, soon exchanged the razor for the pen "while retaining the scissors," for in his literary career he borrowed without either stint or acknowledgment from predecessors. In his small *Lives of the Poets* may be found notice of many minor folk, among them a master of Colchester Grammar School, of whose invaluable verses we might else have remained in ignorance. One flash of unconscious humour the book retains in its royalist author's account of that great Puritan, John Milton, Cromwell's Latin secretary. Writing in 1687, Winstanley says: "His fame is gone out like a candle in a snuff, and his memory will always stink." *Poor Robin's Perambulation from Saffron Walden to London* gives a lively description of the chief ale-houses on the road, in doggerel verse; the thirsty traveller may be partly excused for his frequent calls by the uncommon heat of the month of July in 1678. Poor Robin's *Jest Books* were very popular for many years, and were the forerunners of those favourite *Pocket Books* issued from Bury St. Edmunds and other places, containing enigmas and conundrums, which enlivened the winter firesides of early Victorian dames.

Every educated person will own him or herself familiar with the name of Francis Quarles and his quaint *Emblems*, but how few can tell more about this out-of-the-way poet and meditative writer, much less attribute a single quotation to his works. The truth is that the present generation, unlike their forerunners, find small profit in dwelling on the wretchedness of man's earthly existence—the theme that possessed so vast attraction for the pious-minded of the seventeenth and eighteenth centuries. Quarles, no doubt, owed some of the original popularity of his *Emblems* to his engraver,

FRANCIS QUARLES.

William Marshall, who lavishly illustrated the book. Pope, in his happiest vein of satire, remarked that "the pictures for the page atone, and Quarles was saved by beauties not his own"; but it was the affected fashion of Pope's day to sneer at Quarles as the admired of the plebeian and vulgar. To a later judgment his verses, though often diffuse and dull, are by no means unillumined with flashes of poetic fire.

Francis Quarles—his name should apparently be pronounced to rhyme with Charles—was the third son of James and Joan Quarles, born at his father's manor house of Stewards, near Romford, and baptized in May, 1592. The elder Quarles is described as "a man of account," and held offices in Queen Elizabeth's household, after having been Surveyor-General of Victuals for the Navy. He died when Francis was very young, leaving £50 a year to each of his sons. The two younger, James and Francis, were educated at home, perhaps by that chaplain of Romford who in 1605 bequeathed the lads money to buy a book apiece. Their mother died when Francis, at fourteen, was proceeding to Christ's College, Cambridge. She charged her elder son Robert—who was knighted by James I. at Newmarket, and sat in Parliament for Colchester in 1626—to provide for the payment of his annuity. Francis was a handsome lad, so fond of music that when he was studying law at Lincoln's Inn he sold his Inn-of-Court gown to pay for a lute case. He was persuaded to accept the post of cup-bearer to the Princess Elizabeth on her marriage to the Elector Palatine, and set out with her from England to the Court of the Palatinate at Heidelberg. Thus he was introduced to many court nobles, among them Robert Sidney, Earl of Leicester, to whom Quarles dedicated his first work, which he endowed with the lugubrious title, *A Feast of Wormes set forth in a Poeme of the History of Job* (1620). Unlike some versatile geniuses of his own and our times, he repeated every subsequent performance in the key of the note thus struck. *Pentelogia, or the Quintessence of Meditation ; Sion's Elegies wept by Jeremie the Prophet ; Sion's Sonnets, sung by Solomon the King ; Wine and Oyl for Afflicted Soules ; Midnight Meditations on Death ; Divine Fancies ;* and an *Alphabet of Elegies,* are the titles of some of the works which appealed remarkably to an age when to take a healthy and cheerful interest in common life appeared inconsistent with a taste for heavenly things. The poet was on friendly terms with Fletcher, Drayton, and the chief literary men of his time, but his dearest and closest friendship brought him back into intimate relations with his native county. Edward Benlowes, of Brent Hall, Finchingfield, was something less of a poet than Quarles himself, but famous in his day as the author of *Theophila, or Love's Sacrifice,* and many other books ; still more notorious as an open-handed and too generous patron, a lover of music, plays, and curiosities, who profusely squandered his patrimony on friends and relations, and died at Oxford actually in want of fuel and the warm comforts which his age (73) necessitated, and without other means of honourable burial than a collection made among scholars who remembered his former condition. Undisputed local tradition has always maintained that it was at Brent Hall, whilst partaking of Benlowes' hospitality, that the older man composed the *Emblems.* Close to this old manor and farmhouse lies a wooded knoll overlooking a sloping dell, through which the little river Pant winds ; it is blue with hyacinths in springtime, and thrills to the songs of nightingales in early summer ; the tall trees crowning the knoll are an interception to the level sky-line as seen from many miles around, and the lonely lane that winds through these woods seldom re-echoes to the sound of wheels. Here in the deep and murmuring solitude of the country the Royalist poet is said to have wandered in pious musings, and here composed his *Emblems.*

In this vein of writing he had no equal. But to have attempted to write plays without other equipment than this poetic fervour, already strongly bent into a channel of meditative and devotional ecstasy, was a mistake. His *Argelus and Parthenia*, described by himself as the fruits of broken hours gathered out of the orchard of Sir Philip Sidney and grafted upon a crab stock of his own, seems to us a dull and ponderous fantasy; yet it was acted a good many times. His *Virgin Widow* was as cold and chaste as ice, and could kindle few sparks of enthusiasm in the sensuous atmosphere of the Restoration. His *Shepheard's Oracles* was ushered into the world by a charming Address to the Reader, describing Quarles and his rural pursuits, which, although signed by the printer, is considered to have been written by no less a personage than the gentle angler, Isaak Walton himself. The shepherd's visions were revealed, it says, to the author by a happy accident:—

" He in a summer's morning about that hour when the great eye of Heaven first opens itself to give light to us mortals, walking a gentle pace towards a Brook whose springhead was not far distant from his peaceful habitation, fitted with angle, lines and flyes, flyes proper for that season, it being the fruitful month of May, intending with all diligence to beguile the timourous trout with which that watery element abounded, observed a more than common concourse of shepherds all bending their unwearied steps towards a pleasant meadow where was a large arbour whose walls were made of the yielding willow and smooth beech boughs, covered over with sycamore leaves and honeysuckles."

Linnets, larks, and nightingales made music without, and the poet passed down through a living moving lane of shepherds and pilgrims who had that morning measured many miles to reach this favoured spot. This arbour has somehow always been associated with the wooded dell at Brent Hall, where the *Emblems* were written.

The friendship of the two Essex men was memorialised in a long poem called *Quarleis*, by the lesser poet, addressed to the greater, quaintly prefaced by the phrase " I hang a chaplet on the back door." " The fountain of

R

our love was poetry," says Benlowes; "religion was its close connecting tie." He apostrophises Quarles as "the chosen jewel of our Essex ground," and lauds in flowery language the author of the *Emblems*, with which *Quarleis* was issued. It was signed "Benevolus" (a well-wisher), a punning variant of his name—Benlowes. The *Emblems* opens with a short address to "my much honoured and no lesse truly beloved friend," who has, Quarles tells him,

. . . "put the theorbœ into my hands and I have played. You gave the musician the first encouragement; the musick returneth to you for patronage. Had it been a light Ayre, no doubt it had taken the most and among them the worst. Being a grave strayn, I hope it will please the best, among them you."

Quarles was about forty-seven when he left Essex finally to settle in London as chronologer to the city. This office appears to have brought him a small salary and few encroachments on his time. He continued his output of "Manuals of Piety," many of which were published after his death. "Who dies in service has lived long enough," as he somewhere remarks, and although he was only fifty-two when he departed this life, it had been long enough for him to have married happily and to become the father of eighteen children. Four of them were born and baptized at Roxwell, where he lived for some years. It is worth remembering that Quarles, with his lugubrious muse, was no Puritan but a staunch Royalist, who died before the fortunes of the King had reached their darkest hour. As he says:—

> "What's here to be enjoyed
> But grief and sickness and large bills of sorrow
> Drawn now and crossed to-morrow?"

And again, with a daintier conceit:—

> "And what's a life? the flourishing array
> Of the proud Summer meadow which to-day
> Wears her green plush and is to-morrow hay."

Contemporary with Quarles, but an older man, was the Lord Chief Justice Bramston, the most distinguished member of a notable family. Born at Maldon and educated at the Free School there, he rapidly rose to the highest place in his profession of law, and was celebrated for his learned exposition of it, no less than for his integrity. In spite of his loyal attachment to King Charles, he was much appreciated by the Parliament, and was more than once pressed by Cromwell to again accept office as Lord Chief Justice under the Commonwealth.

He purchased Skreens, in Roxwell, from the Westons, died there and was buried in the church, where a Latin epitaph, by Abraham Cowley, marks his tomb. By his wife, Bridget Moundeford, he was father of another Sir John Bramston, who also followed the profession of law, but is better known by his delightful autobiography, a record of social and domestic life in the seventeenth century, as rare as it is valuable. Bramston represented Essex, Maldon, and Chelmsford in several Parliaments ; he lived at Skreens, and had a town house in Greek Street, Soho. In his *Autobiography* he has left us many portraits of his family and friends, none more vivid and gracious that the following of his eldest daughter and second child, Abigail :—

"She was of a moderate stature and well shaped; handsome but not a beautie; her complexion sanguine which inclined to choller. She was virtuous and pious, neate in her person and house. She began to be my housekeeper when she was very young; loved a liberal table whilst I continued at Skreens, but was never prodigal or wasteful. When I removed to Greek Street she proportioned my expence to my family, but so as we shamed not to be surprised by a friend or two. She was very careful of me, see me in bed at night, visited me in the morning, craved my blessing and assisted me at my risinge, and was very studious to pleasure in my diet and what else was in her power. She died unmarried, having refused some advantagious offers, in the 57th year of her age. . . . After the death of my onlie daughter and nurse I soon took resolution to quit my house in Greek Street and return to my house, Screens. On August 13 I came home bringing with me one maid and a boy. My cousin Colonel John

Bramston left town also and came to Screens. At the expiration of my 83rd year I am very well pleased with God's dispensation and hope I am readie to leave this wretched world at His call."

It is only fair to suppose that Sir John was using the conventional expression of the time, for the cheerful old man seems to have passed through the world without finding it any more "wretched" than an optimistic and prosperous gentleman should. He had a profound belief in doctors—Abigail was an invalid for many years—and spent fabulous sums on apothecaries for her, besides consulting at least eleven physicians, whom her father names. Among them was the famous Sir Thomas Millington, who had then recently bought Gosfield Hall from Lord Grey. However, the hale old man continued keeping his diary right up till ten days before his death, which occurred on February 4th, 1700. Sir John's grandson, Thomas, represented Essex in Parliament, as did the elder son of each of the three following generations, thus making, with Chief Justice Bramston, a singularly long record of county service.

It is seldom, indeed, that genius runs in families. Who ever heard of another Shakespeare or a second Milton? But talent, on the contrary, frequently does, and sometimes a whole group of members of one family elevate it for a generation or two above any previous level of distinction.

The Taylor family, of Ongar, is an example of this, and we like to think that they derived some of their ability from their Essex mother, Sarah Jefferys, of Shenfield. By her marriage to Isaac Taylor, an engraver, of London, she became mother of Isaac, the Nonconformist minister of Ongar, author of many well-read children's books, and an engraver of no mean ability. The names of Ann and Jane, his two daughters, became household words in thousands of nurseries from their verses, and his son and grandson, a couple more Isaacs, attained lasting celebrity as authors of philosophical and ethical works. Another son, Jeffreys Taylor, also wrote children's books; while

Your most obedient humble Servant

Phil: Morant

Charles, his brother, attained considerable repute as an engraver.

Sydney Smith, the witty Canon of St. Paul's, was born on Essex soil at Woodford. Sir William Gull, a physician of some repute during the later nineteenth century, is said to have first seen the light on board a craft of some kind off the Essex coast. Joseph Strutt, the author of many industrious illustrated works on the costume, manners, and sports of England, came of a family of yeomen millers, of Springfield, near Chelmsford, from whom Lord Rayleigh is also descended. Judge Nicholas Tindall is commemorated in his birthplace by Tindall Square at Chelmsford. Lord Western, the well-known Whig, represented the county in Parliament for forty years. Philip Morant, whose name will ever be associated with Essex, though born in Jersey, lived for fifty years in the county, to the history of which (2 vols., fol., 1760-8) he devoted so much of his life, thus completing the elaborate structure, whose foundations had been already laid by earlier Essex antiquaries—Nicholas Tindal, Nathaniel Salmon, Thomas Jekyll, and William Holman. Morant held six benefices in the county, though only two at once. He is buried at Aldham, near Colchester, where he had been rector for twenty-five years. He held the rectory of St. Mary-at-Walls, Colchester, for an even longer period—viz., from 1738 to his death in 1770. Thomas Plume, founder of the Plumian Chair of Astronomy and of an observatory at Cambridge, was born at Maldon, and was a Chelmsford Grammar School boy.

Last of all we come to a name which, if less honoured than any of these, is, at least, more stimulating and romantic, and accorded without dispute a foremost place in the eye of every school boy or girl who loves adventure. Richard Turpin, the immortal " Dick," " our favourite national freebooter," as he has been wittily called, was born in a modest farmhouse in the parish of

Hempstead, near Saffron Walden, on September 21st, 1705. His biographer, Mr. Thomas Seccombe, in the pages of the *Essex Review* (vol. xi., p. 19), humorously suggests the appropriateness of the birthplace of William Harvey, the discoverer of the circulation of the blood, being also the native village " of a man who did so much to stimulate the circulation of all whom he met, even in the most casual of encounters." Dick became the head of a wild gang of highwaymen, robbers, and deer-stealers, who made the life of dwellers in the purlieus of Epping Forest a terror. With a kindred spirit, one Tom King, he lurked in a cave hidden by brambles of the forest. Then he took to lodging in oak trees, and finally moved northwards to continue his predatory career. He was hanged for horse-stealing from gallows on Knavesmire, York, on April 7th, 1739, thus ending a life which has inspired more fictitious narratives, rhymes, and ballads than any other outlaw or freebooter.

DICK TURPIN.

WITCHCRAFT AND SUPERSTITION

By Edward Smith

THE present age is vastly removed from that of our great-grandfathers — in nothing, perhaps, so distinctly as on the subject of superstition. Superstition is not extinct, and there is little hope that the human family will be entirely freed from it for a long, long time. But superstition has little power over the minds of any persons who have a share in the action of the modern world. Mainly in some back-waters of rural life, where local traditions hold a powerful sway, and low conditions of existence exert a paralysing action over body and soul, do we find the bacteria of mental weakness kept alive. Our own county of Essex is, in some parts of it, such a back-water.

There are districts in Essex which are very remote, even now, from the influences of the higher civilization. You may still meet men and women who have never seen a railway; people to whom a newspaper is chiefly the vehicle for police news. The country eastward from Tiptree Heath and the villages lying about the upper waters of the Pant, the Chelmer, and the Roding, are literally far behind the times. Those of us who knew Dengie and Rochford hundreds before the railways got there could testify to some strange and very stupid ways of thought among the people. The present writer has heard dwellers among the villagers about the uplands speak of their entire isolation—not with anger, or even with contempt, but in sorrow for the poor folks remaining unenlightened and unexcited about the world that is outside them. The everlasting round of dulness and stupidity has the force upon their souls which an iron hoop would exert upon their bodies—and this not from the nature of their employment. Far from that. The Essex countryman who is not given over to mental sloth or to frivolous and sensual pleasures can be most joyous and intelligent company. But hide-bound traditions and inherited habits keep many poor people down in the depths; and where these remain practically undisturbed it is not surprising to learn that a belief in witchcraft is still discoverable in such parts as the secluded districts of Essex.

The novelists have not omitted to utilise this low phase of social life. We have tales of modern sorcery galore. A very notable one, where the scene is laid on the Essex shore of the Thames estuary, is that of *Cunning Murrell*, by Arthur Morrison, a writer who knows his Essex as well as the East End of London. The plot of the story is probably familiar to our readers; also the fascinating description of Hadleigh, where the scene is laid at the time of the Crimean War (1854). The most interesting point, however, to us is that the work, so far from being merely fancy, is really founded on fact. It is well known that the source of Morrison's inspiration was found in the neighbourhood of Hadleigh. The real James Murrell passed a long life in this village, which was a singularly unsophisticated place before the Salvation Army settlement was made, and the environs were given up to bungalows and week-enders. Murrell died in 1860 full of years and honours. A shoemaker by trade, he added to his substance by telling fortunes, discovering thieves and witches, and even finding stolen property. He was also something of a herbalist doctor, and administered drugs and potions very extensively. There was great dread of his occult powers, and many people came from a distance to consult him. After his death a prodigious correspondence was revealed. Many of the letters addressed to him were written in a good hand, indicative of educated writers; but mostly persons

steeped in superstitious ignorance—farmers wanting
relief from some evil-disposed persons who are damaging
their crops or flock; women jealous of their husbands;
men suspicious of their rivals; young girls wretched
with longing, miserable and unhappy because luck has
gone against them. By means of much ingenuity,
especially in the making of utensils for practising his
spells, Murrell gained immense influence with the people
within a circuit of thirty miles. He was in the habit of
using a form of prayer to the Deity before beginning
a charm, and on his death-bed he protested to the
assistant-curate of the parish that he was no deceiver,
but firmly believed in the powers attributed to him.

Revelations of similar superstition have been made
repeatedly at a very much later date than the year 1854.
The subject of witchcraft took up some space in *The
Times* newspaper during March, April, and May, 1857,
and from the records and letters of that period it would
appear that a belief in witchcraft was still remaining
in several parts of England. Rugeley, in Staffordshire,
and Hockham, in Norfolk, furnished well attested stories.
In August, 1861, an Essex case was before the Bench at
Castle Hedingham. The police brought a charge of
witchcraft against one Mrs. Legitten. On information
received they had gone to her house and found several
articles which they produced for the inspection of the
magistrates—to wit, brimstone, red ochre, etc. There
was a person at Yeldham, a few miles distant, who had
long been ill, and many of whose neighbours believed
her to have been bewitched. It does not appear that the
magistrates took any action, and it came to be understood
among rational people that the brimstone and the red
ochre were required for ordinary purposes in rural
life. Twenty years later, more than one instance was
made public which showed the tenacity with which these
ideas still lingered in the minds of poor people. A
case from Good Easter, reported June, 1880, has all the

well-known features, a labourer of the village charging a female neighbour with "ill-wishing" himself and his wife, and proposing that she should submit to the time-honoured test—sink or swim—to which the poor woman naturally objected. The late Mr. I. C. Gould (*Notes and Queries*, 7th series, xi., 1886) tells us that "not many years since Sible Hedingham had to plead guilty to drowning a wizard (an innocent old Frenchman, if I remember rightly)."

Now Sible Hedingham is just one of those backward places to which reference has been made. A week spent in chat and gossip with the people in this district will reward any collector of grotesque folk-lore and moribund superstition. A concrete example was furnished in the newspapers of December, 1890, to this effect: There was living in the village an old labourer, popularly supposed to be a wizard. One day he told a man who was in charge of a load of straw that he would not get far with it. A little further on the horse fell, and it was so injured that it had to be killed. The men called upon to assist were so convinced that the horse had been under the influence of the wizard that they refused to move the carcase until a slice of flesh had been cut from the hind quarters of the animal and burned in a bush faggot, the idea being that the person who cast the spell would suffer burning in a corresponding part of his body.

This, of course, is purely the superstitious gossiping story. The real facts were that it was an old horse, probably not even in fit condition for a comparatively light load; that it did break down before getting home; was well taken care of, but got worse, and was killed three days after by advice of a veterinary surgeon. It is true that a man standing at his cottage gate had remarked to a companion that "'e didna' think that 'ere horse 'd du werry much more work." But this poor chap was already under suspicion as a wizard. And the story grew, as stories will.

Mr. Reginald Beckett, in his *Romantic Essex*, states that he found this superstition "still alive" in the extreme north of the county. But there is a more recent record yet. The *East London Advertiser* of August, 1903, contains a remarkably funny story from West Essex:—

"A Bishops Stortford barber was cutting the hair of a customer from a neighbouring village, when he was requested to save a piece of hair from the nape of the neck. The barber ascertained that the man imagined some one in the village had done him an injury, and to have revenge he intended to cast a spell upon him. The hair from the nape of the neck, the lip, and the armpits, the parings of the nails, and other ingredients, mixed with water, were to be corked up in a bottle and placed on the fire at night. Desiring sickness to fall upon his enemy, his wish would be accomplished as the bottle burst, which would be as near midnight as possible."

Even while these pages are passing through the press the London papers have given extended reports of a case heard at Witham Police Court on August 12th, 1908, which affords fresh evidence of the belief in "witches" still to be found in Essex. An old woman living in Tiptree was by many of the villagers accounted to be a witch. This belief led to the alleged assault of the old woman's husband, and on August 19th the person complained against was bound over to be of good behaviour for six months, and ordered to pay the costs of the case.

Once more, it must be understood that, while the distinct belief in witchcraft is existent only among the most ignorant folk, the actual cult is half-recognised, although with contempt, by a good many persons who really know better, but are unable or unwilling to break with a very powerful tradition. They speak and act as if they thought there must have been something once-upon-a-time to justify the genuine faith which formerly existed in the witch's powers. It is not two centuries since the law against witchcraft was in full force. That period is long enough for wiser people to have become well taught; as to the ignorant "and him that is out of the way," it is all too short for any hope of eradicating superstition. Our own county has a bad record in the past, as we will show. At Saffron Walden in the year 1852, in pulling down an old house, the workmen found a small grey-beard jug embedded in the chalk. It was at once pronounced by people in the town to be a "witch jug." At the time that house was built (1610) it was customary to place under the entrance door a jug filled with horse-shoe nails, to prevent the entrance of witches. A similar incident happened in this town some twenty years later, an old witch-bottle being found "below the floor and very near the fireplace." It contained some water, about fourteen horse-nails, and twenty thorns! There was a story of persecution for witchcraft, in the latter part of the eighteenth century, which occurred at Fambridge Ferry. It occurs in the memoirs of Captain Harriott (*Struggles through Life*, London, 1815), who went through many adventures and travelled all over the world, ending his career as a London magistrate. An old couple named Hart lived in a cottage near the ferry. Young Harriott and his brother alternately patronised and teazed the old lady, and presently satisfied themselves by an experiment of their own that she was no witch. But the pair, long after the boy was gone, were wickedly persecuted by their neighbours, and according to Mr. Benton (*History of Rochford Hundred*) they were eventually "swum" in the presence of a great crowd of people. The husband was adjudged innocent, after being nearly drowned, but the wife was tied to a boat by a line, and consequently floated. She was ever afterwards regarded as a witch.

We hear little of sorcery and witchcraft in pre-Reformation annals. The Catholic Church recognised the heinous character of any alleged dealings with the devil, but there does not appear any record of panic or persecution in England on the score of witchcraft before the days of Henry VIII. For some reason now unknown, a law first appeared on the statute-book in 1541 making this crime a felony. This Act was repealed six years later, under Edward VI. In 1562, four years after the accession of Queen Elizabeth, a new Act was passed— Protestantism and Puritanism were making headway, bringing free thought and superstition in their train. In a very few years persecutions for witchcraft became numerous. In 1584 appeared in print the first counterblast against the terror—Reginald Scott's famous *Discoverie of Witchcraft*, in which the author exposed the weakness and absurdity of the usual charges made against the poor victims. He was followed by a preacher of Maldon, George Giffard, who wrote in succession two powerful, but wordy, tracts concerning witchcraft and sorcery. These two men were the first representatives of a class who attacked the superstition with considerable force and angry humour. The literature of this Puritanical period of obsession is largely endowed with more or less futile arguments for and against witchcraft. King James was a firm believer in witchcraft, and foolishly lent himself to the public advocacy of the propriety of witch-hunting. He caused Reginald Scott's book to be burnt whenever a copy could be found.

The county of Essex soon became rather noted for its witches. The earliest circumstantial story that has come down to us is of 1566, and is contained in a rare black-letter pamphlet, the property of the Archiepiscopal Library at Lambeth : " The examination and confession of certain wytches at Chensforde, in the county of Essex, before the quenes maiesties judges, the xxvi. daye of July, 1566, at the assizes held there, and one of them put to death for the same offence." Agnes Waterhouse, of Hatfield Peverel, was the culprit. She had a white spotted cat, which she called " Sathan," and went about with. She recites, under examination, certain vengeful deeds, and what followed, and how the cat presently

changed itself into a toad. In her final confession she
stated that she went to church regularly, said the Lord's
Prayer and *Ave Maria* in Latin, because "Sathan"
would not permit her to do so in English, and appears
to have acquiesced in her conviction; that is to say, she
was insane from first to last. Her execution took place
three days afterwards. Her daughter, Jone Waterhouse,
testified that her mother would teach her this matter,
"but she learned it not." But she did once, in a moment
of anger, experiment with the cat upon a neighbour's
daughter who had been churlish towards her, " and made
her afeard." Jone, who was eighteen years of age, escaped
conviction. After this date there is mention of a poor
woman hanged at Barking in the year 1575. Another
circumstantial account belongs to 1579, when three old
ladies of Maldon were executed at Chelmsford in April
of that year. One of these culprits was Elleine Smithe.
The testimony against her amounts to this : that John
Chaundler, having fallen out with her about some money
owing, "never eate any meate that digested in him but
ever it came up again as soon as it was done," by "which
means he consumed and wasted away to death." The
son of this woman, a boy of thirteen, being refused alms
of a neighbour named Eastwood, went home and told
his mother. After a while Eastwood was taken with
great pain in his body, and presently a rat ran up the
chimney and fell down in the likeness of a toad. Taking
it up with the tongs they thrust it into the fire, and so
held it forcibly. It made the fire burn "as blew as azure,"
and at the burning thereof the said Elleine Smithe was
in great pain, whereupon she "dissemblyngly" came to
Eastwood's house and asked how they all were, and he
said : "Well, I thank God." She said : "I thought you
had not been well, and then came to see how you did."
Also the son of this mother Smithe confessed that his
mother did keep three spirits, whereof the one was called
"Great Dick" enclosed in a wicker bottle ; the second,

named "Little Dick," was put into a leather bottle; and
the third, named "Willet," she kept in a "woole packe";
whereupon the house was searched. The bottles and the
pack were found, but the spirits were banished away.

These later times of Queen Elizabeth seem to have
come hard upon witches. Beside a number of cruel cases
in different parts of England, there were seventeen or
eighteen sufferers in a batch, who were executed at
St. Osyth in 1582; three more at Chelmsford in July,
1589; and some at Brentford in 1595. In the Boreham
parish register appears the entry, under 29th July, 1593,
"Mother Haven suffered for witchcraft." The reign of
James I. was distinguished by great superstitions. But
it was not an unhappy one for the average people of
England, and the absence of popular fanaticisms is
particularly to be marked. Questions of sorcery and
demonology were freely discussed, but all this was done
academically. A stringent law, which almost imposed
the necessity of believing in witchcraft, was passed in the
early part of this reign. But this was really aloof—the
popular mind was unaffected by excitement over the topic.
It required an outside agency and the accumulation of
other superstitions to awaken anything like persecution.
Come it did, however, when Puritanism had become
general; and, among the sectarian feeling which poured
over the land toward the middle of the seventeenth
century, there came a horrid mania for murdering people
under the pretence of witchcraft.

It was in 1645 that this began. One Matthew Hopkins,
son of a Suffolk minister, was settled at Manningtree.
Supposed to have gained a living as a lawyer, he
professed to have become acquainted with women at
Manningtree who were witches. "Every six weeks they
met on a Friday night and offered sacrifices to the
Devil." After obtaining the condemnation of these poor
women he set up as witch-finder general, "a trade never
hitherto taken up in England." This proceeding does

not appear to have excited any other sentiment than horror at the crime. People were too well-prepared for such things, seeing that it was a period of great mental and religious excitement. The belief in the personality of the Devil was never stronger; indeed, alarm at his ostensible familiarity with human beings seems to have made this generation omit the fear of God from its thoughts altogether. The sort of stuff that imposed upon Christian society at this period may be best shown by the "examination" of one of the culprits, Elizabeth Clarke, an old woman, of Manningtree. The plan of Hopkins in dealing with a reputed witch was to prevent her sleeping until she made confession. In Clarke's case he watched with her several nights in the house of a Mr. Edwards, where she was detained, and was not permitted to sleep. After three nights of watching she broke silence and "confessed" that about six or seven years ago she had surrendered herself to the Devil, who came to her in the form of "a proper gentleman with a laced band." Soon after this a little dog appeared, fat and short in the legs, in colour white with sandy spots, which, when she hindered it from approaching her, vanished from sight. She confessed that it was one of her imps, named "Jarmara." Immediately after this had disappeared, another came in the form of a greyhound, which she called "Vinegar Tom," and it was followed by another in the shape of a pole-cat. Hopkins further deposed that—

". . . going from the house of Mr. Edwards to his own house about nine or ten o'clock that night, with his greyhound with him, he saw the greyhound suddenly give a jump, and run as she had been in full course after a hare; and when he made haste to see what his greyhound so eagerly pursued, he espied a white thing about the bigness of a Kythyn (Kitten), and the greyhound standing aloof from it; and that by and bye the said white imp or Kythyn danced about the said greyhound, and by all likelihood bit a piece of the flesh of the shoulder of the greyhound, for the greyhound came shrieking and crying to him with a piece of flesh torn from her shoulder. Further, coming into his own yard that night, he espied a black thing, proportioned like a cat, only it was thrice as big, sitting on a strawberry bed and fixing his eyes on him, and when he looked toward it, it leaped over the pale towards him, as he thought, but ran quite through the yard, with his greyhound after it, to a great gate, which was underset with a pair of tumbril-strings, and did throw the said gate wide open, and then vanished, and the said greyhound returned again to him, shaking and trembling exceedingly."

Elizabeth Gooding and Anne Leech were the remaining culprits. Leech " confessed " that " she had a grey imp sent to her, and that she, together with Clarke and Gooding, did about a year since send their imps to kill a black cow and a white cow of Mr. Edwards, which was done accordingly. Also, about thirty years since, she sent a grey imp to kill two horses of Mr. Briggs, of Mistley, which were killed accordingly, and the cause of her malice was that Mistress Briggs had told her she suspected her to be a naughty woman. Also that she and the said Elizabeth Gooding sent either of them an imp to destroy the child of the said Mr. Edwards. Leech's imp was a white one, Gooding's a black one. And about thirty years ago she had the said white imp and a grey and a black one. And that these imps went commonly from one to another and did mischief wherever they went, and so on.

In company with Hopkins was a colleague whom he enlisted in the good work, one John Sterne, " gentleman," zealous as himself, who assured the world, indeed, long afterward, that " he had no trouble of conscience for what he had done." They had as assistant a woman, who acted as searcher. The career of this wretch Hopkins is one of the most monstrous things in our social history. After his success at Chelmsford Assizes he went about through Suffolk, Norfolk, and Huntingdonshire. The poor, the old, and the ignorant were easy victims to his avarice— for avarice it was. It was a lucky stroke of money-making, and he was well paid while the craze lasted : " Twenty shillings a head for every witch discovered." Hopkins

S

posed as a great judge of Special Marks, and the load of guilt to be attached to them. But as a true criterion of the real witch, he adhered to the traditional mode of discovery—swim or sink. He would tie together the thumbs and toes of the suspected person, and give her a dowsing in a pond. Coming alive out of the water was deemed a certain proof of guilt. Sometimes the accused were tied neck and heels and tossed into a pond; if they floated they were guilty, and forthwith taken out and burnt or hanged; if they were innocent, they were "only drowned." In the end it was long believed that the experiment was tried on Hopkins himself, and coming out alive from the water he was condemned and executed as a wizard. But, according to his friend Sterne, he found himself disgraced; vexation and a tendency to consumption brought him to the grave. He had come home to Manningtree in 1647, and after printing an apologetic in the form of a pamphlet on the *Discovery of Witches*, took to his bed and died.

It should be understood that there was early displayed an antagonism to Hopkins. It was a dangerous time to enter into any controversy; but there were many of the clergy who preached and spoke vehemently against the cruel business. Several curious tracts have come down to us, usually of a non-committal character, which tell us of the alleged magical arts in vogue. Others boldly say there was too much cruelty going on, and without due reason or excuse. In the case of some of the Essex "witches" who were tried at Colchester sessions, there was one bench of five magistrates who petitioned the House of Lords to pardon a set of prisoners who had been convicted in their court on July 17th, 1645. They asserted that the court was "not fully satisfied with the evidence given," and the prisoners were respited for mercy—"and we think them fit for mercy and pardon." The culprits included the following:—Susannah Cocke, of St. Osith, farmer's wife, for feloniously entertaining of evil spirits; Elizabeth

Harvey, of Ramsey, widow, for the like offence; Brigitt Mayes, of Holland, seaman's wife, for the like offence; Dorothea Waters of Clacton, labourer's wife, for the like offence; Anne Therston, of Great Holland, farmer's wife, for the like offence; Mary Johnson, of Wivenhoe, seaman's wife, for the like offence; Mary Sterling, of Langham, yeoman's wife, for the like offence.

If the endorsement, "nothing done," which is written on this paper, means anything, this petition was fruitless. As far as can be seen now, it would appear that these poor creatures were done for as soon as they got within the toils of the law. Public opinion was far more vindictive than any constable. Only a few escaped the actual penalty by death, from fright or despair. There was Margaret Moone, of Thorpe (who had had twelve imps), died on the way to execution; Rose Hallybread, of St. Osyth, and Jane Cooper, of Great Holland, who both died in gaol.

When Hopkins collapsed the great persecution was soon over. But there were incidental trials for witchcraft in England until about 1712. In that year Lord Chief Justice Parker, sitting at the Brentwood Summer Assizes, gave a straight warning: "If any dared for the future to make use of that experiment [*sink or swim*] and the party lose her life by it, all they that are the cause of it are guilty of wilful murther." The latest date among our notes concerning Essex is the following, from a MS. diary of the period (*Essex Archæological Society*, i., 126), belonging to Coggeshall:—

"July 13, 1699.—The widow Comon was put into the river to see if she would sink, because she was suspected to be a witch; and she did not sink, but swim. And she was tryed again July 19th and then she swam again, and did not sink.

"July 24, 1699.—The widow Comon was tryed a third time by putting her into the river, and she swam and did not sink.

"December 27, 1699.—The widow Comon that was counted a witch, was buried."

One feels the tears threatening at this full stop.

Although the belief in witchcraft is so nearly extinct, it appears that the sense of magic art is still fairly widespread in Essex—as, indeed, in many other counties in England. We have a few notes concerning the charms which are still resorted to in some emergencies. "Every man his own wizard," as it would seem, and in a tolerably harmless way. One of the oddest symptoms of this craft is the belief in the power of grease. The idea is a very ancient one. Brand (in his *Popular Antiquities*, under "Divination at Weddings") quotes a classic story of the bride (on nearing her new home) anointing the door-posts with swine's grease, because she thought by that means to drive away all misfortune. In Essex the application of grease is made after the mischief is done, with hopes of a speedy cure. Benton (*History of Rochford Hundred*) mentions a case at Leigh of this sort. "A man named Harvey fell from a wharf, and in his descent came in contact with a long rusty nail, whereby his arm was much lacerated. By the advice of some fellow-workmen the enraged nail causing this damage was mollified by an abundant anointing of grease." Enquiry in the *Essex Review* some years ago raised quite a crop of allied cases—*e.g.*, on Mersea Island a horse trod on some sharp substance and cut his foot. Forthwith a horseshoe nail was stuck into a bit of tallow candle. At Little Dunmow it was stated to be quite common for a man whose horse was hurt or pricked to grease the place, and also the fork or hook that caused the damage. These things are told of A.D. 1894 or thereabouts! One more (of the same period):

"At Lawford recently a lad was killed by the wound of a pitchfork. One of the witnesses in the case being asked if there was any blood on the fork, said he had wiped it off, and greased the fork and laid that by. He added that he was asked by the parents of the deceased lad if he had greased the fork, as they had another son injured by a fork which was greased, and the boy got well."

It was stated by the contributor of this story that it was a common superstition in Essex. The laying-up of the fork was considered essential, the idea being that it should be laid up till the wound caused by it became healed. Not long since an Essex girl, fresh from school, strongly recommended her mistress to grease a tin, which had scratched her finger, as the best method of insuring the speedy healing of the wound.[1]

Bee-keeping is a prosperous industry in this country. There will be some choice fruit from the labours of the folk-lorist who is understood to be now pursuing the topic. Here is one statement which we owe to the late Mr. C. M. Ingleby, of Ilford: —

" I have learned that the superstition about the bees deserting their hives on the death of one of their owner's family is common in the county of Essex. A lady tells me that calling upon some poor people who lived at Hyde Green, near Ingatestone, she enquired after the bees. The old woman of the house replied, ' They have all gone away since the death of poor Dick, for we forgot to knock at the hives and tell them he was gone dead.' "

The late Canon Atkinson (*Forty Years in a Moorland Parish*) tells us that when he was a schoolboy in a country parish near Colchester the rector died. Nothing remained on his mind so much as the putting of the bees into mourning. Strips of a black material were folded round each hive, and as each strip was knotted three taps with the house key were given, and each hive severally informed that the master was dead.

The ceremony of " blessing the geese " is described by a lady who was staying about two miles from Epping some twenty-five years ago (*Folk-lore*, 1903): —

" One morning while standing at my window I saw a flock of goslings come out of a lane, driven by an old woman who was dressed in the style of the pictures of Old Mother Goose. She drove them to a piece of grass at the side of the road, and walked up and down in front of them, spreading her arms over them and bowing first one way and then the

---

[1] Miss Evelyn Carrington, in *Folk-Lore Record*, iii., pt. 2, p. 169.

other, at the same time saying some words which I could not catch, but
they evidently formed some kind of incantation. I asked my maid (a
country girl) if she knew what the old woman was doing. ' Oh yes ' (said
she), ' that is old Mother Jenkins. Otherwise they would never prosper.'
The girl assured me all the breeders of geese patronised this old woman,
who was paid a fee for her services, and that she made the principal part
of her living in this way. ' Now ' (said the girl) ' they will grow strong
and flourish.' I ought to add that the old woman held a kind of wand in
her hand, which she waved over the geese whilst muttering her
incantation."

There are at least two churches in Essex which are
lucky to be married in, or used to be considered so. The
legend at Rayne is that the church formerly possessed
an altar and chapel in the south aisle dedicated to the
Blessed Virgin. The story goes that the wife of John de
Naylinghurst was dying in childbed, on which the women
in attendance flew to the altar of Our Lady to implore
her benevolent interference, and looking up in the fervour
of their devotion they beheld the Virgin smiling assent to
their prayer. Forthwith they hurried back with the news,
and found the lady safe and a little de Naylinghurst added
to the household. At Ashingdon there was a miraculous
image early in the fourteenth century. An image, reputed
to perform miracles, was placed in the church, and numbers
resorted to it, some even crawling up the hill upon their
knees in the excess of their devotion. The intercession of
the saint was supposed to be highly efficacious with
females desirous of heirs. The thing is supposed to have
been a speculation of the rector's. At any rate, the Bishop
of London sent a Commission to report upon it. The result
of this enquiry is not on record, but ever afterwards it
was considered lucky to be married in Ashingdon church.

There are in the county several springs of a medicinal
character, which have been more or less in vogue. Some
of these even obtained modern celebrity, as Hockley Spa,
Witham, Upminster, and West Tilbury. At Chingford,
near the Forest Hotel, there is a spring which feeds the
pond and streamlet. The present writer has, thirty or forty

years ago, talked with people who found this water of benefit for sore eyes. They protested that the fact was known for many miles round. Some other springs have in former days reached the dignity of holy wells, as at Castle Hedingham, where a chapel was built in an adjoining field. At St. Osyth there was a holy well of very great merit; Mr. Beckett (*Romantic Essex*) speaks of it as the Wishing Well, in the present tense.

The mention of St. Osyth reminds us that Essex holds one of the saintliest legends in the South of England. Like St. Winifred, the heroine of Flintshire, St. Osyth was as devout as she was beautiful. In the midst of her career as abbess of the nunnery here, fate came by in the shape of a savage Danish marauder, who cut off her lovely head. As in the case of the other lady mentioned, the head of St. Osyth was carried away in her own arms; and at the place where she fell a fountain gushed out, which long remained famous for its miraculous curative power. There is still talk of a ghost which wanders about occasionally in the "Nun's Wood."

All this water-logged part of Essex is full of superstition. Readers of *Mehalah* will remember the dwellers by the creek. There are few places about here without their ghosts or traditions of them. Tendring Hundred, Dengie, Rochford, have always, until recent years, been districts where the people were easily worked upon by fear. There are two places where the ghost was a woman carrying her head under her arm: at a remote corner of Foulness Island, and near the ferry at Great Stambridge. A long time ago there was a reputed ghost at Rochford Hall; but this one seems to have been laid by a little alacrity on the part of the vicar of the parish. At Leigh there is a house, formerly known as Blackhouse, near the church, which was believed to be haunted. It had been occupied by a physician of some local celebrity. He believed in supernatural visitation, even of a friendly kind. There was nothing of devilry or magic about it, but he was careful not to offend the spirits. After his death his house was long uninhabited, because of the general belief that a troubled spirit haunted it.

There is a haunted tree near Barling, with a good story attached to it, told by Mr. Tompkins (*Marsh Country Rambles*). A baker, who was a good and a successful baker, became miserable about something—whether criminal or not no one knew. One evening he wandered out to a lonely spot and hanged himself from a tree. His spirit found no rest. The countryside was much troubled, and sometimes people would hear his heels knock together as the body hung, especially on windy nights. If you walked round that tree a hundred times you would see the baker working at his kneading-trough. There was one man determined to brave out the thing, and if possible see the ghost, if he perished in the attempt. It was dark, but, nothing a-feared, the man began his task. Ninety-nine times he went round the tree and then slipped and sprained his ankle. It was thought but a right punishment for having derided the treasured local belief.

We will conclude this paper with a return to old times— a story of 1709. There was published in that year an account of the wonderful adventures of Mr. Jan Smagge and his household on Canvey Island. "Certain injurious pranks were played by some restless, unhappy goblin or spirits, or else by their grand chieftain, the Prince of the Power of the Air." The house of Smagge had formerly been occupied by an old couple who got their living, and laid up much store, by fraud and oppression. After the husband's decease a wandering spirit was seen from time to time. Tradition had it that it was to be "laid" at the end of twenty-one years. This period lapsed in September, 1709, and on the 10th, 13th, 14th, 15th, and 16th of this month the house was wofully disturbed. Doors opened and shut, chairs rocked, latches lifted, lights were seen where no candle nor fire existed. Petticoats rustled when no female was nigh. Unaccountable noises were heard. The cats

scuttled away, and the maids were terribly frightened.
The Rev. Mr. Lord, curate of the island, nobly gathered
the neighbours together and entered into an active
investigation of the matter. But all things come to an
end. The only recognisable ghost discovered was an
oldish man with sharp eyes, countenance pale and ghastful,
wearing a short grey coat, whitish hat, and holding a
white stick in his hand.

With the belief in "the devil's intercourse with
humanity," it happens naturally enough that folk were
ready enough to accept any stories of monstrous and
unaccountable shapes prowling about the earth. We have
several fearful and astonishing old tales from Essex to
this effect. The earliest on record is A.D. 1170, when there
was seen at Osyth "a Dragon of Marvellous Bigness,
which, by moving, buried houses." Coming to later times,
we have more circumstantial accounts of such wonders.
There is in King Street, Covent Garden, a tavern bearing
the sign of the "Essex Serpent." It is mentioned as an
old inn in the eighteenth century, and the name doubtless
keeps in record "The Flying Serpent at Walden in Essex."
From the printed account (Lond., 1669) we learn some
details of this monster. It was

". . . a most venemous serpent, which in former times lurked about
the meads near Saffron Walden, who by his very sight killed so many,
as the town became almost depopulated, when a valorous Knight, making
him a coat of Christal glass, boldly went to assail this Cockatrice, but
her venemous nature not able to indure the purity of that fine mettle, she
suddenly dyed, in memory whereof his sword was hung up in Walden
Church, the effigies of the Cockatrice set up in Brass, and a Table hanged
close by wherein was contained all the story of the adventure; but in
these late times of Rebellion, it being taken for a monument of
superstition was by the lawless soldiers broken in pieces, to shew they
were also of a venemous nature as well as the Cockatrice."

Actual dates are impossible. The above was probably
an old story in 1669, when there was also an alarming
appearance at Henham-on-the-Hill, about seven miles
southward, unless the following story was purely an

imaginary one. We know what a credulous age it was. But here is the tale :—

"*The Flying Serpent*, or Strange News out of Essex, being a true relation of a monstrous serpent which hath divers times been seen at a parish called Henham on the Mount within 4 miles of Saffron Walden. Shewing the length, proportion, and bigness of the Serpent, the place where it commonly lurks, and what means hath been used to kill it. Also a discourse of other serpents, and particularly of a Cockatrice killed at Saffron Walden."

This relation has a suspicious look of having been concocted by some ingenious publicist, and may have been merely a satire on the Saffron Walden legend. The minutiæ of the incident are in a style which would not disgrace the ubiquitous reporter of our own days. The facts of the case are attested by the churchwarden, the constable, the overseer for the poor, and four householders :

"In a pasture ground near to a wood called Birchwood hath this monstrous serpent been often seen upon the sides of a Bank, beaking and stretching himself out upon the same at such time as *Sol* did parch the Earth with his refulgent beams."

The first visitation is on a day in May, when a horse-man was so frightened that he put spurs to his horse, "and with winged speed hasted away." The neighbours presently assembled in force, and came near, yet did not dare to strike. The serpent's eyes were very large and piercing, "about the bigness of a sheep's eye"; in his mouth two rows of very white and sharp teeth, and on his back two wings. The creature took things quietly enough, and presently retired into the wood, "and has since been closely watched for by several persons with musquets and fowling-pieces and such like to shoot it, but as yet it hath been no man's good fortune to light on him." The latest report was that folks were still keeping watch for the monster till such time as they hoped to kill it.

THE DUNMOW FLITCH

By Thomas Fforster

MONGST the very many curious customs or tenures found in various parts of the country dating from an early period, the "Dunmow Flitch" is unique and world-renowned. Grose says of it that "among the jocular tenures of England, none have been more talked of than the bacon of Dunmow. By whom, or at what period, this custom was instituted is not certain, but it is generally ascribed to one of the family of Fitz-Walter. The bacon, generally a flitch (sometimes a gammon was given instead), could be claimed by any couple who had been married a year and a day. It might, however, be claimed several years after marriage, provided that during the period the conditions could be complied with. The couple desiring it must have lived together in peace and amity, without even a difference of opinion or desire." The actual person who founded it may be called in question, but the family is fairly clear. Dugdale, in the *Monasticon Anglicanum*, is the clearest, and is allowed to be the most accurate, as the following will prove:

"Robert Fitz-Walter, living long beloved of King Henry, the son of King John, as also of all the realme, betook himself in his latter dayes to prayer and Deeds of Charity, and great and bountifull Almes to the poor, kept great Hospitality, and reedifyed the decayed prison of Dunmowe, which one Juga, a most devout and religious woman, being in her kind his Ancestor, had builded. In which prison arose a custome, begun and instituted eyther by him, or some other of his successors, which is verefied by a common proverbe or saying, viz., 'That he which repents him not of his marriage, either sleeping or waking, in a year and a day, may lawfully go to Dunmowe and fetch a Gammon of Bacon.' It is most assured, that such a custome there was, and that the Bacon was delivered with such solemnity and triumphs, as they of the Priory, and Townsmen could make. I have enquired of the manner of it, and can learn no more, but that it continued till the dissolution of that House, as also the Abbies. And that the party, or Pilgrim for Bacon was to take his oath before Prior and Covent, and the whole Town, humbly kneeling in the Churchyard upon two hard pointed stones, which stones, some say, are there yet to be seen in the Priors Churchyard. His oath was ministered with such long Process, and such solemn singing over him, that doubtless must make his Pilgrimage (as I may terme it) painfull. After, he was taken up upon men's shoulders, and carryed, first, about the Priory Churchyard, and after, through the Town, with all the Fryers and Brethren, and all the Townsfolke, young and old, following him with Shouts and with Acclamation, with his Bacon borne before him, and in such manner (as I have heard) was sent home with his Bacon; of which I finde that some had a Gammon, and others a Fleeke, or a Flitch."

The custom is said to have been instituted in the thirteenth century. The first recorded presentation is some two hundred years later, but from various authors it appears to have been given much earlier. The first reference to it is in *The Vision of Piers Plowman*, supposed to have been written by Robert Langlande about 1326, in which he does not speak kindly of those who claim it :

> "Many a couple since the pestilence
> Have blighted them together;
> The fruit that they bring forth
> Is foul words
> In jealousy without happiness
> And quarrelling in bed,
> They have no children but strife,
> And slapping between them;
> And though they go to Dunmow
> (Unless the devil help!)
> To follow after the flitch,
> They never after obtain it;
> And unless they both are perjured,
> They lose the bacon."

Chaucer, in the Prologue of *The Wife of Bath's Tale*, where she relates how she treated one of her husbands, remarks :

> " The bacoun was nought fet for hem, I trow
> That som men feeche in Essex at Dunmowe."

In a paraphrase on the Ten Commandments, printed in *The Reliquiæ Antiquæ* from a MS., *circa* 1460, is the following :

> "I can fynd no man now that wille enquere,
> Th parfyte wais unto Dunmow;
> For they repent hem within a yere,
> And many within a weke, and sonner, men trow;
> That cawsith the weis to be nowth and overgrow
> That no man may fynd path or gap
> The world is turned to another shap.
>
> .   .   .   .   .   .
>
> Befe and moton wylle serve wele enow;
> And for to secke so ferre a lytill bakon flyk
> Which hath long hanggid, resty and tow;
> And the wey I telle you is combrous and thyk,
> And thou might stomble, and take the cryk
> Therefor bide at home, what so ever hap
> Tylle the world be turned into another shap."

In the *Chartulary of the Priory*, now in the British Museum, six recipients are recorded as having received, but from the above extracts it would appear to have been given earlier. The particulars were either not taken or are lost, therefore these following must not be considered as the first six to whom it was given. The custom, though always mentioned as a flitch (*i.e.*, a side), yet to some was given a gammon (*i.e.*, a leg); why, does not appear.

" First.—That one Richard Wright, of Badbourge, near the city of Norwich, in the county of Norfolk, yeoman, came and required the bacon of Dunmow on the 27th day of April, in the 23rd year of the reign of King Henry VI. (1445) and according to the form of the charter was sworn before John Cannon, Prior of this place and the convent, and many other neighbours, and there was delivered to him, the said Richard, one flitch of bacon.

"Second.—That one Stephen Samuel, of Little Easton, in the county of Essex, husbandman, came to the Priory of Dunmow, on our Lady day in Lent, in the seventh year of King Edward IV. (1467), and required a gammon of bacon, and was sworn before Roger Bulcott, then Prior, and the convent of this place, as also before a multitude of other neighbours, and there was delivered to him a gammon of bacon.

"Third.—That in the year of our Lord, 1510, Thomas Le Fuller, of Coggeshall, in the County of Essex, came to the Priory of Dunmow, and on the 8th September, being Sunday, in the second year of King Henry VIII. he was, according to the form of the Charter, sworn before John Tills, the Prior of the house, and convent, as also before a multitude of neighbours, and there was delivered to him, the said Thomas, a gammon of bacon."

These three are before the Dissolution; the other three are after. Two claimants next appeared—John Reynolds, of Hatfield-Brodoke, Gent., and Anne his wife; and William Parsley, of Much Easton, butcher, and Jane his wife. The trial was at a Court Baron of Sir Thomas May, Knt., on June 7th, 1701, before Thomas Wheeler, Gent., Steward, the "homage," or jury, being five fair ladies, spinsters—viz., Elizabeth, Henrietta, Annabella, and Jane Beaumont, and Mary Wheeler. They found for the claimants, who, "by means of their quiet and peaceable, tender and loving co-habitation for the space of three years last past and upwards, were fit and qualified persons to be admitted by the court to receive the antient and accustomed oath, whereby to entitle themselves to have the bacon of Dunmow delivered unto them according to custom of the maner." A gammon to each. The *Gentleman's Magazine* for 1751 says that on the same day a gammon was given to Mr. Reynolds, Steward to Sir Charles Barrington, of Hatfield Broad Oak, but does not say for what reason.

The next and last of the six given in the *Chartulary* is perhaps the most important, because we have two contemporary illustrations taken by David Ogborne, a local artist. One represents the taking the oath; the other the procession, with the bacon borne before them on a pole.

At a special Court Baron of Mary Hallett, widow, Lady of the Manor, on June 20th, 1751, before George Comyns, Esq., steward, six bachelors and six spinsters constituted the homage. The claimants were Thomas Shakeshaft (sometimes quoted as Shakeshanks, but the Court Roll gives the former), of Wethersfield, woolcomber, and Ann his wife; they had been married over seven years. The verdict was in their favour, in nearly the same words as in the previous case. The illustration represents them kneeling on the pointed stones in a chamber, not near the church door, as before the Dissolution. The oath taken is also recorded in the *Chartulary:*

> "You shall swear, by custom of confession,
> That you ne'er made nuptial transgression,
> Nor since you were married man or wife,
> By household brawls or contentious strife,
> Or otherwise, in bed or at board,
> Offended each other in deed or in word,
> Or since the parish clerk said Amen,
> Wished yourselves unmarried again,
> Or in a Twelvemonth and a Day
> Repented not in thought any manner of way,
> But continued true in thought and desire
> As when you joined hands in the Holy Quire."

Here it appears that the bacon was presented, and the following sentence pronounced :

> "If to these conditions, without all fear
> Of your own accord you freely swear
> A whole gammon of bacon you shall receive
> And bear it hence with love and good leave;
> For this our custom of Dunmow, well known,
> Though the cost be ours, the bacon's your own."

The oak chair in which the pilgrims were carried round, much worn by use and age, is now preserved in the chancel of Little Dunmow Church. It is supposed to have belonged to the priory before the Dissolution, and to have been the one always used on the occasions.

It was certainly used in 1751. Some few years ago
the Dunmow Committee had a new one made, exactly
similar, which is now used by the judge who presides
at the trial. The stones upon which the pilgrims knelt
are now lost. Hone, writing in 1838, says that "they
are still there."

The Spectator, No. 607, October 15th, 1714, discusses
the Dunmow Flitch, and a similar custom at Wichenour,
Staffordshire. The next number continues the subject,
and both are in reply to No. 605. In the first quoted
number the writer states: "I hope your readers are
satisfied of this truth, that as love generally produces
matrimony, so it often happens that matrimony produces
love."

The engraving of the procession, with the church in
the background, represents the loving couple seated in
a chair, with the bacon on a long pole borne before
them. Having, according to custom, been carried round
the churchyard, they are starting on a tour through the
town. The happy couple are known as the pilgrims.
They were attended by a large concourse of people,
including many from the surrounding villages. About
seven thousand gathered together. It was a festive day;
sports and music graced the festival.

Chambers's *Book of Days* mentions its being claimed
and given twelve years later (1763), but says that the
names of the claimants are not now known. In 1772
it was claimed by John and Susan Gilder, of Terling.
On June 12th they made their public entry into Dunmow,
attended by a great concourse of people, and demanded
the gammon of bacon, according to notice previously given,
declaring themselves ready to take the oath. The Lord
of the Manor had caused the priory gates to be nailed
up, and refused to entertain the claim.

About eighty years pass away before any record of
its being given again appears, but that the custom was
not overlooked is proved by a ballad opera, entitled

THE DUNMOW PROCESSION, JUNE 20TH, 1751.

The Flitch of Bacon, written by Henry Bates, son of an Essex clergyman, being performed at the Haymarket Theatre in 1778. It was printed in 1779. Two verses will be enough to quote:

> " Ye good men and wives
> Who have all your lives,
>   And whose vows have at no time been shaken,
> Now come and draw near
> With your consciences clear,
>   And demand a large flitch of bacon,
>
> Since a year and a day
> Have in love roll'd away,
>   And an oath of what love has been taken,
> On the sharp pointed stones
> With your bare marrow bones,
>   You have won our fam'd Priory Bacon."

We can well imagine that the custom was continued; but if so, no record remains. A public holiday does not pass out of sight suddenly; a festival of the nature of a fair would long hold its own. Mr. John Timbs says: "It is reported in the neighbourhood that when our excellent Queen (Victoria) had been married a year and a day, the then Lord of the Manor privately offered the flitch of bacon to Her Majesty, who declined the compliment."

One hundred years now pass before the next authentic presentation takes place on July 16th, 1851, though it was then deprived of its ancient historic associations. Mr. and Mrs. Hurrell, owners and occupiers of a farm at Felstead, adjoining Little Dunmow, claimed the award. The Lord of the Manor of Dunmow Priory refused to entertain the claim, assigning as a reason that the custom had long been dormant. The inhabitants of Dunmow held a meeting to protest against the decision, and in the end agreed to give it themselves. The loving couple were informed that if they would present themselves on July 16th, the gammon would be given at a public fête in Easton Park. A brass band met them at the

T

Market Cross, and preceded their chaise to the park playing "See the Conquering Hero comes"; banners and flags enlivened the scene. The bacon, ornamented with ribbons, was borne on a pole before them. About three thousand persons were present, including members of the aristocracy and gentry in the neighbourhood.

The next presentation occurs on July 19th, 1855, when two couples claim and obtain—James Barlow, of Chipping Ongar, builder, and Hannah his wife; and Mons. Jean Baptiste Ernest de Chatelain (a Frenchman) and Clara his wife. Both the latter were engaged in literary pursuits. Chatelain, in his examination, stated that he came from Paris, met madame in London, and had been married twelve years. He found it a fallacy that a clever woman did not make a good wife. They resided first in France, but then at Grafton Place, Euston Square, London. The next question asked was: "Is this a love match?" To which he replies in the affirmative, and in reference to their residence in France stated that "the difference in habits did not lead to any difference of opinion." They were married in England.

After the trial of 1855 a procession was formed and paraded the principal streets of the town, some in carriages, some on foot. The claimants were seated in two chairs, one couple in each, and carried on men's shoulders. A halt was made at the Market Cross, where proclamation was made by sound of trumpet and drum that the award had been gained. They then proceeded to the Windmill field, and in a tent there the oath was taken and the flitches delivered. They were given by Mr. William Harrison Ainsworth, the well-known author of the historical novel, *The Flitch of Bacon*. He presided on this occasion. Sports and amusements were continued up to a late hour.

On June 25th, 1857, Jeremiah and Sarah Heard, of Bentley, Staffordshire, and John Nichol Hawkins, M.D., of Victoria Place, Regent's Park, and his wife, Ann

Sophia, were the fortunate couples. Mr. Barlow, one of the gainers in the previous contest, acted as crier of the court, and proclaimed silence. Mr. W. H. Ainsworth once more occupied the chair. In his opening remarks, after alluding to the refusal of the Lord of the Manor to continue the custom, he announced that a lady (whose name was not given) had signified her intention of bequeathing a sum of money sufficient to make the custom annual. The proceedings were similar to those of former contests. The first pair received the flitch, the other pair a silver testimonial as a consolation prize. Mr. Bowker, as counsel for the claimants, remarked that out of the nine claims, seven were from natives of Essex, and he observed that "Essex was rather celebrated for matrimonial felicity."

In 1869 advertisements appeared in the papers that claims might be sent in. A goodly number were forwarded, and two were selected—William Casson, wood engraver, and Emma Elizabeth, his wife, of No. 3, Cornwall Road, Victoria Park, London; and Josiah Leaver, jeweller, and Mary Jane, his wife, of Rydon Crescent, Clerkenwell, London. They both received it on August 16th, and the festival was attended by twenty thousand persons. The next presentation was on August 10th, 1874. A large number of claims were sent in, and the committee selected one—Joseph James Clegg, merchant's clerk, and Hannah his wife, of 240, Roman Road, London. They were married at Prestwich Church, Lancashire, on February 12th, 1861, thus having lived in sweet concord for the ill-fated number of thirteen years. Mr. William Casson, to whom was awarded a prize in 1869, presided. The local lodge of Foresters, "Court of Prince Arthur," assisted the celebration, and received towards their funds the profits from the entertainments. Two years later, July 17th, 1876, the flitch was awarded to James Henry Boosey, parish clerk of Holy Trinity Church, Ventnor, Isle of Wight, and Mary his wife. He was born at Standon, Herts.; she at Furneux Pelham, in the same county. Another pair, the Rev. S. M. Smith, Vicar of Harwell, Berks., and his wife, wanted to claim, but a previous engagement for the same day prevented his attendance. He wrote to signify his intention of competing on a future occasion. This trial was presided over by the well-known antiquarian, Mr. William Andrews, of Hull, a frequent writer on historical subjects. In his introductory speech on this occasion, he traces the history of the custom, and adds the following: "You must, I think, all feel with me that the meeting to-day is well calculated to promote matrimonial happiness. We are the great rival of the divorce court. The name of Dunmow, and the remembrance of the flitch, causes the votaries of that court to hide in shame their heads. By the committee I am directed to state that they urge on claimants to remember that the prize must not be estimated by its cost, but by the distinction it offers to those who may be fortunate enough to obtain it. Enviable are the wedded pair on whom the prize is conferred, since the acquisition establishes a claim of honour and respect. To say that a couple 'deserve the flitch' is a high compliment; but to say that 'they have actually won it' is to proclaim them among the best and happiest of mankind."

The *Times* of July 10th, 1877, announced the above Mr. Andrews, of Hull, and his wife to be competitors, with another couple. The prize was given on the 23rd of the same month. The former did not put in an appearance, but the latter, James Barrack, foreman brickmaker, of Dunmow, and Hannah his wife were the fortunate recipients. They had been married twenty-eight years. Mr. Sowill, of Dunmow, was judge. Mr. William Tegg, publisher, appeared for the claimants. After the trial, "the couple, preceded by a band, were carried shoulder high from the Town Hall to a field on the outskirts of the town, where, on an elevated platform, they took the oath, kneeling on sharp stones, and then received the bacon amid the firing of cannon."

The contests are now more frequent, and it has been given from 1892 to the present time with but few exceptions. As the attendant circumstances are similar, it is needless to give them in detail.

Robert Fitz-Walter, spoken of in a foregoing extract, was a descendant of that earlier Robert, Steward of William the Conqueror, who granted to his faithful servant the estates at Dunmow and various other rewards, including the honour or "Soke" of Baynard's Castle in the south-west angle of the city of London. This Robert Fitz-Walter was succeeded by his son, Walter Fitz-Robert, who married, firstly, Matilda or Maud de Beecham, and secondly, Matilda, daughter of Richard de Lucy, the faithful Justiciary of Henry II. His son Robert, by the second marriage, who next follows, is the reputed founder of the custom of Dunmow. He married Gunmor, daughter and heiress of Robert of Valognes. The marriage is said to have been an unhappy one, and is assigned as a reason for his founding it. This Robert Fitz-Walter was high in favour with King John, but from being a leader of the Barons, and taking a prominent part with the French King against the English King, he had to retire from the kingdom, and his possessions were seized. Eventually he was restored to favour and to his estates. He had a handsome daughter, whom it is said King John caused to be poisoned. There is every probability that this Robert is the real founder. It is, however, fully allowed that it was a Fitz-Walter. Valens, in his scarce work upon the Dunmow Flitch, printed in 1743, says: " Hereby appeareth, that it was given according to a Charter, or donation, given by some conceited Benefactor to the House: And it is not to be doubted but that, at such a time, the bordering Towns and Villages would resort and be partakers of their pastimes, and laugh to scorn the poor man's pains," evidently quoted from Dugdale. Morant considers the cost of the flitch a rent charge upon the priory, and that eleven generations of the Fitz-Walters in the direct male line held Dunmow ere it then passed to the female line.

After Dunmow, next in importance comes the custom of Wichenour, in Staffordshire. Here corn and sometimes cheese were added to the bacon. *Notes and Queries*, of December 22nd, 1906, mentions a parchment roll of the reign of Edward III., which gives particulars concerning it. Philip de Somervill held the manor from the Earl of Lancaster upon condition that he kept always hanging in his hall a bacon flitch, except during Lent. Like Dunmow, the couple receiving it must have been married a year and a day. But the oath was less severe:

"Here ye, Sir Philip de Somervile, Lord of Wichenour maynteyner and gyver of this Baconne, that I —— A. —— sythe I wedded, B. —— my wife, and sythe I hadd hyr in my kepyng, and at my wylle by a yere and a day after our mariage, I wold not have chaunged for none other, farer ne fowler; rycher ne powrer; ne for none other descended of gretter lynage; slepyng ne waking at noo tyme; and yf the seyd B. —— were sole and I sole, I wolde take her to be my wife before all the wymen of the world, of what condiciones soever they be, good or evylle, so help me God and hys Seyntys, and this flesh and all fleshes."

As witnesses, we are told: "And hys neghbors shall make othe that they trust verily he hath said truly; and yff it be founde by his neghbours, beforehand, that he be a freeman, there shall be delyvered him half a quarter of wheate, and a cheese; and yf he be a villeyn he shall have half a quarter of rye without cheese." Having received, he is to mount a horse (should he have none, the lord to provide one), and so to depart out of the lordship of Wichenour with "trompetts, tabouretts, and other manôir of mynstralce; and all the free tenants of Wichenour shall conduct hym to be passed the lordship," they to return, but he to continue to the border of the county at the charge of the lord.

Pennant, who visited Wichenour House in 1780, states that it was "remarkable for the painted wooden bacon flitch, still hung up over the hall chimney, in memory of the singular tenure by which Sir Philip de Somerville, in the time of Edward III., held the manor."

Brayley and Herbert, in *Tales and other Poems* (1803), give an imaginary account of one who received the bacon, and who, having answered all the questions required, was asked to explain how he had managed to do it :

> "'Oh ! if that's all,' the Farmer replied with a leer,
>   'I'll inform you, my friend, how it come ;
> You, yourself, will acknowledge the reason is clear,
>   As soon as I tell you that my pretty dear
>   Has been all her life—Deaf and Dumb !'"

The latest imitator of the Dunmow custom is Walthamstow. It was there given for the first time in 1906 to a loving couple residing in that ancient village. There was a fête, trial, etc., as at Dunmow, and it is stated that the custom is to be continued yearly.

INDEX

U

Bemrose & Sons Limited, Derby and London

Selected from the Catalogue of
BEMROSE & SONS Ltd.

Memorials of the Counties of England.

Beautifully Illustrated. Demy 8vo, cloth extra, gilt top.
Price **15/=** *each net.*

MEMORIALS OF OLD OXFORDSHIRE.

Edited by the Rev. P. H. DITCHFIELD, M.A., F.S.A. Dedicated by kind permission to the Right Hon. the Earl of Jersey, G.C.B., G.C.M.G.

"This beautiful book contains an exhaustive history of 'the wondrous Oxford,' to which so many distinguished scholars and politicians look back with affection. We must refer the reader to the volume itself . . . and only wish that we had space to quote extracts from its interesting pages."—*Spectator.*

MEMORIALS OF OLD DEVONSHIRE.

Edited by F. J. SNELL, M.A. Dedicated by kind permission to the Right Hon. Viscount Ebrington.

"A fascinating volume, which will be prized by thoughtful Devonians wherever they may be found . . . richly illustrated, some rare engravings being represented."—*North Devon Journal.*

MEMORIALS OF OLD HEREFORDSHIRE.

Edited by the Rev. COMPTON READE, M.A. Dedicated by kind permission to Sir John G. Cotterell, Bart.

"Another of these interesting volumes like the 'Memorials of Old Devonshire,' which we noted a week or two ago, containing miscellaneous papers on the history, topography, and families of the county by competent writers, with photographs and other illustrations."—*Times.*

MEMORIALS OF OLD HERTFORDSHIRE.

Edited by PERCY CROSS STANDING. Dedicated by kind permission to the Right Hon. the Earl of Clarendon, G.C.B.

"The book, which contains some magnificent illustrations, will be warmly welcomed by all lovers of our county and its entertaining history."—*West Herts and Watford Observer.*

"The volume as a whole is an admirable and informing one, and all Hertfordshire folk should possess it, if only as a partial antidote to the suburbanism which threatens to overwhelm their beautiful county."—*Guardian.*

MEMORIALS OF OLD HAMPSHIRE.

Edited by the Rev. G. E. JEANS, M.A., F.S.A. Dedicated by kind permission to His Grace the Duke of Wellington, K.G.

"'Memorials of the Counties of England' is worthily carried on in this interesting and readable volume."—*Scotsman.*

MEMORIALS OF OLD SOMERSET.

Edited by F. J. SNELL, M.A. Dedicated by kind permission to the Most Hon. the Marquis of Bath.

"In these pages, as in a mirror, the whole life of the county, legendary, romantic, historical, comes into view, for in truth the book is written with a happy union of knowledge and enthusiasm—a fine bit of glowing mosaic put together by fifteen writers into a realistic picture of the county."—*Standard.*

MEMORIALS OF OLD WILTSHIRE.

Edited by ALICE DRYDEN.

"The admirable series of County Memorials . . . will, it is safe to say, include no volume of greater interest than that devoted to Wiltshire."—*Daily Telegraph.*

MEMORIALS OF OLD SHROPSHIRE.

Edited by the Rev. THOMAS AUDEN, M.A., F.S.A.

"Quite the best volume which has appeared so far in a series that has throughout maintained a very high level."—*Tribune.*

MEMORIALS OF OLD KENT.

Edited by the Rev. P. H. DITCHFIELD, M.A., F.S.A., and GEORGE CLINCH, F.G.S. Dedicated by special permission to the Rt. Hon. Lord Northbourne, F.S.A.

"A very delightful addition to a delightful series. Kent, rich in honour and tradition as in beauty, is a fruitful subject of which the various contributors have taken full advantage, archæology, topography, and gossip being pleasantly combined to produce a volume both attractive and valuable."—*Standard.*

MEMORIALS OF OLD DERBYSHIRE.

Edited by the Rev. J. CHARLES COX, LL.D., F.S.A. Dedicated by kind permission to His Grace the Duke of Devonshire, K.G.

"A valuable addition to our county history, and will possess a peculiar fascination for all who devote their attention to historical, archæological, or antiquarian research, and probably to a much wider circle."—*Derbyshire Advertiser.*

MEMORIALS OF OLD DORSET.

Edited by the Rev. THOMAS PERKINS, M.A., and the Rev. HERBERT PENTIN, M.A. Dedicated by kind permission to the Right Hon. Lord Eustace Cecil, F.R.G.S.

"The volume, in fine, forms a noteworthy accession to the valuable series of books in which it appears."—*Scotsman.*

MEMORIALS OF OLD WARWICKSHIRE.

Edited by ALICE DRYDEN.

"Worthy of an honoured place on our shelves. It is also one of the best, if not the best, volume in a series of exceptional interest and usefulness."—*Birmingham Gazette.*

MEMORIALS OF OLD NORFOLK.

Edited by the Rev. H. J. DUKINFIELD ASTLEY, M.A., Litt.D., F.R.Hist.S. Dedicated by kind permission to the Right Hon. Viscount Coke, C.M.G., C.V.O.

"This latest contribution to the history and archæology of Norfolk deserves a foremost place among local works. . . . The tasteful binding, good print, and paper are everything that can be desired."—*Eastern Daily Press.*

MEMORIALS OF OLD LONDON. Two vols. Price 25/- net. Edited by the Rev. P. H. DITCHFIELD, M.A., F.S.A.

CONTENTS : Celtic, Roman, Saxon, and Norman London, by the Rev. W. J. Loftie, F.S.A.—The Tower of London, by Harold Sands, F.S.A.—St. Bartholomew's Church, Smithfield, by J. Tavenor-Perry.—The Charterhouse, by the Rev. A. G. B. Atkinson, M.A.—Glimpses of Mediæval London, by G. Clinch, F.G.S.—The Palaces of London, by the Rev. R. S. Mylne, LL.D., F.S.A.—The Temple, by the Rev. H. G. Woods, D.D., Master—The Inns of Court, by E. Williams—The Guildhall, by C. Welsh, F.S.A.—The City Companies, by the Editor.—The Kontor of the Hanse, by J. Tavenor-Perry.—The Arms of London, by J. Tavenor-Perry.—Elizabethan London, by T. Fairman Ordish, F.S.A.—The London of Pepys, by H. B. Wheatley, F.S.A.—The Thames and its Bridges, by J. Tavenor-Perry.—The Old Inns of London, by Philip Norman, LL.D.—London Clubs, by Sir Edward Brabrook, C.B., F.S.A.—The Coffee Houses, by G. L. Apperson.—Learned Societies of London, by Sir Edward Brabrook, C.B., F.S.A.—Literary Shrines, by Mrs. Lang.—Crosby Hall, by the Editor.—The Pageant of London ; with some account of the City Churches, Christ's Hospital, etc., by the Editor.

MEMORIALS OF OLD ESSEX. Edited by A. CLIFTON KELWAY, F.R.Hist.S.

Among the contributors are : Guy Maynard, Francis W. Reader, Rev. J. Charles Cox, LL.D., F.S.A., C. Forbes, T. Grose Lloyd, C. Fell Smith, Alfred Kingston, Miller Christy, F.L.S., W. W. Porteous, E. Bertram Smith, Thomas Fforster, Edward Smith, and the Editor.

The following volumes are in preparation :—

MEMORIALS OF OLD SUFFOLK. Edited by VINCENT B. REDSTONE, F.R.Hist.S.

Among the contributors will be : F. Seymour Stevenson, M.A., Rev. J. Charles Cox, LL.D., F.S.A., L. P. Steele Hutton, Rev. Rowland Maitland, B.A., B. J. Balding, P. Turner, H. J. Hitchcock, and the Editor.

MEMORIALS OF OLD SUSSEX. Edited by PERCY D. MUNDY.

MEMORIALS OF OLD LANCASHIRE. Two vols. Price 25/- net. Edited by LIEUT.-COLONEL FISHWICK, F.S.A.

MEMORIALS OF OLD YORKSHIRE. Edited by T. M. FALLOW, M.A., F.S.A.

MEMORIALS OF OLD GLOUCESTERSHIRE. Edited by P. W. P. PHILLIMORE, M.A., B.C.L.

MEMORIALS OF OLD MIDDLESEX. Edited by J. TAVENOR-PERRY.

MEMORIALS OF OLD NOTTINGHAMSHIRE. Edited by P. W. P. PHILLIMORE, M.A., B.C.L.

MEMORIALS OF NORTH WALES. Edited by E. ALFRED JONES.

MEMORIALS OF OLD MANXLAND. Edited by the Rev. JOHN QUINE, M.A.

MEMORIALS OF SOUTH WALES. Edited by E. ALFRED JONES.

MEMORIALS OF OLD STAFFORDSHIRE. Edited by the Rev. W. BERESFORD.

MEMORIALS OF OLD MONMOUTHSHIRE. Edited by COLONEL BRADNEY, F.S.A., and J. KYRLE FLETCHER.

MEMORIALS OF OLD WORCESTERSHIRE. Edited by F. B. ANDREWS, F.R.I.B.A.

MEMORIALS OF OLD LEICESTERSHIRE. Edited by ALICE DRYDEN.

MEMORIALS OF OLD CHESHIRE. Edited by the VEN. THE ARCHDEACON OF CHESTER, and the Rev. P. H. DITCHFIELD, M.A., F.S.A.

OLD ENGLISH GOLD PLATE.

By E. ALFRED JONES. With numerous Illustrations of existing specimens of Old English Gold Plate, which by reason of their great rarity and historic value deserve publication in book form. The examples are from the collections of Plate belonging to His Majesty the King, the Dukes of Devonshire, Newcastle, Norfolk, Portland, and Rutland, the Marquis of Ormonde, the Earls of Craven, Derby, and Yarborough, Earl Spencer, Lord Fitzhardinge, Lord Waleran, Mr. Leopold de Rothschild, the Colleges of Oxford and Cambridge, &c. Royal 4to, buckram, gilt top. Price 21/= net.

" Pictures, descriptions, and introduction make a book that must rank high in the estimation of students of its subject, and of the few who are well off enough to be collectors in this Corinthian field of luxury."—*Scotsman.*

LONGTON HALL PORCELAIN.

Being further information relating to this interesting fabrique, by the late WILLIAM BEMROSE, F.S.A., author of *Bow, Chelsea and Derby Porcelain.* Illustrated with 27 Coloured Art Plates, 21 Collotype Plates, and numerous line and half-tone Illustrations in the text. Bound in handsome "Longton-blue" cloth cover, suitably designed. Price 42/= net.

" This magnificent work on the famous Longton Hall ware will be indispensable to the collector."—*Bookman.*
" The collector will find Mr. Bemrose's explanations of the technical features which characterize the Longton Hall pottery of great assistance in identifying specimens, and he will be aided thereto by the many well-selected illustrations."—*Athenæum.*

THE VALUES OF OLD ENGLISH SILVER & SHEFFIELD PLATE, FROM THE FIFTEENTH TO THE NINETEENTH CENTURIES.

By J. W. CALDICOTT. Edited by J. STARKIE GARDNER, F.S.A. 3,000 Selected Auction Sale Records; 1,600 Separate Valuations; 660 Articles. Illustrated with 87 Collotype Plates. 300 pages. Royal 4to Cloth. Price 42/= net.

" A most comprehensive and abundantly illustrated volume. . . . Enables even the most inexperienced to form a fair opinion of the value either of a single article or a collection, while as a reference and reminder it must prove of great value to an advanced student."—*Daily Telegraph.*

HISTORY OF OLD ENGLISH PORCELAIN AND ITS MANUFACTURES.

With an Artistic, Industrial and Critical Appreciation of their Productions. By M. L. SOLON, the well-known Potter-Artist and Collector. In one handsome volume. Royal 8vo, well printed in clear type on good paper, and beautifully illustrated with 20 full-page Coloured Collotype and Photo-Chromotype Plates and 48 Collotype Plates on Tint. Artistically bound. Price 52/6 net.

" Mr. Solon writes not only with the authority of the master of technique, but likewise with that of the accomplished artist, whose exquisite creations command the admiration of the connoisseurs of to-day."—*Athenæum.*

MANX CROSSES; or The Inscribed and Sculptured Monuments of the Isle of Man, from about the end of the Fifth to the beginning of the Thirteenth Century.

By P. M. C. KERMODE, F.S.A.Scot., &c. The illustrations are from drawings specially prepared by the Author, founded upon rubbings, and carefully compared with photographs and with the stones themselves. In one handsome Quarto Volume 11½ in. by 8⅝ in., printed on Van Gelder hand-made paper, bound in full buckram, gilt top, with special design on the side. Price 63/= net. The edition is limited to 400 copies.

" We have now a complete account of the subject in this very handsome volume, which Manx patriotism, assisted by the appreciation of the public in general, will, we hope, make a success."—*Spectator.*

DERBYSHIRE CHARTERS IN PUBLIC AND PRIVATE LIBRARIES AND MUNIMENT ROOMS.

Compiled, with Preface and Indexes, for Sir Henry Howe Bemrose, Kt., by ISAAC HERBERT JEAYES, Assistant Keeper in the Department of MSS., British Museum. Royal 8vo, cloth, gilt top. Price 42/= net.

" The book must always prove of high value to investigators in its own recondite field of research, and would form a suitable addition to any historical library."—*Scotsman.*

SOME DORSET MANOR HOUSES, WITH THEIR LITERARY AND HISTORICAL ASSOCIATIONS.

By SIDNEY HEATH, with a fore-word by R. Bosworth Smith, of Bingham's Melcombe. Illustrated with forty drawings by the Author, in addition to numerous rubbings of Sepulchral Brasses by W. de C. Prideaux, reproduced by permission of the Dorset Natural History and Antiquarian Field Club. Dedicated by kind permission to the most Hon. the Marquis of Salisbury. Royal 4to, cloth, bevelled edges. Price 30/= net.

"Dorset is rich in old-world manor houses; and in this large, attractive volume twenty are dealt with in pleasant, descriptive and antiquarian chapters, fully illustrated with pen-and-ink drawings by Mr. Heath and rubbings from brasses by W. de C. Prideaux."—*Times*.

THE CHURCH PLATE OF THE DIOCESE OF BANGOR.

By E. ALFRED JONES. With Illustrations of about one hundred pieces of Old Plate, including a pre-Reformation Silver Chalice, hitherto unknown; a Mazer Bowl, a fine Elizabethan Domestic Cup and Cover, a Tazza of the same period, several Elizabethan Chalices, and other important Plate from James I. to Queen Anne. Demy 4to, buckram. Price 21/= net.

"This handsome volume is the most interesting book on Church Plate hitherto issued."— *Athenæum*.

THE OLD CHURCH PLATE OF THE ISLE OF MAN.

By E. ALFRED JONES. With many illustrations, including a pre-Reformation Silver Chalice and Paten, an Elizabethan Beaker, and other important pieces of Old Silver Plate and Pewter. Crown 4to, buckram. Price 10/6 net.

"A beautifully illustrated descriptive account of the many specimens of Ecclesiastical Plate to be found in the Island."—*Manchester Courier*.

THE LAST FORMED SEE OF THE ANGLICAN CHURCH.

THE CATHEDRAL CHURCH AND SEE OF ESSEX.

By the REV. J. CHARLES COX, LL.D., F.S.A. This book, written by that well-known ecclesiologist and antiquary, contains an outline story of the founding of Christianity in the Kingdom of the East Saxons in the seventh century, and pursues the history of the Church in Essex up to the completion of the scheme for an Essex Bishopric in 1908, with the selection of Chelmsford as the Cathedral Church. Crown 8vo, with many illustrations. Paper covers, 1/6 net; cloth gilt, 2/= net; postage, 2d. extra.

"To Churchmen generally the little book before us should prove especially interesting."— *Church Family Newspaper*.

GARDEN CITIES IN THEORY AND PRACTICE.

By A. R. SENNETT, A.M.I.C.E., &c. Large Crown 8vo. Two vols., attractively bound in cloth, with 400 Plates, Plans, and Illustrations. Price 21/= net.

". . . What Mr. Sennett has to say here deserves, and will no doubt command, the careful consideration of those who govern the future fortunes of the Garden City."—*Bookseller*.

THE CORPORATION PLATE AND INSIGNIA OF OFFICE OF THE CITIES AND TOWNS OF ENGLAND AND WALES.

By the late LLEWELLYNN JEWITT, F.S.A. Edited and completed with large additions by W. H. ST. JOHN HOPE, M.A. Fully illustrated, 2 vols., Crown 4to, buckram, 84/= net. Large paper, 2 vols., Royal 4to, 105/= net.

"It is difficult to praise too highly the careful research and accurate information throughout these two handsome quartos."—*Athenæum*.

THE RELIQUARY: AN ILLUSTRATED MAGAZINE FOR ANTIQUARIES, ARTISTS, AND COLLECTORS.

A Quarterly Journal and Review devoted to the study of primitive industries, mediæval handicrafts, the evolution of ornament, religious symbolism, survival of the past in the present, and ancient art generally. Edited by the REV. J. CHARLES COX, LL.D., F.S.A. New Series. Vols. 1 to 13. Super Royal 8vo, buckram, price 12/= each net. Special terms for sets.

"Of permanent interest to all who take an interest in the many and wide branches of which it furnishes not only information and research, but also illumination in pictorial form."—*Scotsman*.

LONDON: BEMROSE & SONS LTD., 4 SNOW HILL, E.C.; AND DERBY.